The Complete Tragedies, Volume 1

T0308749

THE COMPLETE WORKS OF LUCIUS ANNAEUS SENECA

Edited by Elizabeth Asmis, Shadi Bartsch, and Martha C. Nussbaum

Seneca

The Complete Tragedies, Volume 1

Medea, The Phoenician Women, Phaedra, The Trojan Women, Octavia

TRANSLATED BY SHADI BARTSCH,
SUSANNA BRAUND, ALEX DRESSLER,
AND ELAINE FANTHAM

EDITED BY SHADI BARTSCH

The University of Chicago Press CHICAGO AND LONDON

The University of Chicago Press, Chicago 60637
The University of Chicago Press, Ltd., London
© 2017 by The University of Chicago
Published 2017
Paperback edition 2022
Printed in the United States of America

31 30 29 28 27 26 25 24 23 22   1 2 3 4 5

ISBN-13: 978-0-226-74823-8 (cloth)
ISBN-13: 978-0-226-82109-2 (paper)
ISBN-13: 978-0-226-37226-6 (e-book)
DOI: https://doi.org/10.7208/chicago/9780226372266.001.0001

Library of Congress Control Number: 2016030088

♾ This paper meets the requirements of ANSI/NISO
Z39.48-1992 (Permanence of Paper).

Contents

Seneca and His World

ELIZABETH ASMIS, SHADI BARTSCH, AND MARTHA C. NUSSBAUM

Seneca once remarked of Socrates that it was his death by hemlock that made him great (*Letter* 13.14). With reason: Socrates' death demonstrated the steadfastness of his philosophical principles and his belief that death offered nothing to fear. When Seneca himself, then, was ordered to commit suicide by Nero in 65 CE, we might well believe Tacitus's account in his *Annals* (15.63) that the Roman Stoic modeled his death on that of Socrates, discoursing calmly about philosophy with his friends as the blood drained out of his veins. In Tacitus's depiction we see, for once, a much-criticized figure living up to the principles he preached.

Seneca's life was mired in political advancement and disappointment, shaped by the effects of exile and return, and compromised by his relationship with the emperor Nero—first his pupil, then his advisee, and finally his murderer. But his many writings say little about his political career and almost nothing about his relationship with Nero except for what can be gleaned from his essay *On Clemency*, leaving us to turn to later sources for information—Tacitus, Suetonius, and Dio Cassius in particular. We know that Seneca was born to a prominent equestrian family in Corduba, Spain, some time between 4 and 1 BCE. He was the second of three sons of Helvia and Lucius Annaeus Seneca (the youngest son, Annaeus Mela, was the father of the poet Lucan). The elder Seneca had spent much of his life in Rome, and Seneca himself was brought to Rome as a young boy. There he was educated in rhetoric and later became a student of the philosopher Sextius. But his entry into political life was delayed, and when he did enter upon the *cursus honorum* late in Tiberius's reign, his ill health (he had asthma and possibly tuberculosis) was a source of difficulty. In any case his career was cut short. He survived Caligula's hostility, which the sources tell us was thanks to his talents in oratory, but was sent into exile on Corsica by Claudius shortly after Caligula's death in 41 CE. The charge, almost certainly false, was adultery with Caligula's younger sister, Julia Livilla. Seneca spent his time in exile in philosophical and natural study and wrote the *Consolations* to Helvia (his mother) and to Polybius (Claudius's freedman secretary), revealing in the latter how desperately he hoped to be recalled to Rome.

When Seneca did return in 49 CE, it was under different auspices. Claudius had recently remarried, to Germanicus's daughter Agrippina, and she urged him to recall Seneca as tutor to her son, the twelve-year-old Nero. Claudius already had a younger son, Britannicus, but it was clear that the wily Agrippina wished to see her own flesh and blood on the throne. When Claudius died five years later, Agrippina was able to maneuver Nero into position as emperor—and Britannicus was dispatched by poison shortly after, in 55 CE.

From 54 until his influence waned at the end of the decade, Seneca acted as Nero's adviser, together with the praetorian prefect Sextus Afranius Burrus. We know he wrote a speech on clemency for Nero to deliver to the Roman senate soon after his accession, and Seneca's own essay *On Clemency* may contain some inkling of his strategy to keep the young emperor from running amok. Seneca's use of the term *rex*, or king, applied to Nero by analogy in this piece, is surprising from a Roman senator, but he seems to have hoped that flattering Nero by pointing to his limitless power and the value of clemency would be one way to keep him from abusing that power. Both Seneca and Burrus also helped with the civil and judicial administration of the empire.

Many historians, ancient and modern, feel that this early part of Nero's reign, moderated by Seneca and Burrus, represented a period of comparative good rule and harmony (the "*quinquennium Neronis*"). The decline started in 59 CE with Nero's murder of Agrippina, after which Seneca wrote the emperor's speech of self-exculpation—perhaps the most famous example of how the philosopher found himself increasingly compromised in his position as Nero's chief counsel. Certainly as a Stoic, Seneca cuts an ambiguous figure next to the others who made their opposition to Nero clear, such as Thrasea Paetus and Helvidius Priscus. His participation in court politics probably led him to believe that he could do more good from where he stood than by abandoning Nero to his own devices—if he even had this choice.

In any case, Seneca's influence over Nero seems to have been considerably etiolated after the death of Burrus in 62. According to Tacitus, Seneca tried to retire from his position twice, in 62 and 64. Although Nero refused him on both occasions, Seneca seems to have largely absented himself from the court after 64. In 65 CE came the Pisonian conspiracy, a plot to kill Nero and replace him with the ringleader, C. Calpurnius Piso. Although Seneca's nephew Lucan was implicated in this assassination attempt, Seneca himself was probably innocent. Nonetheless, Nero seized the opportunity to order his old adviser to kill himself. Seneca cut his own veins, but (so Tacitus tells us) his thinness and advanced age hindered the flow of blood. When a dose of poison also failed to kill him, he finally sat in a hot bath to make the blood flow faster. His wife, Pompeia Paulina, also tried to commit suicide but was saved on orders from Nero.

Because of his ethical writings, Seneca fared well with the early Christians—hence the later forging of a fake correspondence with St. Paul—but already in antiquity he had his fair share of critics, the main charge arising from the apparent contradiction between his Stoic teachings on the unimportance of "externals" and his own amassing of huge wealth. Perhaps for this reason he never gained the respect accorded the "Roman Socrates," the Stoic C. Musonius Rufus, banished by Nero in 65, even though Seneca's writings have had far more influence over the centuries. In Seneca's own lifetime one P. Suillius attacked him on the grounds that, since Nero's rise to power, he had piled up some 300 million sesterces by charging high interest on loans in Italy and the provinces—though Suillius himself was no angel and was banished to the Balearic Islands for being an embezzler and informant. In Seneca's defense, he seems to have engaged in ascetic habits throughout his life and despite his wealth. In fact, his essay *On the Happy Life* (*De vita beata*) takes the position that a philosopher may be rich as long as his wealth is properly gained and spent and his attitude to it is appropriately detached. Where Seneca finally ranks in our estimation may rest on our ability to tolerate the various contradictions posed by the life of this philosopher in politics.

A Short Introduction to Stoicism

Stoicism is one of the world's most influential philosophical movements. Starting from the works and teaching of the three original heads of the Greek Stoic school—Zeno of Citium (335–263 BCE), Cleanthes (331–232 BCE), and Chrysippus (ca. 280–207 BCE)—it became the leading philosophical movement of the ancient Greco-Roman world, shaping the development of thought well into the Christian era. Later Greek Stoics Panaetius (ca. 185–109 BCE) and Posidonius (ca. 135–51 BCE) modified some features of Stoic doctrine. Roman thinkers then took up the cause, and Stoicism became the semiofficial creed of the Roman political and literary world. Cicero (106–43 BCE) does not agree with the Stoics on metaphysical and epistemological matters, but his ethical and political positions lie close to theirs, and even when he does not agree, he makes a concerted effort to report their positions sympathetically. Roman Stoics Seneca, Epictetus (mid-first to early second century CE), Musonius Rufus (ca. 30–ca. 102 CE), and the emperor Marcus Aurelius (121–80 CE, emperor 161–80) produced Stoic works of their own (the last three writing in Greek).

The philosophical achievement of the Greek Stoics, and especially that of Chrysippus, was enormous: the invention of propositional logic, the invention of the philosophy of language, unprecedented achievements in moral psychology, distinction in areas ranging from metaphysics and epistemology to moral and political philosophy. Through an accident of history, however, all the works of all the major Greek Stoics have been lost, and we must recover their thoughts through fragments, reports (particularly the lengthy accounts in Diogenes Laertius's *Lives of the Philosophers*, in Cicero, and in Sextus Empiricus's skeptical writings, since the Stoics are his primary target), and the works of the Roman thinkers—who often are adjusting Stoic doctrines to fit Roman reality and probably contributing creative insights of their own. This also means that we know somewhat less about Stoic logic or physics than about Stoic ethics, since the Romans took a particular interest in the practical domain.

The goal of Stoic philosophy, like that of other philosophical schools of the Hellenistic era, was to give the pupil a flourishing life free from the forms of distress and moral failure that the Stoics thought ubiquitous in their societies. Unlike some of their competitor schools, however, they emphasized the need to study all parts of their threefold system—logic, physics, and ethics—in order to understand the universe and its interconnections. To the extent that a Roman such as Cicero believed he could uphold the moral truths of Stoicism without a confident belief in a rationally ordered universe, he held a heretical position (one shared many centuries later by Immanuel Kant).

Stoic physics held that the universe is a rationally ordered whole, and that everything that happens in it happens for the best of reasons. (It is this position, in its Leibnizian incarnation, that is pilloried in Voltaire's *Candide*.) Rejecting traditional anthropomorphic religion, the Stoics gave the name Zeus to the rational and providential principle animating the universe as a whole, and they could find even in the most trivial or distressing events (such as earthquakes and thunderbolts) signs of the universe's overall good order. This order was also a moral order based on the inherent dignity and worth of the moral capacities of each and every rational being. The Stoics believed that this order was deterministic: everything happens of necessity. But they were also "compatibilists," believing that human free will is compatible with the truth of determinism. They engaged in spirited debates with "incompatibilist" Aristotelians, making lasting contributions to the free will controversy.

Stoic ethics begins from the idea of the boundless worth of the rational capacity in each and every human being. The Roman Stoics understood this capacity to be centrally practical and moral. (Thus, unlike Plato, they did not think that people who had a natural talent for mathematics were better than people who didn't, and they became more and more skeptical that even the study of logic had much practical value.) They held that all human beings are equal in worth by virtue of their possession of the precious capacity to choose and direct their lives, ranking some ends ahead of others. This, they said, was what distinguished human beings from animals: this power of selection and rejection. (Unlike most other ancient schools, they had little concern for the morality of animal treatment, since they thought that only moral capacity entitled a being to respect and good treatment.) Children, they said, come into the world like little animals, with a natural orientation toward self-preservation but no understanding of true worth. Later, however, a remarkable shift will take place, already set up by their possession of innate human nature: they will be able to appreciate the beauty of the capacity for choice and the way in which moral reason has shaped the entire universe. This recognition, they said, should lead people to respect both self and others in an entirely new way. Stoics were serious about (human) equality: they urged the equal education of both slaves and women. Epictetus himself was a former slave.

Stoicism looks thus far like an ethical view with radical political consequences, and so it became during the Enlightenment, when its distinctive emphases were used to argue in favor of equal political rights and more nearly equal economic opportunities. However, the original Stoics maintain a claim of great significance for politics: moral capacity is the only thing that has intrinsic worth. Money, honor, power, bodily health, and even the love of friends, children, and spouse—all these are held to be things that one may reasonably pursue if nothing impedes (they are called "preferred indifferents"), but they have no true intrinsic worth. They should not even be seen as commensurate with moral worth. So when they do not arrive as one wishes, it is wrong to be distressed.

This was the context in which the Stoics introduced their famous doctrine of *apatheia*, freedom from the passions. Defining the major emotions or passions as all involving a high valuation of "external goods," they argue that the good Stoic will not have any of these disturbances of the personality. Realizing that chance events lie beyond our control, the Stoic will find it unnecessary to experience grief, anger, fear, or even hope: all of these are characteristic of a mind that waits in suspense, awestruck by things indifferent. We can have a life that truly involves joy (of the right sort) if we appreciate that the most precious thing of all, and the only truly precious thing, lies within our control at all times.

Stoics do not think that it is at all easy to get rid of the cultural errors that are the basis of the rejected passions: thus a Stoic life is a constant therapeutic process in which mental exercises are devised to wean the mind from its unwise attachments. Their works depict processes of therapy through which the reader may make progress in the direction of Stoic virtue, and they often engage their reader in just such a process. Epictetus and Marcus Aurelius describe processes of repeated meditation; Seneca (in *On Anger*) describes his own nightly self-examination. Seneca's *Letters* show the role that a wiser teacher can play in such a therapeutic process, but Seneca evidently does not think that even he himself is free from erroneous attachments. The "wise man" is in that sense a distant ideal, not a worldly reality, particularly for the Roman Stoics. A large aid in the therapeutic process is the study of the horrible deformities that societies (including one's own) suffer by caring too much about external goods. If one sees the ugly face of power, honor, and even love clearly enough, this may assist one in making the progress toward true virtue. Thus Seneca's *On Anger* is an example of a genre that we know to have been common in Stoicism.

Because of their doctrine of value, the Stoics actually do not propose radical changes in the distribution of worldly goods, as one might suppose equal regard for the dignity of all human beings would require. They think that equal respect does require dignified treatment of each person; thus Seneca urges masters not to beat their slaves or use them as sexual tools. About the institution of slavery, however, there is silence, and worse than silence: Seneca argues that true freedom is internal freedom, so the external sort does not really matter. Musonius, similarly, advocates respectful treatment for women, including access to a Stoic education. But as for changes in the legal arrangements that confined women to a domestic role and gave males power of life and death over them, he too is silent, arguing that women will manifest their Stoic virtue in the domestic context. Some Roman Stoics do appear to have thought that political liberty is a part of dignity and thus died supporting republican institutions, but whether this attention to external conditions was consistent with Stoicism remains unclear. (Certainly Cicero's profound grief over the loss of political freedom was not the attitude of a Stoic, any more than was his agonizing grief over his daughter's death.)

There was also much debate about whether the Stoic norm of *apatheia* encouraged people to detach themselves from bad political events in a way that gave aid and comfort to bad politics. Certainly Stoics were known to counsel retirement from politics (a theme in Seneca's own life as he sought Nero's permission for retirement, unsuccessfully), and they were thought to believe that upheaval is worse than lawless tyranny. Plutarch reports that Brutus (a Platonist) questioned potential coconspirators in the assassination of Julius Caesar by trying to determine whether they accepted that Stoic norm or believed, with him, that lawless tyranny is worse than civil strife; only non-Stoics were selected for the group of assassins. During Nero's reign, however, several prominent Stoics—including Seneca and his nephew, Lucan—joined republican political movements aimed at overthrowing Nero, and lost their lives for their efforts, by politically ordered suicide.

Stoics believed that from the moral point of view, national boundaries are as irrelevant as honor, wealth, gender, and birth. They held that we are, first and foremost, citizens of the universe as a whole. (The term *kosmou polites*, citizen of the universe, was apparently first used by Diogenes the Cynic, but the Stoics took it up and were the real forefathers of modern cosmopolitanism.) What cosmopolitanism meant in practical terms was unclear, for the reasons already given—but Cicero thinks, at any rate (in *On Duties*, a highly Stoic work), that our common human dignity entails some very strict limits on the reasons for going to war and the sort of conduct that is permissible in it. He thus adumbrated the basis of the modern law of war. Cicero denied, however, that our common humanity entailed any duty to distribute material goods beyond our own borders, thus displaying the unfortunate capacity of Stoic doctrine to support the status quo. Cicero's *On Duties* has had such an enormous influence on posterity in this that it is scarcely an exaggeration to blame the Stoics for the fact that we have well worked-out doctrines of international law in the area of war and peace, but no well-established understanding of our material duties to one another.

Stoicism's influence on the development of the entire Western intellectual tradition cannot be underestimated. Christian thought owes it a large debt. Clement of Alexandria is just one example of a Christian thinker steeped in Stoicism; even a thinker such as Augustine, who contests many Stoic theses, finds it natural to begin from Stoic positions. Even more strikingly, many philosophers of the early modern era turn to Stoicism for guidance—far more often than they turn to Aristotle or Plato. Descartes' ethical ideas are built largely on Stoic models; Spinoza is steeped in Stoicism at every point; Leibniz's teleology is essentially Stoic; Hugo Grotius bases his ideas of international morality and law on Stoic models; Adam Smith draws more from the Stoics than from other ancient schools of thought; Rousseau's ideas of education are in essence based on Stoic models; Kant finds inspiration in the Stoic ideas of human dignity and the peaceful world community; and the American founders are steeped in Stoic ideas, including the ideas of equal dignity and cosmopolitanism, which also deeply influence the American transcendentalists Emerson and Thoreau. Because the leading works of Greek Stoicism had long been lost, all these thinkers were reading the Roman Stoics. Because many of them read little Greek, they were primarily reading Cicero and Seneca.

The Stoic influence on the history of literature has also been immense. In the Roman world, all the major poets, like other educated Romans, were acquainted with Stoic ideas and alluded to them often in their work. Virgil and Lucan are perhaps particularly significant in this regard. Later European literary traditions also show marked traces of Stoic influence—in part via the influence of Roman literature, and in part through the influence of philosophers in their own time who were themselves influenced by Stoic thought, but often also through their own reading of the influential works of Cicero, Seneca, and Marcus Aurelius.

Seneca's Stoicism

Seneca identifies himself as a Stoic. He declares his allegiance by repeatedly referring to "our people" (*nostri*)—the Stoics—in his writings. Yet he exercises considerable independence in relation to other Stoics. While he is committed to upholding basic Stoic doctrines, he recasts them on the basis of his own experience as a Roman and a wide reading of other philosophers. In this respect he follows a tradition of Stoic philosophical innovation exemplified most clearly by Panaetius and Posidonius, who introduced some Platonic and Aristotelian elements while adapting Stoicism to Roman circumstances. Seneca differs from previous Stoics by welcoming some aspects of Epicurean philosophy along with other influences.

Seneca is concerned above all with applying Stoic ethical principles to his life and to the lives of others like him. The question that dominates his philosophical writings is how an individual can achieve a good life. In his eyes, the quest for virtue and happiness is a heroic endeavor that places the successful person above the assaults of fortune and on a level with god. To this end, Seneca transforms the sage into an inspirational figure who can motivate others to become like him by his gentle humanity and joyful tranquility. Key topics are how to reconcile adversity with providence, how to free oneself from passions (particularly anger and grief), how to face death, how to disengage oneself from political involvement, how to practice poverty and use wealth, and how to benefit others. All of these endeavors are viewed within the context of a supreme, perfectly rational and virtuous deity who looks with favor on the efforts of humans to attain the same condition of virtue. In the field of politics, Seneca argues for clemency on the part of the supreme ruler, Nero. In human relations, he pays special attention to friendship and the position of slaves. Overall, he aims to replace social hierarchies, with their dependence on fortune, with a moral hierarchy arranged according to proximity to the goal of being a sage.

Seneca's own concerns and personality permeate his writings. The modern reader learns much about the life of an aristocrat in the time of Claudius and Nero, and much about Seneca's personal strengths and weaknesses. At the same time, there is also much in the work that transcends the immediate concerns of Seneca and his period. Some topics that resonate especially with a modern audience are his vision of humans as members of a universal community of mankind, the respect he demands for slaves, his concern with human emotions, and, in general, his insistence on looking within oneself to find happiness. What is perhaps less appealing to the modern reader is the rhetorical elaboration of his message, which features an undeniable tendency toward hyperbole. Most of all, Seneca's own character strikes many readers as problematic. From his own time onward, he was perceived by some as a hypocrite who was far from practicing what he preached. Some of Seneca's writings (in particular, his *Consolations* to Polybius and his mother Helvia, and his essay *On the Happy Life*) are obviously self-serving. As Seneca himself suggests (*Letters* 84), he has transformed the teachings he has culled, in the manner of bees, into a whole that reflects his own complex character.

The Stoics divided logic into dialectic (short argument) and rhetoric (continuous exposition). There is not much to be said on dialectic in Seneca's writings except that he shuns it, along with formal logic in general. Every so often, however, he engages in a satirical display of fine-grained Stoic-type reasoning. The point is that carrying logical precision to excess is futile: it does not make a person any better. Quibbles of all kinds should be avoided, whether they involve carrying through a minute line of argument, making overly subtle verbal distinctions, or indulging in abstruse philological interpretation. While making the point, Seneca makes sure the reader knows he could beat the quibbler at his own game if he wanted to.

We have only sparse details about how the Stoics viewed rhetoric. What is clear about Seneca, however, is that he used the full panoply of Roman rhetorical methods to persuade readers of his philosophical message. His writings are full of vivid examples, stunning metaphors, pointed sayings, ringing sound effects. He knows how to vary his tone, from casual conversation to soaring exhortation and bitter denunciation. He peoples his text with a varied cast of characters: the addressee, the implied audience, hypothetical objectors, friends, opponents, historical figures. He himself hovers over the proceedings as watchful friend and sometime foe. Following Cleanthes, he intersperses poetry into his prose to impel the reader even more forcefully toward the task of self-improvement.

Given Seneca's ethical aims, it is perhaps surprising that he devotes a large work, *Natural Questions*, to physics. Yet the entire work has an overarching ethical aim. As Seneca insists repeatedly, the mind is uplifted by venturing beyond narrowly human concerns to survey the world as a whole. The contemplation of the physical world complements moral action by showing the full context of human action: we see god in his full glory, caring for human lives as he administers the world as a whole. In the spirit of Lucretius (who championed a rival philosophy), Seneca also intersperses ethical messages throughout his physical inquiries. Thus he emphasizes that humans must confront natural events, such as death and natural disasters, with courage and gratitude to god; and he warns against human misuse of natural resources and the decadence that accompanies progress. Of all areas of inquiry, physics affords Seneca the greatest scope for making additions and corrections to Stoic doctrine. He ranges over the whole history of physical inquiries, from the Pre-Socratics to his own time, to improve on the Stoics.

Seneca writes (*Letters* 45.4) that while he believes "in the judgment of great men," he also claims something for his own judgment: previous philosophers left some things to be investigated by us, which they might indeed have discovered for themselves if they hadn't engaged in useless quibbles. Granted that Seneca shows special investigative fervor in his cosmological inquiries, his moral teachings too are a product of his own judgment and innovation. What he contributes is a new vision rather than new theories. Using certain strict Stoic distinctions as a basis, he paints a new picture of the challenges that humans face and the happiness that awaits those who practice the correct philosophy. In agreement with Stoic orthodoxy, Seneca is uncompromising about differentiating between external advantages and the good, about the need to eradicate the passions, about the perfect rationality of the wise person, about the identity of god with fate. What he adds is a moral fervor, joined by a highly poetic sensibility, that turns these distinctions into spring-boards for action.

The Stoic sage was generally viewed by critics as a forbidding figure, outside the reach of human capabilities and immune to human feeling. Seneca concedes, or rather emphasizes, that the sage is indeed rare; he remarks that the sage is like a phoenix, appearing perhaps every five hundred years (*Letters* 42.1). As he sees it, the sage's exceptional status is not a barrier to improvement; it inspires. Seneca gives real-life immediacy to the sage by citing the younger Cato, opponent of Julius Caesar, as an example. Cato, indeed, is not just any sage; Seneca says he is not sure whether Cato might even surpass *him* (*On Constancy* 7.1). In this he is not blurring Stoic distinctions, but highlighting the indomitable moral strength of a sage. Through Cato and numerous other examples from the Roman past, Seneca fuses the Stoic sage with the traditional image of a Roman hero, thus spurring his Roman readers to fulfill their duties by emulating both at once.

Below the level of sage, Seneca outlines three stages of moral progress, demarcated according to our vulnerability to irrational emotions (*Letters* 75). There is the condition very near to that of being a sage, in which a person is not yet confident of being able to withstand irrational emotions (the so-called passions, *pathē*). Just below it is the stage in which a person is still capable of lapsing, and at the lowest level of progress a person can avoid most irrational emotions, but not all. Below these are the innumerable people who have yet to make progress. Seneca has nothing to say to them; he wants to avoid them, lest he be contaminated. What he does allow is that persons who are still struggling to become good may give way to grief initially; but he insists that this period must be brief. The Stoics talk "big words," he says, when they forbid moans and groans; he'll adopt a more gentle tone (*Letters* 23.4). Still, he insists, these words are "true"; and his aim is to lead, as much as he can, to the goal of a dispassionate attitude toward externals. Like everyone, the wise person is prone to initial shocks—reactions that look momentarily like irrational emotions—but these are involuntary responses to be succeeded immediately by the calmness of judgment. Seneca's sage is kind to others and is filled with a serene joy that has nothing to do with the ephemeral pleasure that other people take in externals.

Looking toward Roman heroism, Seneca portrays moral progress as an arduous struggle, like a military campaign or the uphill storming of an enemy's position. The enemy is fortune, viciously attacking its victim in the form of the most cruel disasters. Its opponent may succumb, but he will have conquered fortune if he resists to the end. In reality, the disasters come from other people or simply from circumstances. Seneca commonly cites death (whether one's own or that of a loved one), exile, torture, and illness. His own life is rich with examples. He goes so far as to advocate adversity as a means of making moral progress, but he also allows (with a view to his own wealth) that favorable circumstances are a help to the person who is still struggling to make progress.

To make progress, a person must not only confront externals but also, above all, look within oneself. Drawing inspiration from Plato, Seneca tells us there is a god inside; there is a soul that seeks to free itself from the dross of the body. Seneca invites the reader to withdraw into this inner self, so as to both meditate on one's particular condition and take flight in the contemplation of god. This withdrawal can occur in the press of a very active life. But it's easier when one is no longer fully caught up in politics, and so Seneca associates moral withdrawal with his own attempt to withdraw from politics toward the end of his life. He insists that he will continue to help others through his philosophical teachings, like other Stoics.

Senecan Tragedy

From Seneca's hand there survive eight tragedies (*Agamemnon, Thyestes, Oedipus, Medea, Phaedra, Phoenissae, Troades, Hercules Furens*), not including the spurious *Octavia* and the probably spurious *Hercules Oetaeus*; of the *Phoenissae* there remain only fragments. These dramas have undergone many vicissitudes in fortune throughout the centuries; however, they are no longer criticized as being mere flawed versions of the older Greek dramas in which much of Seneca's subject matter had already been treated. While Seneca's plays were once mined only for the light they shed on Roman Stoic philosophy, for examples of rhetorical extravagance, or for the reconstruction of missing plays by Sophocles and his fellows, the traits that once marked the dramas as unworthy of critical attention now engage us in their own right. Indeed, they are the only extant versions of any Roman tragedy, the writings of other dramatists such as Marcus Pacuvius (ca. 220–130 BCE) and Lucius Accius (ca. 170–86 BCE) having been lost to posterity. It is thus only Seneca's version of Roman drama, translated into English as the *Tenne Tragedies* in 1581, that so influenced the tragedians of the Elizabethan era.

Seneca may have turned his hand to writing drama as early as the reign of Caligula (37–41 CE), although there is no way of determining exactly when he began. Our first reference to the plays comes from a famous graffito from the *Agamemnon* preserved on a wall in Pompeii, but we can only deduce that this was written before the eruption of Vesuvius in 79 CE; it is of little actual use in trying to date the dramas. Stylistic analysis has not provided us with a sure order of composition, though scholars seem to agree that the *Thyestes* and the *Phoenissae* are late efforts. Certainly we are unable to make claims about their dating with respect to the *Essays* and *Letters*, despite the very different tones of Seneca's prose and his poetry—a difference that led some readers, including the fifth-century churchman and orator Sidonius Apollinaris and after him Erasmus and Diderot, to speculate (erroneously) that there might have been two Lucius Annaeus Senecas at work on them rather than one.

This confusion about the authorship of Seneca's writing may seem natural, given the argument that Stoicism fails as a way of life in the dramas. Whether it fails because its adherents are too weak to resist the pull of desire or emotion, because Stoicism itself is too difficult to practice successfully, because the universe is not the locus of a divine providence, or because the protagonists are so evil that they fail to see providence in action, is open to argument; a metaliterary view might even suggest that plotlines inherited from mythology provide the force that condemns a Cassandra or a Polyxena to death at the hands of a Clytemnestra or a Ulysses, with Seneca taking advantage of this dramatic fact to suggest the inexorable workings of Fate and the futility of struggle against it. Consider the *Thyestes* (a topic often dramatized in the Late Republic, though Seneca's version is the only one we have). We meet the eponymous exile as he praises the pauper's life to his children—only the man who drinks out of earthenware cups can be truly happy and without fear, he reminds them—but when invited to return to the palace at Argos by his conniving brother Atreus, the source of his exile, he allows himself to be lured back after only a token hesitation about giving up his newfound equanimity. "Sequor," he says to his son, "I follow you"; but in following his appetite for the luxurious life he does the opposite of the good Stoic.

The rest is, well, the stuff of myth. Dressed in royal regalia, Thyestes sits down to enjoy a hearty stew and some fine red wine, but his satiated belches soon turn into howls of horror as the delighted Atreus informs him of his dinner's provenance: the meal is made up of the dismembered bodies of Thyestes' own sons. Is there an explicit ethical or philosophical message here? If we followed the view of another Stoic, Epictetus (ca. 55–ca. 135 CE), who defined tragedy as what happens "when chance events befall fools" (*Discourses* 2.26.31), we might conclude that the story of Thyestes precisely illustrates the folly of giving in to a desire for power (or haute cuisine). In Seneca's treatment, however, such a clear object lesson seems undermined by a number of factors: the fact that Atreus reigns triumphant as the drama ends; the undeniable echoes of Stoic exhortation in the impotent counsels of Atreus's adviser; and the fragility of civic and religious values—the hellish scene in which Atreus sacrifices the children represents precisely a travesty of sacrifice itself, while *xenia* (the ancient tradition of hospitality) fares still worse. The adviser or a nurse mouthing Stoic platitudes without effect is featured in many of the plays: Phaedra, Clytemnestra, and Medea all have nurses to counsel them against their paths of action, even though their advice is invariably distorted and thrown back in their faces. Creon plays a similar role in the *Agamemnon*.

Other Senecan protagonists have more lasting doubts than Thyestes about the value of earthly success. Oedipus asks: "Joys any man in power?" And unlike his more confident Sophoclean manifestation, he feels the answer is clearly no. From the beginning of the play, the *Oedipus* provides striking contrasts to its Greek precedent, whose emphasis on the discovery of identity yields here to the overwhelming sense of pollution affecting Oedipus. The king, anxious even as the drama opens, worries that he will not escape the prophecy of his parricide, and suspects he is responsible for the plague ravaging Thebes. Despondent, he hopes for immediate death; his emotional state is far different from that of the character at the center of Sophocles' play. Seneca's version also features Creon's report of the long necromantic invocation of Laius's ghost in a dark grove, something absent in Sophocles. Even the sense that the characters' interaction onstage fails to drive the drama makes sense in the context of Seneca's forbidding and inexorable dramatic world. Causality and *anagnorisis* (dramatic recognition) are put aside in favor of the individual's helplessness before what awaits him, and the characters' speeches react to the violence rather than motivate it.

The pollution of the heavens by humans goes against Stoic physics but finds its place in the plays. The Stoics posited a tensional relationship between the cosmos and its parts; according to this view, the *pneuma* or vital spirit that subtends all matter results in a cosmic sympathy of the parts with the whole. "All things are united together . . . and earthly things feel the influence of heavenly ones," as Epictetus (*Discourses* 1.4.1) puts it. But what we see in the dramas is a disquieting manifestation of this *sympatheia*: the idea that the wickedness of one or a few could disrupt the rational and harmonic logos of the entire cosmos represents a reversal of the more orthodox Stoic viewpoint that the world is accessible to understanding and to reason. Thus we see the universe trembling at Medea's words, and the law of heaven in disorder. In the *Thyestes*, the sun hides its face in response to Atreus's crime; in the *Phaedra*, the chorus notes an eclipse after Phaedra's secret passion is unveiled. Horrific portents presage what is to come in the *Troades*. In Seneca's dramas, unlike in Greek tragedy, there is no role for civic institutions or the city to intervene in this relationship. The treatment of the gods is similarly unorthodox. Although Jason calls upon Medea to witness that there are no gods in the heavens, the very chariot in which she flies away is evidence of the assistance given her by her divine father. The gods are there; the problem is that they are unrecognizable.

Seneca's great antiheroes like Medea and Thyestes are troubling not only because they often triumph but because the manner of their triumph can resemble the goal point of the aspiring Stoic: in exhorting themselves to take up a certain stance toward the world, in abandoning familial and social ties, in rejecting the moral order of the world around them, and in trying to live up to a form of selfhood they have judged to be "better," Seneca's tyrants, just like his sages, construct a private and autonomous world around themselves which nothing can penetrate. Not only do they borrow the self-exhortations and self-reproving of the Stoic's arsenal, in which the dialogue conducted with the self suggests a split between a first-order desiring self and a second-order judging self, but they also adopt the consideration of what befits or is worthy of them as a guiding principle—always with a negative outcome.

This leads in turn to a metatheatrical tinge in several of the plays. In the *Medea*, for example, Medea seems to look to prior versions of her own story to discover what exactly is appropriate for her persona, in the same way that Oedipus, after putting out his eyes, remarks, "*This* face befits (an) Oedipus" (*Oedipus* 1000) or that Atreus says of his recipe, "This is a crime that befits Thyestes—and befits Atreus" (*Thyestes* 271). Such metatheatricality seems to draw upon the concern of the traditional Roman elite to perform exemplary actions for an approving audience, to generate one's ethical exemplarity by making sure that spectators for it exist.

And spectators do exist—we, the theater audience or the recitation audience. Scholars have long debated the question of whether Seneca's dramas were staged in antiquity. It is possible, as argued by the nineteenth-century German scholar Friedrich Leo, the tragedies were written for recitation only; inter alia, it would be unusual (but not impossible) to represent animal sacrifice and murder onstage. The question is unresolvable, but whether the original audiences were in the theater or in the recitation room, they shared with us the full knowledge of how the story would turn out, and in this they uncomfortably resembled some of the plotting antiheroes themselves. Indeed, our pleasure in watching Senecan tragedy unfold might seem to assimilate us to the pleasure these characters take in inflicting suffering on one another. In a famous line from the *Troades*, the messenger who brings news of Astyanax's murder reports of the scene of his death—which he has already compared to a theater—that "the greater part of the fickle crowd abhors the crime—and watches it" (1128–29). Here, in the tension between sadistic voyeurism and horror at what the drama unfolds, we can recognize the uncomfortable position of the spectator of Seneca's despairing plays.

Senecan Drama after the Classical Period

The fortunes of Senecan drama have crested twice: once during the Elizabethan period, and again in our own day. Although Seneca himself never refers to his tragedies, they were known in antiquity at least until Boethius (ca. 480–524 CE), whose *Consolation of Philosophy* draws on the themes of Seneca's choral odes. The dramas then largely dropped from sight, to reemerge in 1300 in a popular edition and commentary by Nicholas Trevet, a Dominican scholar at Oxford. Trevet's work was followed by vernacular translations in Spain, Italy, and France over the next two centuries. In Italy, an early imitator was Albertino Mussato (1261–1329), who wrote his tragic drama *Ecerinis* to alert his fellow Paduans to the danger presented by the tyrant of Verona. In England, the Jesuit priest and poet Jasper Heywood (1535–1598) produced translations of three of the plays; these were followed by Thomas Newton's *Seneca His Tenne Tragedies Translated into English* in 1581—of which one tragedy was Newton's own *Thebais*. The dramas were considered to be no mere pale shadow of their Greek predecessors: Petrarch, Salutati, and Scaliger all held Seneca inferior to none on the classical stage. In Scaliger's influential treatise on poetry, the *Poetices libri septem* (1561), he ranks Seneca as the equal of the Greek dramatists in solemnity and superior to Euripides in elegance and polish (6.6).

The Elizabethan playwrights in particular took up Seneca as a model for translation or imitation. T. S. Eliot claimed that "No author exercised a wider or deeper influence upon the Elizabethan mind or on the Elizabethan form of tragedy than did Seneca," and the consensus is that he was right. It is perhaps little wonder that Seneca appealed to an age in which tragedy was seen as the correct vehicle for the representation of "haughtinesse, arrogancy, ambition, pride, iniury, anger, wrath, envy, hatred, contention, warre, murther, cruelty, rapine, incest, rovings, depredations, piracyes, spoyles, robberies, rebellions, treasons, killings, hewing, stabbing, dagger-drawing, fighting, butchery, treachery, villainy, etc., and all kind of heroyicke evils whatsoever" (John Greene, *A Refutation of the Apology for Actors*, 1615, p.56). Kyd, Marlowe, Marston, and Shakespeare all read Seneca in Latin at school, and much of their drama shows his influence in one form or another. The itinerant players at Elsinore in Shakespeare's *Hamlet* famously opine that "Seneca cannot be too heavy nor Plautus too light" (2.2.400–401), but it is Shakespeare's *Titus Andronicus* that shows the greatest Senecan influence with its taste for revenge, rape, decapitation, human cookery, and insanity. Richard III and Macbeth, on the other hand, exemplify the presence of unrestrained, brooding ambition in the power-hungry protagonist. Similarly, in such plays as Thomas Kyd's *The Spanish Tragedy* and John Marston's *Antonio's Revenge* we see the influence of such Senecan fixtures as ghosts speaking from beyond the grave, graphic violence, obsession with revenge, and even structural features such as choruses, use of stichomythia, and division into five acts.

The bleak content of the dramas was often tied to the notion of a moral lesson. Already Trevet's preface to the *Thyestes* argued that the play taught the correction of morals by example, as well as simply offered the audience enjoyment. The Jesuit Martín Antonio Delrio (1551–1608) defended the use of Roman drama in a Christian education by suggesting that it provided a masked instruction in wisdom, as did Mussato before him. Nonetheless, after the middle of the seventeenth century Seneca's drama fell largely into disrepute. The Restoration poet John Dryden (1631–1700) took the opportunity in the preface to his own *Oedipus* to criticize both Seneca's and Corneille's versions; of the former, he wrote that "Seneca [. . .] is always running after pompous expression, pointed sentences, and Philosophical notions, more proper for the Study than the Stage." The French dramatist Jean Racine (1639–1699) used Seneca as a model for his *Phèdre*, but at the same time claimed that his main debt was to Euripides. Not surprisingly, the Romantics did not find much to like in Seneca. Recently, however, an efflorescence of interest in both the literary and the performance aspects of Senecan drama has produced new editions, scholarly monographs, and the staging of some of the plays. Noteworthy here are Sarah Kane's adaptation *Phaedra's Love*, performed in New York in May 1996; Michael Elliot Rutenberg's May 2005 dramatization of a post-Holocaust *Oedipus* at Haifa University in Israel; and a 2007 Joanne Akalaitis production of the *Thyestes* at the Court Theatre in Chicago.

A note on the translations: they are designed to be faithful to the Latin while reading idiomatically in English. The focus is on high standards of accuracy, clarity, and style in both the prose and the poetry. As such, the translations are intended to provide a basis for interpretive work rather than to convey personal interpretations. They generally eschew terminology that would imply a Judeo-Christian moral framework (e.g., "sin"). Where needed, notes have been supplied to explain proper names in mythology and geography.

For Further Information

On Seneca's life: Miriam T. Griffin, *Seneca: A Philosopher in Politics* (Oxford, 1976) and Paul Veyne, *Seneca: The Life of a Stoic*, translated from the French by David Sullivan (New York, 2003). On his philosophical thought: Brad Inwood, *Seneca: Stoic Philosophy at Rome* (Oxford, 2005), and Shadi Bartsch and David Wray, *Seneca and the Self* (Cambridge, 2009). On the dramas: A. J. Boyle, *Tragic Seneca: An Essay in the Theatrical Tradition* (New York and London, 1997); C. A. J. Littlewood, *Self-Representation and Illusion in Senecan Tragedy* (Oxford, 2004); and Thomas G. Rosenmeyer, *Senecan Drama and Stoic Cosmology* (Berkeley, 1989). On Seneca and Shakespeare: Robert S. Miola, *Shakespeare and Classical Tragedy: The Influence of*

Seneca (Oxford, 1992) and Henry B. Charlton, *The Senecan Tradition in Renaissance Tragedy* (Manchester, 1946).

Editor's Note

The ten tragedies attributed to Seneca have been here translated by five different translators. As should be evident from the text, the translators have chosen to follow certain conventions and not others (for example, to avoid archaic language; to use blank verse, but no rhyming verse; and to aim at language that was as literal as possible without being awkward). Apart from this they were left to follow their own sense of what terminology suited their own encounter with the original Latin. All five translators were also invited to write their own short translator's introduction to their plays, focusing on what was of the most interest to them; there was no attempt to provide a general overview of all the scholarship on each play, though a suggested reading section follows each introduction.

The transmitted colometry of Seneca's anapests, even when the manuscript families A and E are in agreement, is often problematic, and two important editors (Zwierlein and Fitch) have hewn their own paths in their editions.[1] In this volume, instead of choosing between different modern understandings of the colometry for the choral odes and non-iambic verse, in the few cases where extra line-breaks create an extra line they have simply been reorganized to eliminate the extra line. This simple measure ensures that the line numbers continue in regular succession throughout the play; and while this has the disadvantage of turning a deaf ear to the metrical niceties of the original Latin (which might accommodate trochees and anapests differently from iambic trimeter), the translation gains the advantage of letting students and teachers refer to specific lines in the translation without having to gesture vaguely at some point between, for example, line 720 and line 730. In rendering all ten plays consistent in this way I have occasionally overridden the line divisions of a particular translator, even when that translator has noted that he or she has used a specific Latin edition.

I want to thank all the translators for their patience and flexibility in this very time-consuming and difficult project. All the translations were vetted by external reviewers for the University of Chicago Press, though probably my voice was the one that my collaborators were the most tired of by the end of this process. I hope our general readers will agree that this joint effort has been rewarded by the final result.

Medea

Medea, daughter of King Aeetes of Colchis, fell in love with the Greek hero Jason and helped him and the Argonauts escape with the famous Golden Fleece. For Jason's sake, Medea was willing to kill both her own brother and Jason's uncle Pelias. The pair settled in Corinth and had two children. But now they are under threat from the advancing army of Pelias' brother. If Jason marries Creusa, the daughter of Creon, king of Corinth, safety is assured—and it seems Jason is willing. Medea is outraged at this betrayal, and the play opens with her speech vowing revenge. After an interlude in which the chorus sings of the royal wedding to come, Medea's nurse enters and urges her to set aside her rage, but her counsel falls on deaf ears.

King Creon appears, impatient to see Medea gone. She pleads her case, arguing that if she must give up Creon's protection so should Jason, who is as guilty as she is. Creon is not persuaded by her argument but allows her one more day in Corinth and promises that her sons will be safe if she leaves them behind.

The chorus now sings of the end of an age of innocence brought about by man's travel over oceans. When Jason enters, lamenting his difficult circumstances, Medea begs him not to leave her and reminds him of the favors he owes her, but Jason scorns her attempt at involving him in guilt and refuses to let her take the children with her. He departs, and she starts the preparations for her vengeance.

The chorus observes that no one hath greater wrath than a woman scorned and expresses its concern for Jason's safety. Indeed, the nurse reports that Medea is gathering toxic poisons. Medea herself sings a long spell to ensure the efficacy of the tainted robe she will give Creusa as a wedding gift.

The messenger enters in shock: Creusa is dead and so is King Creon. The city is in flames. Medea exults at the success of her plan, but it is not complete: Jason must suffer more. She wavers back and forth over the dreadful option of killing their children then finally invites the fury Megaera into her chest and kills one son. Jason rushes in to arrest her just in time to see the slaughter of the second son. As Medea flies off in her winged chariot, Jason calls after her to witness that there are no gods in the skies above.

Introduction

SHADI BARTSCH

As the Medea of Seneca's drama flies off in triumph on her serpent-yoked chariot and the play nears its horrific close, she shouts down to the earthbound Jason standing among the corpses of their children: "Lift your swollen eyes up here, thankless man. Do you recognize your wife?" Jason does not say; but whatever *he* may think has become of his once-loving wife, Medea herself feels by the end of the play that she is finally recognizable as "Medea": the madwoman with the bloody hands, the granddaughter of the Sun, the epitome of a drastic form of vengeance—the murder of one's own children in order to make their father suffer. And while Jason may stare in horror, we in the audience nod in recognition: yes, this is the Medea we know; this is how the story goes. It is a grandly metatheatrical moment, with the added twist that even Medea seems to recognize, anachronously, her place in the mythological and literary tradition.

Seneca's version of the tragedy of the woman who killed her children to punish a wayward husband has much that is unusual about it. Murdering what you love because of your rage at another, just to cause that person pain as well: we can usually only imagine this as a crime of passion, the doings of a woman driven out of her mind (whether temporarily or permanently) by anger and suffering. The Medeas of drama and literature themselves find the crime almost too shocking to commit, and part of the interest of each version of the story is the struggle within Medea, her teetering between the forces of love and hate as she debates the choice before her. Seneca's Medea is no different in this regard: she too has a decision to make between alternatives, and alternates between them. But there is something unusual about this Medea. It is the surprising fact that her language and actions at this point, her self-exhortations, her self-awareness, are all uncannily similar to those Seneca recommends for aspiring Stoic philosophers. For his Medea, Seneca has taken the techniques of self-questioning and character formation that he describes in his prose philosophical works and puts them in the mouth of a woman who seems far from a would-be Stoic. What are we to make of this? The Stoic philosopher's ultimate goal was both supreme self-control and also the calm that accompanied it; what could be less similar to this than the famously passionate character whose love and hate exceeded all bounds?

Seneca's Medea is in this sense a paradox, a master of self-control in carrying out a deranged act. Indeed, even as she carries out the act, she seems to think of it in terms of progress toward an ideal—not a philosophical one, of course, but a mythological and tragic one, the woman who can kill her children. This is a perverse version of progress, to be sure. The Roman Stoics emphasized the idea of accomplishing one's potential to be an ideal version of oneself, a wise man completely at one with the universe, and they urged the use of a model to keep before one's eyes. As Seneca tells us in *Letter* 11.8–10, Epicurus himself told us to take "some man of high character, and keep him ever before your eyes, living as if he were watching you, and ordering all your actions as if he beheld them." Choose therefore, Seneca continues, a Cato or a Laelius, and "picture him always to yourself as your protector or your example." Medea too has such a model, but it is not a famously wise Roman, but Medea. For, faced with Jason's betrayal, she has been planning her revenge from the start in a way that repeatedly evokes the existence of her namesake in myth and literature. Her will to reach this "ideal" permeates her conversation with her quaking *nutrix* (170–71):

NURSE
Flee!

MEDEA
I wish I never had.

NURSE
Medea—

MEDEA
—I will become her!

The tinge of metatheatricality here has been noted ever since the German philologist Wilamowitz commented that Seneca's Medea had obviously read Euripides' play of the same name.[1] Medea will in fact name herself eight times in this play, in comparison to the single self-naming of Euripides' matching play.[2]

Later, when Medea has murdered Creon and his daughter, she signals the end of the process of shaping herself to meet her goal by her famous claim (and the last evocation of her name), "Now I am Medea: my talent's grown through suffering " (910). As it happens, the announcement is premature; Medea will continue to struggle between opposing desires (to kill her sons or let them live) until she has slaughtered both her children, but the metatheatrical implications are unavoidable.[3] We might compare her to Atreus in Seneca's play *Thyestes*, who is similarly driven to match himself to a negative exemplar—he has his family, whose precedent in the art of cooking children stands before him like a mockery of more traditional ancestral masks: "Look at Tantalus, at Pelops," he exhorts himself, "these are the archetypes my hands are called to match" (242–43). Where the Stoic aspirant can look to the model of a Cato or imagine what the sage would do in trying circumstances, Medea and Atreus seem to look to the history of their selves and their family line. It is Seneca's manipulation of this and other parallels to Stoic procedures in the *Medea* that raises the question of just what Medea's self-transformation can be taken to suggest.

There are many examples in the play that we could turn to. Medea's promise "I will become Medea" presages a process much like that of the philosopher who strives to become fully "himself" by embarking on a series of mental operations to bring him to his wiser self. As she prepares herself to "become Medea" in her great final monologue, she turns several times to address herself and to deliberate on which of her desires is correct, borrowing the self-exhortations and self-reproving of the Stoic's arsenal. Urging herself onward to the climactic murder of her sons, she starts with a reproof of her *animus* for shying away from the task: "Why are you faltering, my mind? Follow up this happy start!" (895). This and lines such as "Why do you delay now, my soul? Why hesitate?" ring with the sound of the Stoic addresses to the self, both in urging to action and in self-criticism, that we find scattered throughout the prose works.

Indeed, as Medea continues to harangue herself into action and lays claim to coming into her own, she stiffens her resolve by another Stoic practice, a review of her actions to date (911–14):

> I'm glad—so glad—I ripped my brother's head off,
> I'm glad I hacked his limbs up and robbed my father
> of his secret treasure, I'm glad I gave those daughters
> means for their father's murder. Seek inspiration,
> anger: you won't bring unskilled hands to any crime.

Her introductory formula here—"I'm happy to have done X"—is familiar as a component of the Stoic self-review, occurring even in the comments that Seneca puts in Nero's mouth at the beginning of the *De clementia* and appearing frequently in the letters as a form of encouragement (e.g., *Letters* 78.14 and 108.7).

One of the rules that the aspiring Stoic must remember is to conduct himself in a manner worthy of himself. There seems to be some flexibility in terms of the behavior this might actually designate for a given individual, as shown by Epictetus' famous refusal to cut off his beard rather than lose his head (*Discourses* 1.2.29); conversely, a Roman Stoic might argue that all sorts of demeaning behavior is appropriate when it comes to preserving the integrity of mind over matter. More generally, however, the consideration of what befits each individual or what is worthy of him or her serves as a guiding principle to the forms of behavior that suit the *persona* one has adopted, and this rule holds equally valid outside the dramas and within them.[4] In the *Medea*, as in the other plays, the question of what exactly befits Medea's *persona* or is worthy of it also arises, as when she comments of her role as parent that "now that I'm a mother, what befits is—greater crimes" (50). In the same way, Oedipus remarks after putting out his eyes that "*This* face is right for Oedipus" (*Oedipus* 1003) and Atreus comments on his plan for child-cookery that it is "A crime that matches Atreus, and fits Thyestes too" (*Thyestes* 271).[5]

These formulations of self-address in the drama add up to a form of self-preparation that smacks of the Stoic's training in the service of an entirely different ideal: reaching philosophical wisdom and equanimity. The result is that at points in the drama our heroine's assertions cannot be distinguished at face value from that of a Stoic.[6] This is particularly striking in dialogue as well, such as a stichomythic passage early in the play in which she and the *nutrix* duel in maxims. When the nurse bids her keep quiet in the face of the outrage done her, Medea responds boldly: "Fortune fears the brave and treads the cowards under foot" (159). And to each further comment, she has a Stoic reply (160–63):

NURSE
Bravery deserves approval only when it has a place.

MEDEA
Bravery can never fail to have a place.

NURSE
Hope offers no way out in your afflictions.

MEDEA
If you have nothing left to lose, then why fear loss?

Elsewhere, she will defend her behavior by allusion to how far above circumstance her spirit stands, indomitable and unable to be crushed. To Jason: "Every form of Fortune has always been beneath me" (520). Or, again to her nurse: "Fortune can take my wealth, but not my spirit" (176).[7] Like the good Stoic, Medea scorns the vagaries of fortune, believes that virtue should always be a guide for behavior, and recognizes the illusory pull of hope. Rich or poor, successful or a failure, what is important is her "spirit," the one thing that is in her control.

Of course, all of these coincidences of language and behavior fail to mask the massive ethical difference that when Medea chastises the part of herself that she feels has gone awry or urges herself to action, what she is chastising is what most societies and stoics would call basic morality, while the voice that urges her to select murder as her choice takes on the role of the "moral" voice that usually warns one *not* to transgress despite the presence of the desire to do so ("I really shouldn't be eating this cake . . ."). The irony with Medea is that these roles are so upside down: the desires she has to argue against are precisely those that we would consider normative, such as not wanting to kill one's children. And yet, like Seneca, she, too, seems to believe that these forms of reflection on one's desires are the best means of effecting a change in her ruling faculty.[8] This Medea in the grip of the "wrong" form of reflection on her original emotions and desires is comparable, say, to a murderer hesitating outside the house of his victim: "Get a grip on yourself!" he might say. "Be a man! Do the job, and don't act like a coward! Don't listen to the voice telling you to run away while you still can! What would so-and-so think?"—an effort at self-control that entails urging the agent to live up to the expectations of a watching self even if the larger framework of this ideal is "bad." Medea is the perfect mirror to the Stoic sage, but one whose final goals wreak havoc with the idea that such self-transformation and self-control is automatically a good. Seneca certainly never considers the question of whether self-control can be a bad quality in his prose works; to work toward this via self-transformation is always treated as a plus. But his drama seems to occasionally open the back door to a world in which an informed self-control has nothing to do with a willful movement toward virtue.

What might Medea illustrate for us about the conditions under which philosophical solipsism might go astray? Most obviously, she is isolated in her situation, and in this she parallels to some degree the isolated Stoic philosopher whose judgments are not necessarily informed by common morality. Seneca himself had mostly a pack of depraved men for company at the imperial court: he often fantasized about withdrawing and tried unsuccessfully to do so at least twice. And Seneca seems to highlight the way in which Medea's framework for judging her actions is solitary by a number of innovations. The chorus of the *Medea* is far less sympathetic to our Colchian exile than its Euripidean counterpart, generally deploring her behavior and singing, near the beginning of the play, the idealistic marriage-hymn for Jason and Creusa. And Seneca also innovates here as in the *Phaedra* by supplying his heroine with a nurse who represents the voice of normative morality and is emphatically rejected. All of the nurse's advice to Medea is turned on its head by its recipient.[9] Moreover, Medea increases her own isolation by rejecting her role as a family member, stripping from herself the role of not only wife but also mother ("anger leaves, and the mother takes its place," 927–28—and then the same thing in reverse). As Fitch and McElduff (2002, 26) note: "The process of 'becoming Medea' . . . involves destroying the self-in-relationship, viz. as mother of Jason's children and therefore still connected to him." Her very monologues reveal her sense of solitude, so that, as Gill (1987, 36) observes: "This conflict centres on Medea's thinking about herself (turning on the question of whether she can sustain her image of herself as the perpetrator of ultimate evil) rather than on her responses to others; and so the 'madness'—or solipsism—of 958ff. provides an appropriate context for its resolution."

It seems Medea lives in a solipsistic world by the end of the play, a situation that poses an important problem—as yet unsolved—for ethical philosophy. She has only her own ideals to rely on for judgement, and in this case we might find them problematic. True, her decision is grimly personal—but, for me at least, it resonates with questions about morality, murder, and self-righteousness that are present in today's world as well.

Suggested Reading

Boyle, Anthony J., ed. 1983. *Seneca Tragicus*. Berwick.
———. 2014. *Seneca:* Medea. Oxford.
Costa, Charles D. N., ed. 1973. *Seneca:* Medea. Oxford.
Fitch, John F., and S. McElduff. 2002. "Construction of the Self in Senecan Drama." *Mnemosyne* 55: 18–40.
Fyfe, Helen. 1983. "An Analysis of Seneca's *Medea*." In Boyle 1983, 77–93.
Gill, Christopher. 1987. "Two Monologues of Self-Division: *Euripides, 'Medea'* 1021–80 and *Seneca, 'Medea'* 893–977." In *Homo Viator: Essays for John Bramble*, edited by P. Hardie and M. Whitby, 25–37. Bristol.
Henry, Denis, and Elisabeth Walker. 1967. "Loss of Identity: Medea Superest: A Study of Seneca's *Medea*." *Classical Philology* 62: 169–81.

Hine, Harry M. 2000. *Seneca:* Medea, *with an Introduction, Text, Translation and Commentary.* Warminster.

Littlewood, Cedric A. L. 2004. *Self-Representation and Illusion in Senecan Tragedy.* Oxford.

Star, Christopher. 2012. *The Empire of the Self: Self-Command and Political Speech in Seneca and Petronius.* Baltimore.

Medea

LUCIUS ANNAEUS SENECA

TRANSLATED BY SHADI BARTSCH

DRAMATIS PERSONAE

MEDEA, wife of Jason and daughter of King Aeetes of Colchis
NURSE of Medea
JASON, captain of the Argo
CREON, king of Corinth
MESSENGER
CHORUS of Corinthians

The drama takes place outside the palace of King Creon at Corinth, where Jason and Medea have recently arrived after fleeing Colchis. Their quarters are adjacent to the palace itself.

ACT 1

(Enter Medea.)

MEDEA

O marriage gods![1] And you, Lucina, guardian of the spousal
bed, and Athena, you who taught the Argo's pilot Tiphys
to steer his novel ship, destined to tame the seas,
and Neptune, cruel ruler of the ocean's depths,
and you, the Sun,[2] apportioning bright daylight for the world,
and you, triform Hecate, who casts complicit light
upon your silent rites—you all, you gods by whom
Jason once swore to me, and those to whom Medea
has greater right to pray: Chaos of eternal night,
regions hostile to the gods, impious shades, and Hades,   10
master of a gloomy realm, your consort like me kidnapped
but by a spouse more loyal: in foreboding tones I pray to you.[3]

Now, now, appear, goddesses avenging crime,[4]
your filthy serpent-hair unbound, clutching
sooty torches in your bloody hands; appear,
just as once you did to me, when you stood bristling
by my bridal bed. Make death your gift to the new wife,
Creusa; death is the gift her father gets, and all the royal line.[5]
What is left? To pray for worse for the new groom:
I pray he lives. May he stray in want through unknown towns,
an exile, fearful, hated, his home in doubt;
may he be a tiresome guest at strangers' doors;
may he wish for *me* as wife; and here's the worst thing
I can pray: may he hope his sons take after father
and mother both. My vengeance is obtained already
—because I've given birth.[6] Why waste words and accusations?
I should attack the enemy! I'll strike the torches from their
     hands,
the light out of the sky! Does the Sun, who sired my family
     line,
see this, and is he seen, and does he, sitting in his chariot,
traverse his customary track across the cloudless sky?
Won't he turn back to the dawn and retrograde the day?
Father, grant to me to ride the air in my ancestral
chariot, give me the reins, entrust to me to drive
with blazing harnesses the steeds who pull the Sun.
Corinth, who parts a pair of gulfs on either side
must burn, and make her two seas meet.
One thing remains, for me to take the nuptial torch
into their room myself, and after sacrificial vows
to kill the victims at the dedicated altars.
If, my soul, you are alive, if any of your former vigor's
left, then find a path to punish them, through
their very innards. Dispel a woman's fear, take up
the spirit of the harsh Caucasian range.[7]
Whatever horrors Phasis saw, or the Pontic sea,[8]
Corinth too will see. Savage acts, unheard of, grim,
ills at which the sky and earth will tremble,

20

30

40

my mind within me stirs: wounds and butchery,
death that spreads throughout the limbs. No, this is
    insignificant;
I did this as a girl. Let my rage well up more strongly;
now that I'm a mother, what befits is—greater crimes.   50
Equip yourself with rage, prepare to deal out death
with undivided fury. The story told of your divorce
should match that of your marriage. How do you leave Jason?
The same way that you joined him. Break off these slow
    delays now:
the home you got by crime must be lost by crime as well.

                        (*Exit Medea. Enter the Chorus.*)

CHORUS
At this wedding of royals, with favoring omen,
may the gods who rule skies and those who rule seas
attend with the people duly approving.
First, to the Thunderers holding their scepters[9]
a bull with white hide must bring his high neck;   60
a heifer new to the yoke, snow-white of flesh,
must please the goddess Lucina; and for her who restrains
the blood-splattered hands of truculent Mars,
who gives treaties to nations at war,
and holds in her hands a rich horn of plenty,
a delicate offering comes, since she is gentler.[10]
And you, who preside over marriage that's lawful,[11]
dispersing the night with an auspicious hand,
languid and drunkenly staggering, approach,
wreathing your head with a garland of roses;   70
you too, star, who precedes the dawn and the dusk,
perpetually rising too slowly for lovers.[12]
Mothers and newlyweds eagerly want you
to cast your bright night-gleam as soon as you can.
The young woman's beauty outdoes by far
brides from the city of Athens, and those
whom Sparta, town without walls,

sends out to train in the manner of men
on the ridges of Taygetus mountain,
and those whom the rivers of Thebes
and holy Apheus cleanse.
If he wished to be judged on appearance,
Jason, the son of Aeson,
would outdo the child born of criminal
lightning, who keeps tigers harnessed to his chariot;[13]
and even Apollo, who inspires the tripods,
brother to stern virgin Diana;
he'd defeat even Pollux, better
at boxing than Castor his twin.
This is the way that I pray to you, gods:
Let this woman outdo other wives,
let this man far surpass other men.
When she stands in the chorus of women,
the face of one girl outshines all the rest—as
the beauty of stars disappears in sunlight,
and the close-knitted clusters of Pleiads go dark
when the moon is filled in with a light not her own,
and forms a full circle by uniting curved horns.[14]
Her blush is the color of snow when it's steeped in
red dye, it's the gleam of the sun when it dawns
while a dew-dampened shepherd looks on.
Free of the bed of that horrible Phasian,[15] you who
always felt fear when you handled the breasts
of your wildcat wife with unwilling hands,
happy now take your Aeolian bride,
the first time you've married with your in-laws' assent.
Young men, crack jokes with indulgence for insults
and launch into song on this side and that;
being outspoken with rulers is rarely allowed.
Fair, noble child of Lyaeus who carries the thyrsus,[16]
it's high time to kindle the torch of split pine;
brandish the nuptial flame in your indolent hand.
Let fescennine wit freely sound with festive abuse,

let the crowd crack its jokes; any fugitive wife
of a foreigner spouse should slink off in shadow and silence.

ACT 2

(*Enter Medea and the Nurse.*)

MEDEA

I'm ruined: the wedding song has reached my ears.
I can scarcely yet believe it true myself, or credit such a blow.
Could Jason have brought this about—to leave me in a foreign
    place,
my father and my country and my royal power lost—
all alone, the cruel man? Has he scorned my services,   120
though he's seen me tame both fire and sea with sorcery?
Does he really think my evil's all used up?
Confused, maddened, out of my mind, I'm borne
in all directions. Where can I get vengeance?
I wish he had a brother![17] He has a bride—the sword
can cut her down. Does this suffice for what I've suffered?
If there's some crime your hands find unfamiliar,
some crime barbaric cities and those of Greece have found,[18]
now is the time to do it. Your own misdeeds should urge
    you on,
and all recur to you: the famous stolen fleece, glory   130
of the realm; the little brother of a wicked girl
dismembered by the sword, the corpse tossed at his father,
his body scattered on the sea,[19] and the limbs of old Pelias
stewed down in a cauldron. How often I have fatally, impiously
spilled blood—and not a single crime did I commit
in rage: it was ill-fated love that acted savagely.
—But what could Jason do, subjected to another man's
authority and rule? —He should have offered up his chest
to meet the sword! —Ah, speak more kindly, raging anger,   140
speak more kindly. If he can, let my Jason live
the way he used to be; if not, let him still live,
recalling me and sparing his own life—my gift!

All the fault is Creon's; deranged with royal power
he breaks up marriages and drags a mother from
her children; he splits apart a loyalty that tight bonds
tie together. Let him be the target, let him pay alone the price
he owes. I'll bury his home in heaps of ash;
the furthest point of the Peloponnese,[20] a long delay for ships
that round its coast, will see the black plume raised by flames.

NURSE

150   Be quiet, I beg, hide your complaints, lock them up
in hidden pain. One who suffers grievous wounds
in silence, with equanimity and patience,
can pay them back; it's rage concealed that inflicts harm.
Hatred you make open loses any chance of vengeance.

MEDEA

A rage that can deliberate or hide itself
has not struck deep. Great anguish does not lie in ambush.
My wish is to attack.

NURSE

       Control your raging impulse, child.
Even silence and inaction can barely keep you safe.

MEDEA

Fortune fears the brave and treads the cowards under foot.

NURSE

160   Bravery deserves approval only when it has a place.

MEDEA

Bravery can *never* fail to find a place.

NURSE

Hope offers no way out in your afflictions.

MEDEA

If you have nothing left to lose, then why fear loss?

NURSE

Colchis is lost, your husband isn't faithful,
and from all your wealth nothing survives.

MEDEA

Medea survives. In her you see the land and sea,
swords and fire and gods and thunderbolts.

NURSE

The king is to be feared.

MEDEA

My father was a king.

NURSE

Don't you fear his weapons?

MEDEA

Not even if they sprang from earth.[21]

NURSE

You'll die.

170

MEDEA

I want to.

NURSE

Flee!

MEDEA

I wish I never had.

NURSE

Medea—

MEDEA

—I will become her!

NURSE

You are a mother.

MEDEA

Thanks to whom, you see.

NURSE

Do you hesitate to flee?

MEDEA

I'll flee, but first I'll be avenged.

NURSE

An avenger will pursue you.

MEDEA

Perhaps I'll find delays for him.

NURSE

Don't say these things; give up your threats now, crazy one,
and stifle rage: adapt yourself to circumstance.

MEDEA

Fortune can take my wealth, but not my spirit.

(*Enter Creon and attendants.*)

—Whose banging makes the palace doors creak open?
It's Creon himself, puffed up with Greek authority!

CREON

Medea—that noxious child of Colchian Aeetes!

180 Has she not yet removed herself from my realm of Corinth?
She has some scheme: her trickery's familiar, as is her skill.
Who will she spare, or leave alone in peace?
I was prepared, myself, to kill this foulest pestilence
quickly and by the sword, but the prayers of my son-in-law
    won out.
I've let her live. Let her release this land from fear
and go away in safety. —She's coming at me fiercely,
she wants to talk more closely, with menace in her look.
Servants! Keep her away from contact and from getting close!
Tell her she must be quiet! Let her learn, though late,
to heed the orders of a king!

(*To Medea.*)

190 Be off at once,
remove at last your monstrous vile and savage self!

MEDEA

For what crime or fault of mine must exile be the penalty?

CREON

Ha, a blameless woman asks the reason for her banishment.

MEDEA

If you're passing judgment, learn the facts; if you're a king, give
orders.

CREON

Right or wrong, you have to bear a king's authority.

MEDEA

Unjust kingdoms never last forever.

CREON

Take your whines back to the Colchians.

MEDEA

I'm going, but let the man who brought me take me back.

CREON

You ask too late; my decree is final.

MEDEA

A decision made without one side being heard
cannot be just, even if the outcome's just.   200

CREON

I suppose you heard Pelias' side before he paid his penalty?
But go ahead and speak; such a noble cause should have a
chance.

MEDEA

How difficult it is to turn one's mind from anger
once riled up; how regal it's considered by one
who's grasped the scepter in his haughty hand
to continue on his chosen course—I learned this in my palace.
For though I'm now laid low by pitiable loss,
expelled, a supplicant, abandoned and alone, on every side
afflicted, I once was eminent thanks to my noble father,
and traced my famous lineage from my grandfather the Sun.   210
All the land made moist by Phasis' slow meandering,
all that the Scythian Pontus sees on its further side,

where waters from the marshes freshen the salt sea,
all the land bound by the banks of Thermadon, that fears
the unwed throngs armed with their crescent shields,
all this my father rules with kingly power.
I shone in regal beauty then, happy, nobleborn
and powerful; suitors sought to marry me, who now
themselves are sought. Fast-moving Fortune, headlong,
fickle, snatched me from my power, delivered me to exile.
Keep trusting in your kingdom, then, though skittish chance
delivers giant riches to this side and that! *This* is what a king
can do that's massive and magnificent, that time cannot remove:
help the wretched and protect the suppliant with a trusty home.
This is all I've taken with me from the realm
of Colchis: the fact *I* saved Greece's grandest glory,
its fabled flower, protectors of the Argive race and offspring
of the gods.[22] It's my gift that Orpheus is safe,
who soothes the stones with song and makes the forests follow;
Castor, Pollux are my gift of twins, as are the sons
of Boreas, and he who spots what's even far across
the Pontus, when he directs his gaze on it, Lynceus,
and all the Minyans too. I don't speak of these chieftains' chief
to whom nothing is owed: I don't bill *him* to anyone.
I brought the others back for you, but him alone for me.
Reproach me now, fling all my shameful acts at me:
I'll grant they're mine. But one crime only I confess to:
I brought the Argo back. Suppose that maidenhood had
    pleased me
as a girl, and to save my father's life: the whole of Greece
would go to ruin with its leaders. This son-in-law of yours
would be the first to fall at the brutal bullock's fiery breath.[23]
Let Fortune trample on my case as much as she would like;
I'm not sad I saved the majesty of so many kings.
Whatever benefit I gained from all this guilt
is in your hands. If you want to, sentence the defendant,
but give me back the man I killed for. I'm guilty, Creon, I
    admit it;

220

230

240

just as you knew then, when I touched your knees as suppliant
and sought protection at your guardian hand.
In this land I seek some nook, a resting place for misery,
a worthless hiding-hole. If you want to drive me from the city,   250
may some distant spot be granted to me in your realm.

CREON

I think I've demonstrated with no small clarity that I am not
the type to wield my power violently, nor stomp on
misery with a supercilious foot, by choosing as
my son-in-law an exile, and one in trouble, who shakes
with no small fear, since Acastus, king of Iolcos,
seeks him out for punishment and death.
He charges that his father—trembling with feeble age, and
heavy in his years—was put to death; that the dead man's
body was dismembered when his two loyal daughters,   260
snared by your duplicity, dared something most unloyal.
If you separate your case from his, Jason can
defend his own: no spilled blood stained his
innocence, his own hand never grasped the sword,
pure, he kept afar from fellowship with you.
You—you mastermind of evil acts, with
a woman's wickedness in daring everything,
a man's strength, and no mindfulness of reputation—
get out now, make clean my land, and take away
your deadly herbs. Free my citizens from fear,   270
settle in another land, disturb the deities there.

MEDEA

You force me to depart? Then as I go, give back to me my ship,
or give me back my mate. Why order me to flee alone?
I didn't come alone. If you're scared to endure wars,
expel us both from your preserve. Why draw distinctions
between two guilty parties? Pelias lies dead on *his* behalf, not
     mine.
Add to this my theft and flight, abandoning my father,
my brother chopped to bits, and what the husband's teaching

his new wife even now: none of this is mine. I took
the blame so many times, never acting for myself.

CREON

You should have long since gone. Why draw out the time with
talk?

MEDEA

As I leave I beg you, as a suppliant, for one last thing:
don't let the mother's guilt drag down her guiltless sons.

CREON

Go. I'll receive them like a parent in my fatherly embrace.

MEDEA

I pray you by the happy outcome of this royal union,
by your future hopes and the status of the realm,
which changing fortune agitates this way and that,
let me as I leave have but a brief delay,
to plant my final kisses on the children as a mother,
perhaps a dying one.

CREON

You ask for time to lay some trap!

MEDEA

What trap could be contrived in this small space of time?

CREON

No time is short enough to block the harm the wicked do.

MEDEA

You won't allow me in my grief a little time for tears?

CREON

Deep-rooted fear fights against your prayers—and yet—
I'll grant a single day for you to plan your exile.

MEDEA

A day's too much, you may prune something from it;
I'm in a hurry too.

CREON

Death will be your penalty,
if you don't leave the Isthmus before the sun brings up

the shining dawn. The wedding rites now summon me,
the day sacred to Hymenaeus calls me to prayer. 300

(*Exit Creon, Medea, and the Nurse; the Chorus enters.*)

CHORUS

He was far too daring, the man who first broke
the treacherous waves with so fragile a boat,
who glanced at the land he was leaving behind
and entrusted his life to the changeable winds;
who, cutting the seas on a dubious course,
could confer his trust to thin planks of wood,
too narrow a boundary drawn up between
the pathways of life and the pathways of death.
Not yet did anyone know constellations,
no use was being made of the stars 310
with which the high sky is painted;
not yet could a boat shun the rainy Hyades;[24]
or the rays of Capella the she-goat,[25]
or the wagon of Attica,[26] followed and steered by
its ploughman, the tardy old fellow Boötes;
not yet did the winds called Zephyr and Boreas
have names.
Tiphys dared unfurl his sails[27]
on the vast open sea,
and to write new laws for the winds: 320
now to pull tight the ropes on billowing sails,
now to capture the southern cross-winds
with a sheet set in front, now to fasten the yards
so they're safe at midmast,
now to tether them right at the top,
when the too-eager sailor is trying to catch
all the gusts, and the rubicund topsails
flutter above the tall canvas.
Bright were the ages our forefathers saw,
when deceit had been distanced afar. 330
Each of them, keeping to his shore alone,

unaspiringly aged on the land of his father;
rich with but little, they were
unversed in wealth, except for
the crops that their home soil bore.
The Thessalian ship confused all the rules
of a world formerly well-portioned out,
forcing the sea to bear lashings of oars,
and the ocean—once set apart—to become
a part of our fears.

340   That criminal ship paid an onerous price
as it sailed through a sequence of horrors,
when two peaks,[28] the gates to the infinite sea,
suddenly smashing from this side and that
groaned with a sort of heavenly sound,
and the sea caught between them
sprinkled the crags and even the clouds.[29]
Brave Tiphys paled and dropped all
the guide-ropes, with faltering hand;
Orpheus fell silent, his lyre now still
and the Argo itself lost its voice.

350   What about when the woman of Sicily's coast
beset with mad dogs encircling her waist,[30]
reared all her jaws open at once?
Who did not tremble in all of his limbs
at the multiple barking of one monster alone?
Or the time when those terrible plagues with
melodious tones soothed the Ausonian sea,[31]
when Thracian Orpheus
playing in counterpoint a Pierian lyre
almost compelled a Siren to follow—though

360   accustomed to hold back ships with her song?
What was the prize of this journey by sea?
The fleece made of gold
and Medea, an evil worse than the sea,[32]
rewards worthy of the first ship.

By our time the ocean has yielded, and obeys
all commands.
We don't need an Argo
built by the hand of Pallas Athena
coming home famous with kings at its oars.
Any old skiff can wander the deep.
Every boundary's gone, and
cities have put down their walls on new land.   370
The world marked by access has nothing
that stays in its previous place;
the Indian drinks the Araxes' cold water,
the Persians the Elbe and Rhine.
An era will come in late years
in which Ocean will loosen the chains
of the world, huge Earth will lie all exposed,
Tethys will show us new realms,[33]
and Thule won't be the far edge of land.

ACT 3

(Enter Medea and the Nurse.)

NURSE

Child, where are you rushing, as you leave the house at such   380
    a clip?
Stop and check your rage, control your frenzied dash.
—Like a confused maenad, when she raves
with the god inside her, and takes divinely driven steps
on the peak of snowy Pindus or the heights of Nysa,[34]
so she hastens back and forth with wild movements,
showing on her face the marks of frantic madness.
Her face is flushed, she's breathing heavily,
she shouts, her eyes are wet with floods of tears,
she smiles. Every sort of feeling finds a home in her.
She's at a loss, she's menacing, she seethes, she grieves,   390
    she groans.

To which side will her mind's weight sink? To what side assign
her threats? Where will that torrent break? Her rage is
   overflowing.
She doesn't mull an easy crime, nor one that's middling-hard;
she will surpass herself. I know the signs of that old rage.
Something large is looming, a savage cruel impious deed:
I see the face of Fury. May the gods disprove my fear!

MEDEA

(*To herself.*)

If you ask, poor wretch, what limit to impose on hate,
then imitate your love. The thought that I should tolerate
royal wedding-torches unavenged! Will this day pass in
   idleness,
400 a day sought for and granted with so much importuning?
While the centered earth will bear the balanced sky,
while the shining universe will cycle through fixed changes,
while the sands stay countless, while day will follow sun,
and the stars the moon, while the pole will spin the
   constellation
Bear and keep it dry, and rivers spill into the sea,
my fury for their punishment will never cease,
but always grow. What monstrousness of wild beasts,
what Scylla, what Charybdis draining Sicily's sea
and the Ausonian, what Etna overlying a
410 gasping Titan will seethe with threats as great?
No rapid-coursing river, nor the stormy sea,
nor the ocean wild with northwest gales, nor the force
of fire whipped up by wind, could check my impetus
and rage. I'll destroy and overturn all that exists.
Perhaps he feared Creon, war with the king of Thessaly?
But real love does not fear anyone.
—But say he yielded and surrendered under duress.
Still he surely could have met with me and comforted
his wife with final words. The fierce hero feared even this.
420 Certainly as son-in-law he had the chance to mitigate

the hour of exile; one day alone was given
for my two children. I don't lament the shortness of this time:
it allows for much. This day will perpetrate, will perpetrate
a deed all future time will talk about. I'll attack the gods
and shake the universe.

NURSE
   I beg you, mistress, control these feelings
stirred up by suffering, and moderate your anger.

MEDEA
   The only peace is if
I see all things destroyed together with my downfall;
let all things die with me. It feels good, as you go down, to take
  all with you.

NURSE
Think upon how many dangers there will be if you persist.
No one can attack the powerful yet remain safe.   430

              (*Enter Jason.*)

JASON
How hard fate always is to me, how harsh my lot—
rotten just the same when it's cruel and when it spares me.
God how often finds for me relief that's worse
than any danger it replaces! If I wanted to be loyal
to my deserving wife, I would have had to offer up
my head for execution; if I were disinclined to die,
I'd sadly have to break my vows. Fear didn't overcome our bond,
but anxious father-love: after all, the parents' death
would be followed by the children's. O holy Justice,
if you dwell within the skies, I summon your divinity   440
and call on it to witness: it was the sons who won over the father.
Why, even she, even if she's fierce of heart and hard to tame,
would dwell upon the children's good and not the marriage's—I
  think.
My mind's resolved to press her angered self with entreaties.
But look! She's seen me and leaps up, she rages,
she displays her hatred openly; all her anger's in her face.

Jason, I've fled before and I am fleeing. This isn't new,
changing my home. What's new is why I'm fleeing now:
I used to flee for you! I'm leaving, I'm going away,

450   a woman you compel to take flight from your home.
But to whom do you return me? Should I head for Phasis and
the Colchians, my father's realm and the fields soggy
with my brother's blood? To what countries would you have
    me go?
What seas are you pointing out? The gate to Pontus' strait,
through which I guided back a noble band of princes,
trailing an adulterer through the Clashing Rocks?
Should I make for your uncle's Iolcos,[35] or Tempe in Thessaly?
Whatever paths I opened up for you, I closed those for myself.
Where do you send me back to? You bid an exile into exile,

460   but you don't provide it. "Let her go": the royal son-in-law
    has spoken.
I object to none of it. Heap dreadful tortures on me:
I have earned them. Let the anger of the king oppress the
    whore
with bloody retribution, let him weight her arms with chains,
let him bury her, imprisoned, in a cave of endless night:
I'll suffer less than I deserve.

(Turning on Jason.)

    Ungrateful wretch!
Let your mind reflect upon the bullock's fiery breath,
and—among the savage terrors of that untamed race—
Aeetes' flaming beast in a field that spawned armed men,
and the weapons of a sudden enemy, when at my bidding

470   the earthborn soldiers fell in mutual slaughter.[36]
Add the far-sought spoils of Phrixus' ram,[37]
and the sleepless monster forced to yield his eyes
to novel slumber, and my brother, given up to death,
(in that single crime, a multiplicity of crime);

and, snared by my deceit, the daughters daring
to chop their aged father's limbs—he could not be revived.[38]
By your hopes for your sons and for a safe home,
by the monsters defeated and these hands which never I
spared for your sake, by the terrors we passed through,   480
by the sky and the sea, who witnessed our marriage,
show the suppliant pity, recompense me for your joy.
From the wealth which the Scythians steal from afar,
as far as the sun-darkened peoples of India,
treasures my crammed home can barely contain,
so that we festoon our orchards with gold, I took nothing
for exile but the limbs of my brother; and these too I spent
on you. You took the place of country, father, brother,
virtue. I married you with *this* dowry; return what is mine as
    I flee.

JASON

When hostile Creon wanted to destroy you,   490
my tears overcame him, and so he granted exile.

MEDEA

I thought it was a punishment; now I see that exile is a gift.

JASON

Make your escape while you still can go, get yourself away
from here; the rage of kings is always vehement.

MEDEA

        This is what you urge on me,
but it's for Creusa: you remove her hated rival.

JASON

Medea charges me with love?

MEDEA

        And murder and deceit.

JASON

But in the end, what crime can you accuse me of?

MEDEA

Whichever I committed.

JASON

     This is the final straw,
that I should be made guilty for your crimes as well.

MEDEA

500   They're yours, they're yours: whoever benefits from crime
committed it. They all condemn your wife as infamous:
it's yours alone to protect her, and name her innocent!
Let her who takes the blame for you be blameless in your eyes.

JASON

Life's a worthless gift if one's ashamed to take it.

MEDEA

There's no point in living if one's ashamed to take it.

JASON

Why don't you rather tame your heart, riled up in anger,
and make up with your sons?

MEDEA

     I disown, reject, renounce them!
Will Creusa provide brothers for *my* children?

JASON

A queen for sons of exiles, an advocate for the oppressed.

MEDEA

510   May such an evil day never arrive for the distressed,
a day to mix a noble line with one that's base,
the children of the Sun with those of Sisyphus.

JASON

What, in your misery you'd drag both of us to death?[39]
Leave, I beg you.

MEDEA

     Creon listened to my plea.

JASON

Tell me what I can do.

MEDEA

     On my behalf, even a crime.

JASON

Here a king, and there as well.[40]

MEDEA

There's a greater terror than even them:
Medea. Bring us together,[41] let us compete, let
Jason be the prize.

JASON

I yield, exhausted, to misfortune. You too
should fear fate's vagaries, which you've experienced often.

MEDEA

Every form of Fortune has always been beneath me.   520

JASON

Acastus presses me.

MEDEA

Creon's the closer enemy:
flee both of them. Medea does not make you arm yourself
against your spouse's father, nor stain yourself
with kindred blood: stay guiltless, flee with me.

JASON

And who'll fight back, if double wars beset us,
if Creon and Acastus unite their forces?

MEDEA

Throw in the Colchians, and Aeetes too as leader,
join Scythians to Pelasgians: I'll overwhelm them.

JASON

I'm afraid of lofty scepters.

MEDEA

Watch that you don't desire them.

JASON

Cut short this long discussion, in case it seems suspicious.   530

MEDEA

Now, highest Jupiter, thunder through the sky!
Extend your hand, prepare avenging flames,

break through the clouds and convulse all the world!
The hand that brandishes your weapons need not choose
between myself or him: whichever of us falls
will die guilty; the thunderbolt hurled at us
cannot stray from the mark.

JASON

>Start thinking sanely
and speak calmly. If any solace from my in-law's house
can ease your exile, ask for it now.

MEDEA

540 >As you well know, my mind can scorn, and generally does,
the wealth of kings. Just let me have my children
as companions to my flight, in whose embrace
I'll weep my tears. For you, new children are in store.

JASON

I confess I'd like to satisfy your pleas: but
paternal love forbids it. Neither the king himself
nor Acastus could make me endure *that*.
They are what I live for, they are the consolation
for a heart that's scorched by suffering. I could sooner
give up breath, or limbs, or light.

MEDEA

>*(Aside.)*

>He loves his sons that much?
550 >That's good—he's caught, the place to strike is clear.

>*(To Jason.)*

>But surely as I leave you'll let me offer them
some final guidance, and give a final hug.

>*(Jason nods.)*

>—I'm grateful. I ask this also in my last words,
if I rashly blurted anything in my distracted anger,
that it not linger in your mind. Let the memory

of a better me remain with you; let the words I said
in rage be canceled out.

JASON

    I've banished all of it from thought.
And I myself ask too, that you control your fiery mind
and behave quietly. Calm soothes unhappiness.

(Exit Jason.)

MEDEA

    He's left. And can this be? You walk out, forgetting me,   560
and all my many crimes? I've vanished from your memory?
I'll never vanish.

(To herself.)

    Come now: summon all your strength
and talents. The fruit of all your crimes is to believe
nothing is criminal. But there's hardly room to plot:
they're scared of me. Attack along the path where
none can fear anything. Come on, be daring now, begin
what Medea can do, and whatever she cannot.

(To the Nurse.)

You, my loyal nurse, companion of my sorrow
and of my changing fortunes, assist my cheerless plans.
I have a robe, a gift from my ethereal home,   570
the treasure of the realm, a pledge of parentage
the Sun gave to Aeetes. I also have a necklace
that gleams with woven gold, and a golden band
that shining gems adorn, which usually binds my hair.
Let our children carry these as my gifts to the bride,
but first let them be smeared and steeped by my black arts.
Let Hecate be summoned. Prepare the murderous rites.
Let altars be set up, let flames soon crackle in the house.

(Exit Medea and the Nurse; Enter Chorus.)

CHORUS

580

There's no force of fire, no force of gale winds,
no fearful force of a spear in midflight,
that matches a wife who's been robbed of her marriage,
when she burns and she hates:
Not when south wind brings mist-laden rains
in the winter and Danube rushes in torrents
and splits once-joined bridges, and strays
from its bed;
not when the Rhone hurtles into the deep
nor when Mount Haemus thaws,
its snows dissolved into streams, and

590

the sun now strong in midspring.
The flame that is kindled by fire is blind,
it shakes off control, refuses the reins,
does not fear death; it's eager to dash
right up to the swords.
Spare us, O gods: we ask for your pardon;
let the man who conquered the sea live unharmed.
But the lord of the deep is enraged
that the second kingdom is vanquished.[42]
The young man who dared to direct the

600

immortal chariot and forgot the paternal bounds,[43]
madly showered the heavens with flames
that he himself felt.
The way that is known costs no one too dear:
go where it's safe for earlier folk, and
don't violate, rash man, the sacrosanct
laws of the universe.
Any who handled the illustrious oars
of that too-daring ship, and ransacked from Pelion
the ample shade of its consecrate grove,[44]

610

who passed through the wandering rocks
and endured on the sea so many toils, then
tied mooring-ropes on a barbarous coast,
to return as thieves of foreigners' gold,

have atoned for the profaned rights of the sea
with a terrible death.
The ocean, provoked, demands restitution.
First of all, Tiphys, who tamed the deep sea,
abandoned the steering to a guide with no training.
Far from his family's country he lies
on an alien shore, lifeless and covered   620
by a trifling tomb and with ghosts he knows not.
Since then the city of Aulis, remembering the loss
of its king, holds back the boats in its delaying harbors;
they complain at their custody.
Orpheus, son of the lovely-voiced Muse,
at the sounds of whose strings and melodious pick
rivers stopped still, the winds didn't howl,
and birds ceased from their song and, with whole
forests in tow, came to pay court—
he lay torn into bits through Thracian fields,   630
while his head floated down the unhappy Hebrus;
he reached Styx and Tartarus, seen once before—
this time he would not return.
Hercules slew the sons of Aquilo,[45]
he murdered the son who had Neptune for father,
who used to take multiple shapes;[46]
but after he pacified both land and sea,
after he harrowed the realms of harsh Dis,
he lay, still alive, on a pyre on Oeta,
and surrendered his limbs to pitiless flames,   640
eaten up by the venom of two mingled bloods,[47]
the gift of his wife.
A fierce bristly boar laid Ancaeus low
with a thrust;[48] Meleager, impious, slew his mother's
own brother and died at the hand of a mother
outraged. They all deserved what they got:
but what crime did young Hylas atone for
with death, dragged down in safe waters, poor thing,
whom intrepid Hercules could not recover?

650	So go ahead, brave ones, plough through the sea,
	when even a wellspring is risky!
	A snake buried Idmon in Libya's sand dunes
	although he knew well the future:
	he told truth to all and was only false to himself.[49]
	Mopsus fell dead far from his Thebes.
	If he prophesied truly the future,
657	the husband of Thetis will wander in exile,[50]
661	while the son of Oileus, killed by lightning and sea,
600a	will pay back the price
600b	for his crimes and those of his father.
658	Nauplius,[51] planning a treacherous beacon
659	to wreak harm on Greeks, will tumble headfirst
662	into the sea; Alcestis will offer her life for her spouse,
	redeeming the death of her husband from Pherae.[52]
	Even Pelias, who ordered the plunder and booty
	of gold to be fetched by that first of all ships,
	was boiled as he wandered in restricted waters.[53]
	By now you've avenged the sea quite enough;
	spare a man under orders, O gods.

(Exit Chorus.)

ACT 4

(Enter the Nurse.)

NURSE

670	My soul fears and trembles: a huge atrocity is near.
	It's monstrous how her anger grows and fans
	itself afire and renews its past brutality.
	I've often seen her raging and taking on the gods,
	drawing down the sky: she's planning something
	greater, an abomination worse than these. After rushing out
	with frantic steps and getting to her deadly inner sanctum,
	she pours out all her resources, and prepares the things
	that even she has feared so far, and sets in place
	an entire host of evils, secret, hidden, and obscure.

With her left hand on the altar, she invokes a cursed rite,   680
and calls down all the monsters which the sand
of burning Libya births, and which the Taurus,
icy with the Arctic frost, locks in eternal snow,
and everything ill-omened. Drawn by magic spells
a scaly throng approaches, abandoning their lairs.
Here a savage serpent drags along its immense bulk,
flickers its forked tongue and looks for a victim
to kill; it freezes when it hears the spell,
and twists its swollen body into heaped-up coils
and forces it in a spiral. "These evils are but small," she says,   690
"paltry are the weapons forged by the earth's interior.
I'll look for poison from the heavens. It's long since time
to stir up something bigger than ordinary crime.
Let Draco come down here, that snake who sprawls
like a gigantic river-course, whose massive coils
two wild beasts know—the Greater and the Lesser Bear—
(the greater useful to the Greeks, the lesser to Sidonians);[54]
let Ophiuchus now at last loosen his grip and
permit that the venom flow;[55] let Python too attend
my chant, who dared insult twin deities,[56] and   700
Hydra too, with all the snakes that Hercules
hacked off, which grew back where he cut them.
You too abandon Colchis and come here, wakeful
snake, whom my chants first lulled to sleep."
Once she'd summoned every kind of serpent,
she heaped together all the banes of toxic plants:
whichever ones Mount Eryx lets grow on its rocks,[57]
those which the Caucasus begets on ridges covered
by perpetual snow and sprinkled by Prometheus' blood,
and those with which the wealthy Arabs smear their arrows,   710
as do the Medes, fierce with bows, and light-armed Parthians;
or the sap which Suebian wives cull under winter's sky,
a tribe that's famous for the forests of their homeland,[58]
or what the Earth brings forth in nesting time in spring
or when the freezing winter has already stripped the leafage

of the groves, and all is bound by snowy cold;
and any plant that's toxic in its deadly flowers,
and the dreadful juice that breeds the cause of harm
in twisted roots: all these she wields within her hands.
Mount Athos in Thessaly supplied some of these banes,
huge Pindus others, others still her bloody sickle cropped of
their tender leaves upon the ridges of Pangaeus.[59]
Some the Tigris fed, which hides its deep stream
    underground;
some the Danube, some the gem-rich Hydaspes
traversing arid regions with its lukewarm waters,[60]
some the Baetis river, which gave its land a name,[61]
and beats the west Atlantic with its languid flow.
This plant felt the knife, while Phoebus was preparing day,
the stalk of another was sliced in deepest night,
this one's stem was snipped by fingernail and spell.
She snatches up the lethal herbs and squeezes out
the venom of the snakes, mixes in ill-omened birds,
a brooding owl's heart and the disemboweled guts
of a living screecher owl. Certain things this artisan
of crime keeps separate: some have fire's devouring force,
some the chilly iciness of numbing cold.
She adds to the poisons words that should be feared
no less than them. Look! I hear her maddened steps,
her incantations. The world shudders at her opening words.

(*Enter Medea.*)

MEDEA

I call upon the voiceless throng, and you, gods of the dead,
and Chaos without sight and the shaded home of gloomy
    Dis, and
the caves of ugly Death, bound by the banks of Tartarus.
Ghosts: your punishment's suspended. Run to the bridal
    chamber:
the wheel that twists the limbs may stop, Ixion may touch the
    ground,

Tantalus may gulp Pirene's stream without a care.⁶² May one
   alone
receive worse punishment—my in-law Creon, the new wife's
   father.
May the slick stone roll his forebear Sisyphus back down the
   rocks.
You too, daughters of Danaus,⁶³ whom pointless toil derides
with leaky pitchers, gather here: this day demands your hands.
And come, O moon, the star of night,⁶⁴ summoned by my   750
   rites,
showing your most hostile face, a threat in every look.
For you I have loosened my hair from its band in the way of
   my folk,
and circled through desolate groves with no shoes on my feet;
summoned the moisture from waterless clouds
and forced the sea down to its bed; the Ocean recalled
its ponderous waves, since its tides were defeated;
the laws of the heavens were thrown into confusion, the world
saw stars at the same time as sun, and you Bears
dipped into the forbidden sea. I warped the sequence of
   seasons:
the summertime earth turned frosty under my spell,⁶⁵   760
Ceres was forced to behold winter harvests.
Phasis' strong current flew back to its source;
the Danube, divided in so many deltas, checked
stubborn waves and was still along every bank.
Without a murmur of wind, waves have resounded,
the sea's madly swollen; the home of the primeval forest
has lost all its shade at my voice's command.
Phoebus has stopped in midcourse, giving up on the day,
the Hyades are shaken because of my spells and slip down.
The time has come, Phoebe, to attend your sacred rites.   770

                                    (*In a chant.*)

I offer to you these garlands woven with butcherous hands
entwined with nine serpents,

I offer to you these snake-parts which disloyal Typhoeus wore,[66]
who undermined Jupiter's realm.
Here is the blood which the treacherous ferryman
Nessus donated while dying;[67]
the pyre on Mount Oeta expired with these embers
which soaked up Hercules' blood-rot;
you see the torch of avenging Althaea, loving as sister,
unloving as wife;
a Harpy abandoned these feathers in her hard-to-reach lair
when she fled from the Argonaut Zetes.
To these add the plumes of the wounded Stymphlian, man-
    eating bird,
pierced by the poisonous arrows from Lerna.
You've resounded, O altars: I note that my tripods
have shaken, showing the goddess' favor.
I see Trivia's hastening chariot,[68]
not the one she drives through the night,
bright with full face
but the one of a gloomier aspect she drives when,
sallow and harried by Thessalian threats
she skirts the sky's edge with reins held more tightly.
Like this, pour your desolate light through the air,
pale-faced, scare people with new-fangled horror,
let precious Corinthian cymbals
clang in your aid, Dictynna.[69]
For you, I perform the consecrate rites
on sod soaking with blood,
for you, the torch snatched from the midst of the pyre
keeps up its nocturnal flame,
for you, I have spoken, bending my neck and tossing my head,
for you, a funereal fillet's laid out
to bind my loose hair,
for you, I brandish an ill-omened branch
from the waters of Styx,
for you, I will beat my arms with the ritual blade,

780

790

800

my breasts exposed, like a Maenad.
Let my blood flow on the altar:
Hands! Accustom yourselves to unsheathing the knife,
to allowing loved blood to be spilled.   810
Striking myself, I've offered my own sacred fluid.
But if, Hecate, you complain that you're summoned
by my prayers too often, forgive me, I beg.
The reason I call on your bows overmuch
is one and the same,
always Jason.
Now you: poison the clothes of Creusa
so the moment she dresses herself, a flame
slowly spreading will burn her down to her marrow.
Enclosed in a tawny gold box lurks hidden   820
a flame which Prometheus gave me,
who atones for his theft from the sky with
a regrowing liver. He taught me to
store up its strength with his art, and Mulciber too[70]
gave me fire hid in finely ground sulfur,
and from Phaethon my kinsman I took
the flames of live lightning.
I have gifts received from Chimaera's midsection,[71]
I have flames I took from the bull's
toasted throat,   830
which, mixed with the bile of Medusa,
I have ordered to hide its power to harm.
Add goads, Hecate, to these poisons,
And conceal in my gifts the seedlings of fire:
let them fool the vision and ignore the touch;
let heat enter her heart and her veins,
let her limbs melt away and her bones become smoky,
let the new bride outshine the nuptial torches
with her own blazing hair.
My prayers are heard: three times has bold   840
Hecate howled and sent out

sacred flames from her grief-bringing torch.
The power of the potion is ready. Call here your sons, so
through them you may send precious gifts for the bride.

(*Enter the sons.*)

Go, children go, born of an ill-fated mother,
win over with gifts and much prayer
your mistress and step-mother. Leave, and quickly
come home, letting me cherish one final hug.

(*Exit the Nurse, Medea and the sons; Enter Chorus.*)

CHORUS

What inhuman love
850   drives headlong the blood-ridden
maenad? With what ungovernedExit
rage does she prepare her crime?
Her face, riled up, is set firm
in fury; shaking her head with wild
motion, she haughtily threatens
even the king.
Who'd think her an exile?
Her cheeks blaze and flush red,
then pallor routs crimson.
860   No color stays long
on her changing complexion.
She rushes this way and that,
as a tigress deprived of her cubs
roams through the jungles by Ganges
at a mad pace.
How to check her anger,
Medea doesn't know; her love's the same.
Now her love and her anger have joined
their causes; what will come next?
870   When will this cursed woman of Colchis
depart from Pelasgian fields and release
both the kingdom and king from their fear?

Phoebe, deliver your chariot *now*,
don't let reins slow you down;
let merciful darkness envelop the light,
let Hesperus, bringer of night,
submerge this terrible day.

ACT 5

(Enter the Messenger.)

MESSENGER
Everything's over! The kingdom has fallen!
Father and daughter lie dead, their ashes commingled!   880

CHORUS
Caught by what trick?!

MESSENGER
    The one that always catches them:
By gifts!

CHORUS
    What sort of trickery could lie in *them?*

MESSENGER
I'm stunned at it myself, and even now the evil's done,
I hardly think it possible.

CHORUS
    What was the means of destruction?

NUNTIUS
A greedy fire rages on command, invading every corner of
the palace; the entire house has perished,
we're worried for the city.

CHORUS
    We need water for the flames!

MESSENGER
This too is amazing in this catastrophe:
the water feeds the flames, and the more the fire's checked,
the more it burns; it exploits the defences!   890

(The messenger and Chorus exit; Medea and the Nurse enter.)

NURSE

Get out of the land of Pelops, quick, Medea,
make for any place you can, and rush!

MEDEA

You think that *I* should flee? If I had fled before,
I would return for this. I'm watching new-style nuptials!

(To herself.)

Why are you faltering, my mind? Follow up this happy start!
That scrap of vengeance you enjoy—how small it is!
You still love him, insane woman, if it's enough for you
that Jason's single. Seek out the sort of punishment
that's most unusual, and now prepare yourself accordingly.
900   Every sense of right must yield, honor, driven out, must go;
vengeance taken by pure hands is insignificant.
Apply yourself to rage and goad your sluggish self,
and wildly, deeply, drink from the bottom of your heart
your former violence. The crimes committed up to now,
let's call "love of family." Come on! I'll make them see
how paltry were the crimes I did for him, and of
what common stamp. My rage was simply practicing
with those. What great deed could unskilled hands
dare undertake, or the fury of a girl?
910   Now I am *Medea*: my talent's grown through suffering.
I'm glad—so glad—I ripped my brother's head off,
I'm glad I hacked his limbs up and robbed my father
of his secret treasure, I'm glad I gave those daughters
means for their father's murder. Seek inspiration,
anger: you won't bring unskilled hands to any crime.
Where then are you heading, fury, and what weapons
are you aiming at the faithless enemy? The mind inside me
has fixed upon some savagery, but doesn't dare confess it
to itself. Fool that I am! —I went too fast. I wish
920   my enemy had fathered some children
by his whore! Those you had by him now have Creusa

as their mother. This line of vengeance pleases me,
and rightly so: I must prepare the ultimate in crime
with great resolve: you children who were mine before,
pay the price for your father's culpability.

(Recoiling from her thoughts.)

Horror's struck my core, my body's numb with cold,
my heart has lurched. My anger has retreated,
the wife's expelled and all the mother reinstated.
Should *I* pour out the lifeblood of my children and
my offspring? Mad fury, keep to better thoughts!   930
Let that unknown crime, that vile abomination,
be distant from me too. What crime will the poor boys pay for?
Their crime is having Jason as their father; a worse crime still,
Medea as their mother. Let them perish—they're no longer
    mine.
No, let them die *because* they're mine. They're free of guilt and
    blame,
they're innocent, I grant: so was my brother.
Why do you vacillate, my mind? Why do tears wet my face,
and as I waver, why does rage now pull me one way, and love now
in another? Ambivalent emotions drive me in all directions—
like when powerful winds wage war with one another,   940
and clashing waves drive the sea two ways at once,
and the ocean seethes in chaos: this is how my heart
is carried on the tide: rage routs my mother-love,
and mother-love routs rage. Anger, yield to love!
Here, sweet children, sole consolation of a shattered
home, come here, enclose me in a tight
embrace. Let your father have you safe and sound,
as long as your mother may as well. But exile and escape bear
    down on me:
all too soon they will be torn away and snatched from my
    embrace,
weeping and lamenting. Let them be lost to the kisses of   950
    their father,

as to their mother's. My fury swells again,
my hatred seethes, the ancient Erinys calls once again
for my unwilling hand. Anger: where you lead, I follow.
I wish that proud Niobe's throng of kids had issued
from my womb, and that I'd borne and parented
twice times seven offspring! I've been too barren for revenge.
And yet I've produced two—one each for my father and my
    brother.
Where is that maddened band of Furies heading?
Who are they looking for? For whom are they preparing fiery
    blows?
At whom does the hellish throng thrust its bloody
torches? There's a huge snake wound around a lashing whip
that's hissing. Who's Megaera hunting down with her hateful
bludgeon?[72] Whose ghost approaches, indistinct, his limbs
all disconnected? It's my brother! He wants justice!
We will provide it—all of us. Stab your torches in my eyes,
butcher me and burn me—I bare my chest, look, to the Furies.
Brother: tell the vengeful goddesses to leave me be,
and to return with minds at rest down to the shades,
to leave me to myself. Use this hand of mine
that's drawn the sword. With this victim I pacify
your ghost.

(She kills the first son.)

    What's that sudden clamor?
Weapons are prepared, they're coming here to kill me.
I'll clamber up the high roof of our house, now that
the killing has begun.

(To the living son.)

    You, come up here now with me.

(To the dead son.)

I'll take your corpse away with me as well.
Come on, now, my mind: you shouldn't waste your heroism
where it can't be seen; let the people praise your handiwork!

(*Medea climbs onto the roof with the corpse, dragging
the remaining son along. Jason enters with an armed guard.*)

JASON

All you faithful folk who mourn the royal family's fall,
rally here, so we can seize the perpetrator
of this grisly crime. Over here! Bring your weapons over   980
here,
brave party of armed men, raze the building to the ground!

MEDEA

Already I've regained my scepter, brother, father,
and the Colchians possess the spoil of the golden ram.
My kingdom has come back, my stolen virginity.
O gods benign at last, O time of celebration,
O wedding day! Go: your crime has been completed—
but not your vengeance yet. Finish it, while you're still at work!
Why do you delay now, my soul? Why hesitate? Has your
mighty fury flagged already? I repent of what I did, it's
shameful!
Wretch, what have I done? —Wretch? I may repent, but still   990
I did it. A massive pleasure's creeping over me, though I resist
—and look, it grows! I was lacking this one thing,
that man as spectator. I now consider nothing done:
any crime I did without him was a waste.

JASON

Look, there she is, looming over us from the roof's very edge.
Someone bring a torch here quick, so that she can fall, burnt
up by her own flames.

MEDEA

Heap up a final pyre, Jason,
for your sons, and build a burial mound for them.

Already your wife and her father have what's owed
1000   the dead, laid in earth by me. This son has met his end,
this one will die a matching death, and while you watch.

JASON

By every god, by the exile that we shared, and by
our marriage bed, which my vows have not betrayed,
now spare our son. If there is any crime, it's mine:
I consign myself to death: sacrifice this guilty head.

MEDEA

Where you resist it, where it hurts—that's where
I'll plunge the sword. Go on, you swaggerer,
seek out virgins' beds, abandon mothers.

JASON

        One boy is punishment enough!

MEDEA

If my hand were sated with a single death,
1010   it would have aimed at none. And even if I slaughter two,
the number's still too limited to satisfy my pain.
If some fetus from our love still lurks inside this mother,
I'll probe my womb by sword and abort it with the steel.

JASON

I won't beg any further—just finish what you started.
Give up this prolongation of my punishment, I beg you.

MEDEA

Enjoy your drawn-out crime, my rage, and do not rush.
The day is mine: I'm using up the time I was allotted.

JASON

You monster! Kill *me*!

MEDEA

        Your request is one for mercy.

(She kills the second son.)

1020   All's well, it's over. I had no more which I could sacrifice
for you, my rage. Jason, lift your swollen eyes up here,

thankless man. Do you recognize your wife?
This is how I always get away. A path lies open to the heavens:
twin serpents bend their scaly necks to fit
the chariot yoke. Retrieve your sons now, father;
I'll ride through the winds in my wing-borne chariot.

JASON

Ride on high through the heaven's lofty void—
and bear witness where you go that the gods do not exist.

The Phoenician Women

The play starts just after Oedipus, king of Thebes, learns the terrible truth about himself: he caused the plague that has devastated Thebes by unwittingly killing his father Laius and marrying his mother Jocasta. In the version of Sophocles (known as *Oedipus the King*, *Oedipus Tyrannus*, or *Oedipus Rex*), Jocasta commits suicide and Oedipus blinds himself, leaving Creon as the ruler of Thebes. In this version, however, Jocasta is still alive and will try to stop the imminent battle between her two sons. Oedipus meanwhile has gone into voluntary exile.

As Seneca's drama opens, Oedipus is wandering in the wild, blind and in exile, accompanied only by his daughter Antigone. He wants to die, but Antigone points out that real heroism under such terrible circumstances is to stay alive. In addition, he must stay alive to control his two sons, who are fighting each other for control of Thebes in Oedipus' absence. However, when a messenger from Thebes arrives to enlist his help, he rejects the request and chooses to stay in the wild countryside.

Meanwhile, Jocasta looks down upon the battle lines from the ramparts of Thebes and contemplates her dilemma—a son on either side! She eventually decides to descend to intervene between the two brothers. She pleads with both of them in turn, but neither will give up his position, and at this point the play cuts off abruptly.

Introduction

SUSANNA BRAUND

Seneca's *Phoenician Women* (*Phoenissae* in Latin) is an oddity. First of all, the play is far from complete: it has no choral odes at all and the surviving 664 lines form only a couple of episodes, with two changes of scene. It has even been argued that what survives is actually the openings of two different plays (by Adolf Paul; reported in Frank 1995, 7). Secondly, there are no Phoenician women in the play as it stands. The title relates to the identity of the chorus that the play would have had were it complete, as Euripides' *Phoenician Women* shows. It is, then, a fragment of a play, and it is, perhaps unsurprisingly, the most neglected of Seneca's dramas. That said, it still deserves attention because it is part of the Oedipus story and because it exercised an influence on later European literature.

Euripides' *Phoenician Women* is the longest surviving Greek tragedy and covers a good deal of this material, starting with the quarrel between Eteocles and Polynices, then portraying the attack on Thebes by Polynices and the Argive army, followed by the single combat between the brothers which results in their mutual slaughter and in turn precipitates Jocasta's suicide. Creon, who in this play has just lost his younger son Menoeceus as a voluntary sacrifice to preserve the city, now issues his decree forbidding the burial of Polynices' corpse. At the end of the play, Creon banishes Oedipus, and Antigone defies Creon's instruction to marry his other son Haemon. Instead, she departs into exile with Oedipus, vowing that she will return to bury Polynices.

The title of Euripides' play derives from the chorus of women from Phoenicia (modern Lebanon) who are on their way from Tyre to Delphi as dedications at Apollo's temple there. They play no part in the action beyond observing the events that unfold at Thebes. Although it is far from certain that Seneca was using Greek tragedies as his models or sources (as Tarrant [1978] argues), it seems likely that

Seneca planned to use the same chorus as in Euripides' play. And yet, this fragmentary play has two different titles in the two manuscript traditions of Seneca's tragedies: the manuscripts collectively designated as E call it *Phoenissae* while the A manuscripts call it *Thebais*, meaning "Theban play." Seneca may also have been influenced by a treatment of the story by Accius (c. 170–86 BCE), the leading Roman tragedian of the Roman Republic. The surviving fragments of his *Phoenician Women* (about twenty lines only) depict Oedipus and Jocasta still alive in Thebes during the battle between Eteocles and Polynices.

We should note that the *Phoenician Women* may well have been Seneca's last play, which might explain its incomplete state.[1] The incomplete text might be attributed to damage during transmission, but the lack of choral odes suggests more powerfully that Seneca died or set the play aside before he could complete it. There are other indications of incompleteness. For example, Antigone's remark at 417–18,

> And look, you can believe they've been affected by my tears,
> so slowly does the force arrive with weapons held at rest,

might imply that Antigone has already attempted to plead with her brothers, yet no fragment of this episode survives.

The portion of the Oedipus story depicted in Seneca's play is organized into perhaps two or three episodes involving two changes of scene. In the first episode (1–362), Oedipus and Antigone deliver long speeches in which they strike opposing positions. Oedipus starts by trying to dismiss Antigone so that he can seek death on Mount Cithaeron, where he was abandoned as a baby, but Antigone insists on accompanying him, whatever lies ahead: "If you die, then I precede you; if you live, I follow" (76). Oedipus persists in his aim, which is framed in the Stoicizing language of self-determination typical of Seneca (103–5):

> Young girl, stop trying: power over my own life and death
> resides with *me*. I've left my kingdom willingly;
> my kingdom of myself I keep.

He repeats the idea of self-sufficiency in death later in the same long speech (151–53):

> Death is everywhere. God has made this excellent
> provision: anyone can rob you of your life, but no one
> of your death. A thousand routes lie open.

In reply, Antigone tries to redefine heroism, saying that it consists in *not* feeling resentment or giving up in the face of misfortune. But despite her argument that he is actually innocent, she cannot reduce Oedipus' self-loathing for the awful crimes he has committed. Her final argument for Oedipus to stay alive is that he alone can stop his sons from fighting with each other. Although Oedipus initially rejects this idea, he seems to weaken in response to Antigone's tears and offers to obey her commands (308–19). But when a messenger arrives to summon Oedipus to help preserve Thebes from his sons, Oedipus flies into a rage (352–55):

> My spirit swells with rage, resentment seethes, ever greater.
> What I desire's beyond the random scope
> of young men's madness. Warfare between citizens
> is not enough: I want brother to fight with brother.

He even envisages the possibility that, as a still worse crime, they might follow in his footsteps and commit incest on Jocasta (356–58). He then withdraws into hiding in the wild countryside to await events in Thebes.

In the next episode (363–64, if this is a single episode), we meet Jocasta, who in this version is still alive, on the ramparts of Thebes looking down at the battlefield and lamenting her dilemma (377–82):

> I don't know what to choose or to support.
> He [Polynices] wants his kingdom back: his case is good, but
>   not his way
> of seeking it. As their mother, what should be my prayers?
> On either side I see a son: there's nothing I can loyally do
> with loyalty intact. My blessing
> to the one will to the other be a curse.

An attendant, seconded by Antigone, interrupts her inward self-pitying and urges her to go down and intervene before the fighting commences, and Jocasta decides to do so. There follows an odd moment in which first Jocasta expresses the wish to move from the battlements to the battlefield, and then, in a moment of what seems to be magic realism, she is transported in real time down among the troops (420–35):

> What whirling wind will carry me through airy breezes,
> transporting me in the mad storm's maelstrom?
> What Sphinx or what Stymphalian bird, its black cloud
> curtaining the daylight, will take me flying high on greedy
>   wings?
> What Harpy, watching over the cruel king's hunger,
> will race me through the high paths of the air
> and hurl me down between the battle lines?

This change of scene is unusual and one might have expected the two episodes to have been separated by a choral ode.[2]

The next episode begins with Jocasta inviting both sides to target her (443–44):

> Point your weapons and fires at *me*, let all the warriors
> as one make *me* their target. . . .

She tries to dissuade her sons from fighting, initially by persuading them both to disarm and then by engaging in shorter bursts of dialogue, first with Polynices and then with Eteocles. In the course of this dialogue, as one of her arguments, she imagines the sack of Thebes in terms strongly redolent of the many representations in Greco-Roman tragedy of the sack of Troy (571–85). Neither her favored Polynices (she stated her bias earlier at 383–86) nor the ruling Eteocles shows himself in a good light. Polynices is desperate to hold power of some kind (586–98), and Eteocles voices maxims about power which echo the tyrants in Seneca's earlier plays—for example (654–56):

The man afraid of hatred has no desire to rule:
god, the founder of the world, joined together these two things:
power and hatred.

And "The man who longs for adoration rules with feeble hand" (659);
likewise, "Power's a handsome purchase at any price" (664). At this
point, amid a typically Senecan exploration of the nature of kingship
and tyranny, the text breaks off.

I noted above that Seneca's play covers some of the same ground
as earlier tragedians, but this is not to claim direct or profound influence. It is important to remember that there were many other
treatments of the Oedipus story in ancient literature, including in
the Greek epic cycle, which have not survived and which may have
influenced Seneca. Ideas that may come from other strands in the
tradition include the idea that Oedipus might commit incest on
Antigone (49–50) and Jocasta's decision to position herself as a human buffer between her two sons on the battlefield (407–14). It is
also possible that Seneca was influenced by patterns or story lines
in other texts in terms of how he frames his material here. For example, it has been suggested that the way that Seneca's Jocasta tries
to prevent Eteocles and Polynices from fighting might be prompted
by the Roman historian Livy's narrative of Coriolanus, in which his
mother Veturia persuades him not to attack Rome (Livy 2.40).

That said, it is equally possible that the novel elements are Seneca's own inventions or twists. The larger idea of combining the two
strands of the legend, that of Oedipus and Antigone in exile and of
the conflict between his sons, could easily be Seneca's. So too the very
specific idea that occurs as the climax to Oedipus' crazed catalogue
of crimes that he urges his sons to commit, where he appears to
propose incest with their mother (356–58, as seen by Marica Frank
and Elaine Fantham [1983, 65]); perhaps the play went on to explore
that idea, given that the text breaks off leaving Jocasta in dialogue
with her two hostile sons.

A highly unusual feature in the *Phoenician Women* is that characters do not address one another by name. For example (36–39):

Carry out my father's order,
now my mother's too. My mind is eager to perform the ancient
punishment. My daughter, why do you detain me, chained
by love abhorrent? Why detain me? My father summons.

The closest case to an exception comes at line 554, where Jocasta refers
to Oedipus by name while she is addressing Polynices. Instead, characters indicate their kin relationship when addressing one another
and speaking of one another. The incidence of the words "daughter,"
"son," "parent," "mother," "father," "wife," "husband," "brother," and
"sister" is more intense than in any other play of Seneca's. Indeed,
Marica Frank in her commentary calculates the incidence of familial
terms as once every 4.2 lines; the next highest incidence is once every
7.2 lines (1995, 258). As she writes, the effect is "to sustain the theme
of the genetic chaos which reigns in the Theban royal house" (1995,
78). This emerges in extreme form when the blind Oedipus expresses
his abhorrence of any familial language at all (224–25):

Does my ear hear any sounds
which might include the name of child and parent?

Connected with this is the theme expressed repeatedly by the Latin
noun *pietas* and its cognates, the adjectives *pius* and *impius*, words
which occur no less than seventeen times in the play. This quintes-
sentially Roman concept, which lies at the heart of Virgil's *Aeneid*,
has no direct equivalent in English, but involves a complex of ideas
concerning the obligations due to gods, parents, and fatherland. The
noun *pietas* can be translated by words such as "devotion" or "loyalty."
I have used both of these words in my translation, along with "love,"
"natural love," "family love," and "sacred love." And I have translated
the adjectives *pius* and *impius* as "good" and "wicked," "religious" and
"irreligious." In using this root so insistently, Seneca is clearly interested in exploring appropriate and inappropriate familial affections.
Tellingly, in his 1580 play *Antigone ou La Piété* (*Antigone or Piety*), the
French tragedian Robert Garnier built his conception of the role of
Antigone primarily on Seneca's *Phoenician Women* and on the Roman idea of piety.

In his *Phoenician Women*, Seneca appears to revisit themes that he elaborated in his much earlier *Oedipus*. Rather wonderfully, Seneca has Oedipus construct himself as a new Sphinx who propounds a new riddle (131–39):

> That cruel scourge of Thebes,
> combining grief-producing words in hidden measures,
> what such riddle did she pose, so hard to solve?
> "A son-in-law to his own grandfather, rival to his own father,
> to his own children brother, to his own brothers father;
> a grandmother in a single birthing bearing children for her
>   husband,
> for herself grandchildren too." Who can disentangle such
>   monstrosities?
> Even I, who won the prize for conquering the Sphinx,
> will falter, slow interpreter of my own fate.

Though neglected these days, the play exerted a significant influence on European literature. George Steiner observes in his important book *Antigones* that Seneca's *Phoenician Women* was "one of the most often imitated texts in the history of western drama" (Steiner 1984, 139). After Seneca, Steiner says, "epic or rhetorical-dramatic variants on the Theban cycle, such as in the twelfth-century *Roman de Thèbes*, in Boccaccio's *Teseida*, and its two English imitations, Chaucer's 'Knight's Tale' and Lydgate's 'The Story of Thebes,' contain distant elements of Sophocles, but derive primarily from the *Phoenician Women*" (181). Another scholar, Simone Fraisse, remarks of the opening of the play that its "grandiloquent dialogue between Oedipus and Antigone" was "a scene which created a strong impression on Renaissance humanists" (Fraisse 1974, 15), including on Robert Garnier. A close examination of Garnier's *Antigone ou La Piété* (1580) alongside Seneca's *Phoenician Women* demonstrates that both plays are constructed as a series of static tableaux within which the characters engage in debates with one another or at times with themselves (see Braund 2017). This is one of many cases of the special role of the Oedipus myth in French literature (see Braund 2016, 94–108).

Suggested Reading

Braund, Susanna. 2016. *Seneca: Oedipus*. London.

———. 2017. "Tableaux and Spectacles: Appreciation of Senecan Tragedy by European Dramatists of the Sixteenth and Seventeenth Centuries." In "Senecan Poetics," edited by Mike Sampson and Chris Trinacty. Special edition of *Ramus*. (Forthcoming.)

Davis, Peter J. 1991. "Fate and Human Responsibility in Seneca's *Oedipus*." *Latomus* 50: 150–63.

Fantham, Elaine, 1983. "*Nihil iam iura naturae valent*: Incest and Fratricide in Seneca's *Phoenissae*." In *Seneca Tragicus: Ramus Essays on Senecan Drama*. Edited by A. J. Boyle, 61–76. Berwick.

Fitch, John G. 1981. "Sense-Pause and Relative Dating in Seneca, Sophocles and Shakespeare." *American Journal of Philology* 102: 289–307

Fraisse, Simone. 1974. *Le mythe d'Antigone*. Paris.

Frank, Marica, ed. 1995. *Phoenissae: Introduction and Commentary*. Leiden.

Steiner, George. 1984. *Antigones*. Oxford.

Tarrant, Richard J. 1978. 'Senecan Drama and Its Antecedents." *Harvard Studies in Classical Philology* 82: 213–63.

Phoenissae

LUCIUS ANNAEUS SENECA

TRANSLATED BY SUSANNA BRAUND

DRAMATIS PERSONAE

OEDIPUS, blinded former king of Thebes

ANTIGONE, his daughter

MESSENGER from Thebes

JOCASTA, mother and wife of Oedipus

ATTENDANT of Jocasta

POLYNICES and ETEOCLES, Oedipus' sons, who both want to
rule Thebes

*The action is initially set in the countryside around Thebes. The second half
of the play takes place on the battlefield near the city walls.*

(*Oedipus and Antigone enter.*)

OEDIPUS

Rudder of your blinded parent, your weary father's
only comfort—Daughter!—it means so much to have produced
   you,
no matter how it happened: now, desert your luckless father!
Why steer my wandering step to make it straight?
Let me stumble. On my own I'll better find the path
I seek, a path to extricate me from this life
and to relieve the sky and earth of looking at this
monstrosity. How little I accomplished with this hand of mine.
The light that witnessed my offence is invisible to me,
but *I* am visible. From now on, drop your clinging hand   10
and let my blind foot travel where it will.
I'll go, I'll go where my Cithaeron stretches out
his shorn-off crags,[1] where swift Actaeon
after roving through the rocky mountain lay

as strange prey for his own dogs,[2] where through the dusky
    grove
and shady valley's forest a mother led her sisters
roused by the god and then, delighting in her evil act,
impaled the head on shaking thyrsus and put it on parade.[3]
Or where Zethus' racing bullock dragged along
the hated body, where through bristling brambles
blood betrays the rampage of the bull, ferocious.[4]
Or where Ino's cliff with its immeasurable summit
looms above deep waters,[5] where a mother, shunning
one strange crime, performed another, and leapt into the strait
to drown her son and self: blessed are those
granted such good mothers by a better fortune.
In that forest is another place that's *mine*,
which demands my presence: there I'll head with urgent pace.
My footsteps will not falter—that's my destination,
bereft of any guide. Why keep my own place waiting?
Cithaeron, give me back my death, restore to me
that lodging-place of mine, so that as an old man I can die
where I should have as a baby. Recuperate the punishment
    of old.
Ever bloody, savage, cruel, ferocious,
when you kill and when you spare, this corpse of mine
was yours already, long ago. Carry out my father's order,
now my mother's too. My mind is eager to perform the ancient
punishment. My daughter, why do you detain me, chained
by love abhorrent? Why detain me? My father summons.
I am coming, I am coming, spare me now. Laius rages
with the bloodied symbol of his stolen realm.
Look, see, with hands of hatred he attacks my empty face,
digging at it. My daughter, do you see my father?
I do. At long last spit out this hated breath,
my craven mind, only brave against one body part.
Be done with slow delays of long-due punishment;
recuperate my death in its entirety. Why do I protract
what life I have? There is no crime I can accomplish now.

20

30

40

But yes, there *is*—in my misery, I proclaim: leave your father,
get away, while still a virgin. After my mother, there is
    everything to fear.   50

ANTIGONE

No force will ever loose my grasp upon your body,
Father; nobody will ever rob you of my
company. The glorious house and wealthy realms
of Labdacus[6]—my brothers can fight for *them*; the prize
possession in my father's mighty realm belongs to *me*—
my father, and he will not be taken from me,
not by the brother who seized the realm and holds the Theban
    scepter,[7]
not by the other, captaining his Argive squadrons.[8]
I would not release your hand, no, not if Jupiter
would rip apart the sky and thunder and his bolt would fall,   60
sundering our bond. My father, though you forbid it,
though you resist I'll steer you and direct your steps unwilling.
Making for the plains? I'll walk with you. Heading for the
    hills?
I'll not prevent you, but I'll lead the way. Use me as your
    guide,
wherever; every pathway picked is for the two of us;
without me death cannot be yours, with me it can.
Here, there rises from the crag a towering cliff,
looking far out at the spread of sea below:
is this your chosen goal? Here, there hangs the naked flint,
here yawns the earth torn open with its throat agape: 70
is this your chosen goal? Here falls a greedy torrent,
rolling chunks it's eaten from the tumbled mountain:
into this are we to plunge? I'll go where you wish, provided I
    go first:
no hindrance, no encouragement. Extinction,
Father, is your wish? Your dearest prayer is death?
If you die, then I precede you; if you live, I follow.
Come, change your mind, and summon up that heart of old,

and overcome and tame your troubles with your mighty
    courage.
Fight back: in such enormous trials to die is to surrender.

OEDIPUS

80   How, in such a monstrous house, did such a shining paragon
      arise, yes, this young girl so different from her line?
      Fortune, are you weakening? Is anyone I've fathered good?
      It couldn't ever be, I well know my own fate,
      unless that "good" were harmful. Nature will adapt herself
      to novel laws: the river will turn back and steer
      his quickened stream toward the source, and Phoebus' lamp
      will bring the night,[9] and Hesperus will make it day;[10]
      to add to my afflictions, I too will be
      good. For Oedipus the one salvation is
90   to not be saved. Allow me to avenge my father
      as yet unavenged. My hand, why do you, sluggish, shrink
      from carrying out the punishment? Any punishment to date,
      that was a gift to your mother. You courageous girl,
      release your father's hand: you're drawing out my death
      and lengthening the rites of your father while he still lives.
      At last, conceal my hateful body in the earth;
      you sin with good intent—devotion you are calling it,
      to drag your father around unburied. Stopping someone keen
        to die
99   is just the same as forcing death on one unwilling—
101   yet they are not the same: I think the former worse.[11]
      I'd rather death be forced on me than stolen from me.
      Young girl, stop trying: power over my own life and death
      resides with *me*. I've left my kingdom willingly;
      my kingdom of myself I keep. If you're a loyal comrade,
      hand a weapon to your parent—the weapon famous for
      my father's death. You have it? Or perhaps my sons possess
      that also, with my kingdom? Its job it will perform, wherever.
      Let it stay there; I relinquish it. My son can keep it—
110   both my sons. Instead, construct a mighty flaming

mound. I'll hurl myself into the raised-up pyre,[12]
and melt my hardened heart, and turn to ash
what little life I have. —Where's the savage sea?
Lead me where the crag juts out with towering rocks,
where swift Ismenos takes his pitiless waters,[13]
lead me where the beasts are, where the sea, the precipice,
if you really are my guide. That is where a man intent on death
desires to go, where on her high-up cliff the Sphinx sat
weaving tricks with half-wild words.[14] Point my footsteps there,   120
there settle your father. To fill that dreaded place, establish
there a worse monstrosity. Crouching on that rock,
I'll speak the words of my own fate, riddling,
solvable by none: pay attention, anyone that ploughs
the places held by the Assyrian king;[15] that worships
as a suppliant at the grove of Cadmus,[16] famous
for its snake where sacred Dirce hides;[17] anyone
that drinks Eurotas and inhabits Sparta glorious
for the brother-twin;[18] the farmer who shears Elis
and Parnassus and Boeotia's fields   130
with their fertile soil.[19] That cruel scourge of Thebes,
combining grief-producing words in hidden measures,
what such riddle did she pose, so hard to solve?
"A son-in-law to his own grandfather,[20] rival to his own
    father,
to his own children brother, to his own brothers father;
a grandmother in a single birthing bearing children for her
    husband,
for herself grandchildren too." Who can disentangle such
    monstrosities?
Even I, who won the prize for conquering the Sphinx,
will falter, slow interpreter of my own fate.
Why squander words anymore? Why try to soothe   140
my wild heart with your entreaties? My mind is set
on pouring out my life—it's struggled for a long time now
with death—and heading for the dark: this night of mine's
not deep enough for my offence. My wish is to be buried

down in Tartarus,[21] or anything beyond. At last my choice
    accords with
what should've happened long ago. I can't be kept from death.
A weapon you deny me? Will you close off paths
with risks of falling, keep the tight noose
from fitting round my neck? Remove death-dealing herbs?
What good will all your efforts in the end achieve?
Death is everywhere. God has made this excellent
provision: anyone can rob you of your life, but no one
of your death. A thousand routes lie open. There's nothing
that I need. My mind has used my hand to good effect
before now, even weaponless. Now to work, my hand,
with all your energy, your anger, all your strength.
For the wound, I do not designate a single place:
the whole of me is guilty. Inflict death wherever.
Break apart my breast, tear out the heart encompassing
so many crimes, expose entire the innards of my guts.
Let my shattered gullet gasp at the ferocious blows,
let fingernails attack and rip the veins until they flow.
Or else direct your anger to the usual place: reopening
these wounds, drench them with abundant blood and gore.
This is the path for dragging out my life so tough, invincible.
And you, my father, wherever you are, witnessing
my punishments: I did not think that such a heinous crime
could be atoned for properly by any punishment,
not ever. I was not contented with this death of mine—
by this part-payment I did not redeem myself: I wished to die
    for you
one part at a time. So, finally, exact your debt.
Now I pay the penalties; before was just my death-offering to
    you.
Come close, and thrust in deep my sluggish hand
and sink it deeper still: before, it timidly just grazed my head
with a small libation, hardly had to draw the eyes out
in their wish to follow. That mind of mine, it hesitates;
it hesitated when my eyeballs thrust themselves upon

150

160

170

my shrinking hand.[22] Oedipus, you'll hear the truth:
your digging out your eyes was less brave than your vow
of suicide. Now plunge your hand into your brain   180
and finish death exactly where it was begun.

ANTIGONE

Great-souled parent, I beg you soothe your mind
and hear a few words from your pitiable daughter.
It's not my aim to take you back to the splendor
of your former home or kingdom powerful with glory's bloom.
It's not my aim to ask you to endure with mild, calm heart
your rage, unbroken even by time's passing.
But what befits a man of such enormous strength
is this: to *not* be subject to resentment, *not* retreat,
beaten by misfortunes. Father, heroism is not,   190
as you believe, the fear of living,[23] but facing
huge misfortunes without turning away or retreating.
A man who's trampled on his fate, who's severed
and cast away the benefits of life, who's aggravated
his bad luck, who has no need of any god—
why should he desire death, or seek it?
Both are coward's ways: no one who desires death
undervalues it. A person whose misfortunes
can progress no more is safely situated.
Which of the gods can now increase your miseries,   200
suppose he wished? You cannot now yourself
increase them, except by thinking you deserve to die.
You don't deserve it: this heart of yours is free of guilt.
And, my begetter, call yourself Not Guilty all the more,
because despite the gods' intentions you are innocent. What
is it that has wilded you, has stuck your pain
with brand new goads? What drives you to the house
of hell, what pushes you away from here? To be lightless?
You are already. To flee your fatherland and home, famous
for its lofty walls? While you still live your fatherland is gone.   210
Do you flee your progeny and mother? Fortune has removed

you from the sight of everyone; whatever death can steal
from anyone, already life has stolen from you.
Kingship's ferment? Your former mob of fortune
has vanished, on your orders. My begetter, who are you running
   from?

OEDIPUS

Myself I run from, my heart I run from, haunted by all my
crimes, this hand of mine I run from, and this sky, the gods,
the awful crimes that I committed in my innocence.
Do I still tread this earth where fruitful crops
220   arise?[24] Do I still draw this air in through my noxious mouth?
Am I sated with a draught of water? Do I enjoy any of
our nurturing mother's benefactions?[25] Am I touching your
   pure hand,
monstrous and incestuous and accursed
as I am? Does my ear hear any sounds
which might include the name of child and parent?
If only I could split these channels wide apart
and, driving in my hands, dig out completely
any path for sounds and every narrow passageway
that opens up for words. Then, Daughter, your unlucky father
230   would have escaped his consciousness of you,
one among my crimes. The wickedness clings tight,
breaks out again repeatedly; my ears force on me all
that you have spared me, eyes. Why don't I plunge this
darkness-heavy head down to the everlasting shades of
   Dis?[26] Why
do I keep my ghost up here? Why am I a burden on the earth
and wander mingling in the upper world?[27] What evil is there
   left?
Gone are power, parents, children, heroism
too, and the remarkable renown of my resourceful
intellect.[28] My hostile fate has taken everything away.
240   Only tears were left—but I have robbed myself of even these.
Stand back: my mind admits no pleas

but seeks a novel punishment to match my crimes.
But what could match them? Even as a baby
I was marked for death. Whoever was allotted
a fate so grim? I had not yet seen daylight,
not yet loosed the closed womb's barriers,
but I was a source of terror. Some as soon as they are born
are seized by night and robbed of newfound light;
in my case, death preceded me. Some suffer
death that's premature inside their mother's guts—   250
but have they sinned already? No. The god put me on trial[29]
for a crime unspeakable while I was hidden, buried,
undefined.[30] On god's testimony father damned me,
had my tender feet sewn through with scalding iron
and sent me deep into the forest as fodder
for the beasts and cruel birds that harsh Cithaeron
nurtures, often stained by kingly blood.
But the person damned by god, rejected by his father,
death has now deserted. I've shown good faith to Delphi:
I attacked and felled my father in irreligious slaughter.   270
That act will be atoned by this religious act: I killed
my father but loved my mother. To speak about my
        wedding-song
and ceremony shames me.[31] Force yourself to undergo
this extra punishment, against your will: name the crime,
unheard of, beastlike, unexampled; one to make the world
flinch, one every generation would deny the truth of,
one to shame a father-killer: I took into my father's bed
my hands still spattered by my father's blood
and as crime's prize embraced a greater crime.
The father-crime was trivial. I took my mother   270
to bed and then, to maximize my crime, I made her
pregnant. Nature can endure no greater wickedness
than this. But if there is yet something more,
we have produced the ones to do it. The scepter, prize
for father's slaughter, I have thrown aside, but this
has strengthened other hands in turn.[32] I know full well

my kingdom's fate: none will have it without shedding
sacred blood.[33] My mind, a father's mind, foresees
immense misfortunes. Sown already are the seeds
280   of catastrophe to come. The treaty's pledge is disregarded.
The one refuses to relinquish the power he has seized.[34]
The other cries his rights as granted by the sealed pact,[35]
the gods who witnessed it; from exile he mobilizes Argos
and the towns of Greece to fight.[36] Exhausted Thebes is facing
no trivial destruction: weapons, flames and wounds
are imminent, along with any evil worse than those,
so none can fail to know that they were born from me.[37]

ANTIGONE
My parent, if you have no reason left to live,
this alone is plenty—to control your sons as their father
290   in their heavy rage. You alone can turn aside
their threats of irreligious warfare. You alone can check
these wild young men, grant citizens peace,
the fatherland tranquility, the damaged pact validity.
If you rob yourself of life, then you rob many others too.

OEDIPUS
No. Do *they* have any love for me, their father, or for what is
          fair,
in their greed for blood and power and war and tricks?
They're terrible and criminal and, in a word, they're sons of
          mine.
They compete in crime of every kind,
not caring where their anger goads them, headlong.
300   Born through wickedness, they think nothing wicked.
No feeling for their broken father moves them, nor their
fatherland. Their frenzied hearts are crazed for power.
I know their goal, the efforts they're prepared to make,
and that is why I seek a route to death, and soon,
and why I'm hurrying to die, while no one in my home
is guiltier than me. My daughter, why prostrate yourself
at my knees in tears? Why tame with pleading the untamable?

Fortune has one means alone to catch me,
otherwise invincible: only you can melt
my hardened feelings, only you in this our house 310
can teach me natural love.[38] Nothing that I know you want
is onerous or painful for me. Just give the word:
this Oedipus will swim across Aegean waters
at your command;[39] he'll swallow down the flames
that earth spews from the Sicilian mountain,[40]
rolling out the fiery balls; he'll face the dragon
raging savagely at Hercules' ransacking of the grove;[41]
at your command he'll offer up his liver to the vultures,[42]
at your command he'll even stay alive.

MESSENGER

In terror at the brothers' fighting, Thebes beseeches you 320
and begs you keep their fires from the houses of your
    fatherland,
you, who were born of royal stock to be a great example.
These are no mere threats—calamity has already arrived.
The brother laying claim to his turn in power as agreed
is driving all of Greece's peoples into war.[43]
Seven war camps are menacing the walls of Thebes.[44]
Come help, and stop a war that's equally a crime.

OEDIPUS

Am *I* the one to naysay acts of crime?
To teach that hands be kept away from blood
of kin? Am *I* a guru of the law and family 330
love? It's *my* deeds they are emulating,
me they follow now. I praise them and acknowledge them with
    joy,[45]
I urge them to achievements worthy of their father.
To work, my glorious children, prove by your deeds
our noble character. Surpass my glory
and renown. Do something that will make your father
happy to have lived this long. You will, I know it:
that's your heritage. It takes a name as great as ours

to carry out a crime beyond the trivial and banal.

340 Bring weapons, shoot your firebrands at the household gods
and reap with flame your native soil's crops,
create universal chaos and destruction,
tear down all the walls and raze them to the ground,
crush the gods in their own temples, melt the hearth-gods,
stained as they are, and let our whole house collapse in ruins.
Let the city burn in its entirety—and let the fire begin
with my marriage-bed.

MESSENGER

Let pass the violent outburst of resentment.
Let yourself be swayed by the misfortunes of the people.
Come and sanction tranquil peace for your children.

OEDIPUS

350 Do you *see* an old man given to thoughts of moderation?
Are you enlisting a lover of tranquil peace?
My spirit swells with rage, resentment seethes, ever greater.
What I desire's beyond the random scope
of young men's madness. Warfare between citizens
is not enough: I want brother to fight with brother.
And *that* is not enough: what ought to happen, to create
an outrage in *my* style, to fit my choice of bed:
assault your mother![46] Nobody will dig me out of these
forests.[47] I will hide in the hollow of an eroded cliff
360 or I'll shelter, hidden in thick underbrush.
From here I'll catch at roaming rumor's words
and hear, as best I can, about the brothers' savage wars.

JOCASTA

Fortunate Agave: she carried her horrendous crime
in the hand that did the deed. The bloodied maenad
bore the trophy of her son all torn to pieces.
She performed the crime, but afterward the miserable woman
did not *meet* her crime. The guilt that's mine is trivial:
I made others guilty. This as well is trivial:

I bred guilty children. The one thing missing from my troubles
  was
to love my enemy as well. Three times has winter has dropped   370
  its snows
and three sickles now have laid the harvest flat
while my son the exile wanders, of his fatherland deprived,
a refugee who asks the kings of Greece for help.
He's son-in-law to king Adrastus,[48] who with his sway
commands the sea cut by the Isthmos. Here he brings
with him his peoples and the seven realms to help
his son-in-law. I don't know what to choose or to support.
He wants his kingdom back: his case is good, but not his way
of seeking it. As their mother, what should be my prayers?
On either side I see a son: there's nothing I can loyally do   380
with loyalty intact. My blessing
to the one will to the other be a curse.
But though I love them both with like affection,
my spirit, always favoring the weak, inclines toward
the pull of better case and lesser luck.
Misfortune brings the wretched closer to their loved ones.

ATTENDANT
  My queen, while you are raising tearful lamentations,
  wasting time, the savage battle-lines are in position,
  weapons bared. The trumpets are already raising warfare.
  The standard bearer has advanced his eagle to signal battle.   390
  The kings in sevenfold positions each prepare to fight.
  With matching courage Cadmus' progeny advances.[49]
  With quickened step the soldiers charge from both directions.
  See how a black fog hides the daylight with its dust
  and how the plain lofts skyward clouds resembling
  smoke, sent up by earth now shattered by the horses'
  hooves. And if people who are terrified can see the truth,
  the standards gleam hostility, the front lines with their weapons
  raised are in position, the banners bear

their leaders' names, written clear in golden letters.
Go, restore devotion to the brothers and peace to all of us:
by a mother's opposition stop the wicked warfare.[50]

ANTIGONE

Mother, hurry up, and quickly speed your step,
restrain their weapons, knock the steel from my brothers,
hold your naked breast between their hostile swords:
either end the fighting, Mother, or be first to feel it.

JOCASTA

I'll go, I'll go and set myself to face their weapons.
I will stand between them. The one who wants to kill his
    brother
must kill his mother first. The one who feels devotion
410   must set aside his weapons when his mother asks. The one who
    doesn't,
he must start with me. I, a crone, will hold the blazing young
    men
back. No wickedness will happen while I'm watching,
or, if wickedness can be committed while I watch,
it will not be the only one.

ANTIGONE

         The standards glitter
face to face with standards,[51] the battle cry is roaring,
the crime is imminent. Mother, get your prayers in first!
And look, you can believe they've been affected by my tears,[52]
so slowly does the force arrive with weapons held at rest.

ATTENDANT

The line's advancing tardily, but the leaders hasten forward.

JOCASTA

420   What whirling wind will carry me through airy breezes,
transporting me in the mad storm's maelstrom?
What Sphinx or what Stymphalian bird, its black cloud
curtaining the daylight, will take me flying high on greedy
    wings?
What Harpy, watching over the cruel king's hunger,

will race me through the high paths of the air
and hurl me down between the battle-lines?[53]

ATTENDANT

She moves like someone crazed—or maybe crazed she *is*.
As an arrow launched by Parthian hand
travels swiftly,[54] as a ship is whirled along when overwhelmed
by the mad gale, as a shooting star falls   430
headlong from the sky, skirting heaven
while forcing its straight path with speeding fires,
so in her frenzy she's raced away and in no time
has separated the twin battle-lines. Conquered by a mother's
    prayer
the fighting's ceased. The men from either side,
just now intent on joining battle for mutual slaughter,
hold back their weapons, poised in frozen hands.
They vote for peace: everybody's blade is sheathed and hidden,
idle—except the pulsing steel in the brothers' hands.
Their mother shows and tears her whitened hair.   440
She begs them as they shake their heads. She floods her cheeks
    with tears.
If he hesitates this long, he can refuse his mother.

JOCASTA

Point your weapons and fires at *me*, let all the warriors
as one make *me* their target,[55] spirited warriors
from Inachus' city-walls and fierce warriors descending
from the Theban citadel:[56] citizen and enemy together   448
tear me limb from limb and scatter wide the pieces.[57]
I bore you both: do you not disarm more quickly?
Or shall I mention who your father was? Give your mother
    your hands,   450
yes, while they're unpolluted still. So far, ignorance has
    made us
guilty unwillingly. All the fault was Fortune's,
when she wronged us. This evil is the first
to be committed knowingly. It's in your hands

to choose, the two of you: if sacred love's your choice,
grant your mother peace.[58] If crime's your choice,
a greater crime is facing you: your mother sets herself
    between you.
So—dispense with war or with war's obstacle.

(Aside.)

Which one first shall I address with prayers in turn,
460   a troubled mother? Which one embrace first, in my misery?
I'm tugged in both directions with like affection.
This one was absent. But if the brothers' deal holds,
now the *other* will be gone. So from now on, shall I
never see the both of them except like this?

(To Polynices.)

      Embrace me first:
you have endured so many hardships and misfortunes–
worn out with lengthy exile, you're looking at your mother.
Come closer, sheathe that wicked sword and fasten
in the ground your quivering spear which even now
desires to be hurled. Your shield is stopping
470   your mother from closing breast to breast with you:
this too set down. Unbind your brow: lift off
from your warring head the grim protection;
let your mother see your face again. Why do you look away
and watch with fearful gaze your brother's hand?
I'll prostrate myself to cover your entire body.
The only path to your lifeblood will be through mine.
Why hesitate and waver? Don't you believe your mother's
    promise?[59]

POLYNICES

Yes: the laws of nature do not any longer hold.
After those examples set by brothers, not even a mother's
promise can be trusted.

JOCASTA

Put your hand back on your sword-hilt,   480
fasten on your helmet, clasp your shield with your hand:
while your brother lays down his arms, stayed armed.

(To Eteocles.)

You, the first cause of the sword,[60] put down your sword.
If you hate peace, if frenzied warfare is your choice,
your mother begs you for a little truce,
so she can give her son returned from exile kisses—
first of many, or the last.

(To both.)

Listen to my plea for peace
without your weapons. Does he fear you? And you fear him?
I fear you both—but for both your sakes.

(To Eteocles.)

Why do you refuse
to sheathe the sword you've drawn? You should delight in any   490
   delay:
the war you both desire to wage is one in which defeat
is best. You fear your hostile brother's tricks?
Whenever the choice is cheat or let yourself be cheated
by your family, better suffer rather than inflict the crime.
But do not be afraid: your mother will chase off treachery
from this side or the other. Am I succeeding? Or must I
be envious of your father? Did I come to stop an outrage,
or to witness it up close? He has put away his sword,
his shield's resting, leaning on the spear that's fastened in the ground.

(To Polynices.)

To you, my son, I'll now direct a mother's prayers,   500
but first, her tears. I'm holding the face I've longed to see

for such a time. You, exiled from your native soil,
are sheltered by the house-gods of a foreign king.
You were driven, wandering, across so many distant seas, so
    many
hazards. You weren't led to your marriage-chamber's threshold
by your mother in procession; she didn't decorate with her own
    hand
the house of celebration or bind the joyful torches
with their sacred ribbons. As gifts the father of your bride has
    given you
not treasures heavy with gold, not lands, not cities:

510   warfare is your dowry. You have married into enemies,
distant from your fatherland, a guest at someone else's hearth,
possessed of alien things but cast out from your own,
an exile for no crime. So that you would not omit
any of your father's fate, this too you've inherited:
a mistaken marriage. My son, returned to me
after many dawns, my son, your anxious mother's
fears and hopes: I always begged the gods
to let me see you, though your return would take
away from me as much as your arrival

520   could bestow. "When shall I cease to fear
for you?" I said; the god said, mocking me: "When it's
him you fear." For sure, if it weren't for the war,
I'd be without you. For sure, if you weren't here,
I'd be without the war. The price of seeing you
is grim and harsh, but as a mother I will pay it.
Only let your troops withdraw while savage Mars
dares no wickedness: even *this* is wickedness enough,
to have come so close. I'm appalled and pale and trembling,
when I see the brothers two facing off like this,

530   on the brink of crime.[61] My limbs are quivering with fear:
how nearly I as mother saw wickedness greater
than your miserable father could not bear to see.
Though now I'm freed from fearing such a heinous deed
and see nothing of the kind, I am still unhappy

because I nearly saw it. I pray you, by the heavy ten-month
labors of my womb, and by the love of your
renowned sister, and by your father's face,
when, angered with himself, he drained it,
guilty through no crime, exacting harsh self-punishment
for his mistake: turn aside the monstrous firebrands   540
from your ancestral walls, steer backward the warring army's
standards. Even if you withdraw, yet your crime
is mostly done:[62] your fatherland has seen its plains
filled by hostile hordes, it's seen the squadrons
glittering far off with weapons, it's seen Cadmus' meadows
trampled by the fleet-foot cavalry and captains flying past
high up on chariots, it's seen logs asmoke,
ablaze with fire, seeking to reduce our homes to ashes,
and it's seen brothers—even for Thebes a novel crime[63]—
attacking one another. This sight has been witnessed   550
by the entire army, by all the people, by both
your sisters and by me, your mother; your father has himself
to thank for missing this display. Think now
of Oedipus, who judges punishment appropriate,
even for mistakes. Do not, I pray, destroy with steel
your fatherland and house-gods, do not overthrow
the Thebes you seek to rule. What madness has you in its grip?
Is your quest for fatherland also its destruction? You want
it annihilated so it can be yours? No, this very action—
ravaging the earth with enemy troops and flattening   560
ripened crops and emptying the entire countryside—
damages your case: no one wreaks such havoc on what is his.
The things you order to be burned and mown down by the
        sword
you think another's. Find out which of you is king,
but leave the kingdom standing. Will *these* homes be the targets
of your flames and weapons? Will you dare to shake
these bastions of Amphion?[64] No hands constructed them
by dragging weary weight with creaking crane,
but stones were mustered by the sound of voice and lyre

570 and of their own accord climbed to the tower tops:
these rocks you'll smash in victory?⁶⁵ From *here* you'll carry off
your spoils, and lead away in chains your father's peers?
Will savage soldiers grab mothers even from
their husbands' arms and drag them off in shackles?
Are Theban virgins, fully grown, to travel in the herd
of prisoners as gifts for Argive brides?
And me—am I, your mother, to ride as booty, bound, with
    hands
behind my back, in your triumph over your brother?
Can you bear to watch the citizens consigned to death
580 and destruction all around? Can you bear to bring
the enemy so close to your own city walls? Can you bear to fill
your Thebes with blood and fire? Are you so wild, with heart
so harsh and cruel for anger? And you are not yet king!
How will power affect you? Shed, I pray, the crazy turmoil
of your mind and return yourself to loyalty.

POLYNICES

To roam, an exile always? To be barred from fatherland
and as a stranger seek support from a foreign race?
What worse would I be suffering if I had broken faith,
or violated an oath? Am I to pay the penalty for someone
590 else's treachery, while he enjoys his crimes' reward?
You tell me, "Leave!"? I obey my mother's order—
but give me a destination. Let my brother occupy
the proud palace, let a little hut conceal me.
Grant me this in banishment. Let a tiny home be
compensation for a kingdom. Given as a chattel to my wife,
shall I endure the harsh rulings of a wealthy marriage
and like a low retainer attend upon her domineering father?
It's hard to fall from regal power into slavery.

JOCASTA

If you seek a kingdom, if your hand must hold
600 a cruel scepter, any land in all the world
will offer many kingdoms to be won:⁶⁶

in one place Tmolus lifts his ridges,[67] known to Bacchus,
where broad wide spaces stretch with fruitful lands,
where river Pactolus trails his wealthy waves
and floods the fields with gold,[68] and in acres no less
flourishing Meander winds his roaming waters,[69]
rushing Hermus cuts the fertile plains.[70]
Elsewhere there is Gargara,[71] delight of Ceres, and the rich soil
that Xanthus,[72] swollen with Mount Ida's snows, surrounds.
From where the sea abandons its Ionian name,   610
where Sestos, facing Abydos, dominates the strait,
to where the sea turns closer to the east
and looks on Lycia, secure thanks to its many harbors:
seek a kingdom *here* with steel, let your bride's brave father
wage war against *these* folks, let him take *these* tribes
and hand them over to your scepter. But *this* realm—consider it
as still your father's. Better banishment than coming back
like this: it is another's crime makes you an exile,
but yours if you return here. Better use your troops
to seek a different realm that's stained by no sin.   620
Why, even your own brother will go to war for you,
accompanying your army. Go, and wage a war
that your father and your mother can support
your fighting. A guilt-fraught kingdom's harder
than any exile. Now, picture to yourself War's
misfortunes and the fluctuating shifts of fickle Mars:
though you trail behind you the entire strength of Greece,
though your soldiery deploys its weapons far and wide,
war's fortune's always hanging in the balance.
Everything is Mars' decision: two unequal fighters   630
are levelled by the sword; both hopes and fears
are in blind Chance's vortex. The prize you seek is not
guaranteed; the crime is. Suppose your prayers are granted
by the gods in unison, suppose the citizens have yielded
and turned away and fled, and troops, prostrate in deathly
     carnage,
are covering the fields: though you exult and bear

the spoils taken from your ousted brother, your victor's palm
must be broken. What kind of war do you think this is,
in which the victor commits abominable wickedness
640   if he celebrates? Misguidedly, you want to conquer him,
but you will grieve him once you've won. Please, end
your cursed battles, free your fatherland from terror
and your parents from their grief.

POLYNICES

     So my monstrous brother
can avoid the punishment for his deceit and crime?

JOCASTA

Don't worry. He'll have his punishment, a heavy one:
he'll be king. This is punishment. If you doubt it, trust
your grandfather, trust your father: Cadmus and his progeny
will tell you this.[73] No Theban ever bore the scepter
with impunity, nor will anybody hold it
650   by breaking faith: among such you can already
count your brother.

ETEOCLES[74]

     Let him! It's worth this much to me
to lie with kings. *You* I number among the crowd
of exiles.[75]

JOCASTA

     So rule, but, inevitably, hated by your people.

ETEOCLES

The man afraid of hatred has no desire to rule;
god, the founder of the world,[76] joined together these two
     things:
power and hatred. I regard it typical of a mighty king
to subdue that hatred.[77] His people's adoration much
constrains a master; when they're angry he has much more
     scope.
The man who longs for adoration rules with feeble hand.

JOCASTA

660   Hated power never lasts for long.

ETEOCLES
Kings are better at explaining power.
Exile's *your* prerogative. For kingship, I'd be willing–

JOCASTA
—to burn your fatherland, your house-gods and your wife?

ETEOCLES
Power's a handsome purchase at any price.[78]

Phaedra

The drama opens with Hippolytus, Theseus' son and Phaedra's step-son, heading out to a hunt with the support of his patron goddess, Diana. After Hippolytus leaves, Phaedra appears onstage, sick with despair. She confesses to her nurse that in Theseus' absence she has fallen in love with Hippolytus. In Venus' inexorable grip, she cannot stem her feelings; she compares herself to her own mother Pasiphae, whose consummated lust for a bull produced the monstrous Mino-taur. Unable to change Phaedra's mind, the nurse resolves to help her rather than let her kill herself.

When Hippolytus returns from the hunt, the nurse approaches him with wheedling words about the pleasures of women and wine, but Hippolytus, who hates all women and abjures human sexuality, praises instead his own pure lifestyle in the woods and claims it was the primeval state mankind enjoyed before degeneration set in.

Phaedra appears, faints, and comes to. Asked by Hippolytus what ails her, she confesses. Hippolytus is aghast. He nearly kills her with his sword but instead runs off in disgust when she welcomes death. At this point the nurse improvises and starts shrieking "Help! Rape!" using Phaedra's battered state and the abandoned sword as evidence. There is an interlude in which the chorus sings about beauty and its dangers.

Suddenly Theseus himself arrives, having escaped from his mis-sion to the underworld to help his friend Pirithous kidnap Perseph-one. Seeing his wife in distress, he demands to know why. Phaedra cryptically says she was "threatened" by the sword and her body suf-fered violence. Theseus sees Hippolytus' sword and draws the obvious conclusion. Cursing his son as a hypocrite and pervert, he prays to Jupiter to destroy him.

A messenger arrives with grim news: as Hippolytus was galloping away in his chariot, a bull-like monster emerged from the sea and threw his horses into a panic. Thrown off and tangled up in the reins, he was mangled and torn to pieces. Phaedra is shown Hippolytus' corpse, confesses the truth to Theseus, then kills herself. Theseus laments his rashness, orders Hippolytus' burial, and hopes bitterly that the weight of the soil over Phaedra's corpse will crush it altogether.

Introduction

SHADI BARTSCH

The story of Phaedra was a well-known one in antiquity and had parallels in other early literatures as well, such as the account of Potiphar's wife in the book of Genesis. The stepmother who falls in love with her stepson then punishes his rejection of her by accusing him of rape was the subject of at least one (lost) drama by Sophocles, two by Euripides, and others by less well known dramatists. Euripides' reason for writing two versions of the same drama is apparently that the first one was overly scandalizing: we are told that in Euripides' original version, the *Hippolytos Kalyptomenos* (*Hippolytus Veiled*, given this name in the Alexandrian period), a lustful Phaedra openly propositioned Hippolytus. This so outraged the Athenian audience that Euripides wrote a second drama as a repudiation of the first. The second drama, in which Phaedra and Hippolytus never confront each other, but only learn of each other's reactions through the nurse as intermediary, has survived as the play we know simply as Euripides' *Hippolytus*. It took the first prize in the Athenian dramatic contest of 428 BCE.[1]

This Euripidean Hippolytus is different in several significant respects from Seneca's later version. Because the Euripidean play is bracketed by monologues from two goddesses—Aphrodite and Artemis (Roman Venus and Diana)—who take responsibility for human action, much of the question of causality is muted. As Coffey and Mayer (1990, 7) point out, "there is a complex and sometimes uneasy interaction between divine intervention and human action and moral responsibility. The action takes place within the framework of the intrusion into human affairs of two goddesses." At the drama's opening, Aphrodite explains that she will punish Hippolytus for refusing to honor her by making his stepmother Phaedra fall in love with him; at its ending, Artemis appears to tell Theseus the truth and to take vengeance on Aphrodite for killing her favorite. In

Seneca's version, however, not only are these goddesses physically absent, but Phaedra's nurse even pooh-poohs the idea that Eros is a god (195–203):

> I know that lust, vile and fond of human fault,
> pretends that love's a god, and in order to enjoy more liberty
> has bestowed on lust the false name of divinity.
> As if Venus sends off her son to wander
> all the lands, and he goes flying through the sky
> with mischief-making arrows in his childish hand
> and though he's small has so much might, of all the gods above!
> Love-mad minds have taken up these empty claims
> and invented Venus' power and the weapon of her son.

Phaedra, however, seems unconvinced and continues to refer to the inexorable power of passion, as does the choral ode that follows this exchange. The exchange suggests that we are deliberately left to wonder about the source of Phaedra's passion; while the nurse thinks such claims are made up to excuse bad behavior, the references in the play to Phaedra's mother Pasiphae leaves the question open and suggests a third possibility, a weakness handed down from generation to generation.

Seneca's innovations also appear in the drama's weighted use of particular images that reveal to us latent flaws in the characters of all the main protagonists.[2] Particularly striking is the duality of *nature* as both nurturing and destructive, both the site of a primeval stage of mankind in which food grew spontaneously and the locus of vicious animal hunts, both a pure realm free of exorbitant passion and yet a place where "natural" sexual love is necessary for the propagation of the species.[3] Civilization, too, is both corrupt and yet a means of controlling nature that Hippolytus is completely open to. His hunting ode opens the drama, and here these themes are already detectable. He both celebrates the beauty of his natural surroundings and exemplifies his mastery of them by naming each spot to which his men and hounds must go, reminding us of how one of the features of civilization is precisely naming and mapping nature. In the lines that follow in which he invokes Diana's aid in the hunt, he characterizes her too as primarily a huntress, tracking down and killing animals in far-flung regions with her terrifying arrows. Killing and civilization are linked when civilization, its crafts, and its violent ways work their way back into the ode: Hippolytus will capture deer by penning them in with finespun nets and lines sporting red feathers, a human trick to deceive the deer with vain fear. Knives and different kinds of tools are there to disembowel the dead animals, and the outcome of the hunt will be "much blood," another link between man's inventions and their cruelty. Somehow the "natural" and technological slaughter end up tangled with each other in Hippolytus' celebration of his own craft.

All this is striking, especially in retrospect, when Hippolytus praises the golden-age life lived in the primeval era at lines 483–564. In this bygone time, he says wistfully, there were no city walls, no blood on men's altars, and—despite the presence already of cunning snares for animals—man was sated by the fruits of the woods. Only in a sort of postlapsarian era did humans develop weapons and spill human blood. As Cedric Littlewood (2004, 292) has remarked, "Hippolytus' opposition to civilization is undermined: the violent art of hunting here and elsewhere has more in common with the world he rejects than with the delicate innocence of the Golden Age which he prefers." And only at this point, it seems, did women suddenly join the picture, procurers of evil each and every one of them, typified by none other than Medea herself. One might ask where women were in the primeval golden era, but Hippolytus so loathes all women that he is incapable of including them in his vision: they seem to enter the picture at the same time as the evils of civilization. He must know that human beings could not have reproduced down to the present era via an asexual self-replication, but he chooses not to acknowledge it even though the nurse draws his attention to it (469–74):

Come now, let's suppose that love abandons humankind,
love which fills out and restores our worn-out race.
The world will lie rotting in gross neglect,
the sea will stand empty without a single fish,
birds won't populate the sky nor beasts the woods,
only breezes will traverse the upper air.

Hippolytus loves nature, but he does not love nature's fertility, the mating of animals, the spawning of future generations. He seems to prefer nature when it is dead: when his dogs have ripped out the throats of the animals he hunts and they lie dead as a sign of his mastery over the realm he claims to love.

Nature has also turned Phaedra into—Phaedra. There seems to be no escaping the character she inherited from her mother Pasiphae, who fell so madly in love with a bull that she had a trick created for him in the shape of a beautiful hollow cow; climbing inside this cow and positioning herself carefully, she was able to lure the bull into having sex with her and the heifer simultaneously (surely a triumph of both engineering and yoga). Here the way in which the bull is "captured" to service Pasiphae's love creates a disturbing precedent that emphasizes the notion of the hunt and of control over the object of love, and here, of course, the outcome of this desire conflated with mastery is a monstrous and unnatural hybrid: the Minotaur, half-man, half-bull. The Minotaur is put to death by none other than Theseus himself—though Phaedra never rebukes him with the murder of her half-brother. She is too busy realizing that the *un*natural element she has inherited is rising in her as well. In her very first appearance on stage, Phaedra speaks sarcastically about Theseus, who is absent on a mission to the underworld to help his rapist friend Pirithous, and no model of chastity for anyone. She also speaks of her own suffering in the grip of passion. But most of all, she recognizes herself (113–19):

> I see my wretched mother's fatal illness:
> our kind of love knows how to sin in forests!
> O Mother, I pity you. Gripped by lust too vile to name,
> with too much bravery, you loved the fierce leader
> of a wild herd of cattle. Grim-looking and unyokeable,
> that lover-bull of yours, the ruler of an untamed herd—
> but at least he could love *something!*

Phaedra recognizes that she has replicated her mother in her love for an "unyokeable" object of desire—Hippolytus, compared implicitly here to a wild animal himself. But in her eyes, there is a difference:

her mother may have loved an animal, not a human, but at least he was able to be tricked into "love" by his amorous pursuit of the fake heifer. But Pasiphae's own situation, she laments, is still worse: not only is she Hippolytus' stepmother (although she mentions no names in this first speech), but Hippolytus is entirely without passion, and literally unyokeable in the yoke of love.

Yoking is in fact a major theme of the play, and the term itself bridges (we might say yokes) two very different referents, both of which appear throughout the drama: the yoke of love, and the crest of a mountain, both *iugum* in Latin (on this topic, see Paschalis 1994). Hippolytus' first words are to send his men to the mountain crests (*iuga*) to hunt animals, and he repeats the term near the end of his speech (69). But the next time it crops up, it is in Phaedra's mouth as she describes her mother's taurine affair: that bull was "impatient of the yoke" (117), fierce and surly, but he still "loved." Then the nurse chimes in to warn Phaedra that if one does not resist love at the very outset, one ends up under its yoke (134) and repents too late. Too bad, responds Phaedra; the god of Love can subdue anyone, including Vulcan, who tends the fires on the ridges/yokes of Mt. Etna. Of course, a volcano's flames are inside it not on its peaks, but the complex of usages here now tie together master, yoking, fire, love, and hunting. And the yokes keep coming, at least once every hundred lines until the pause in its usage after line 617. There are many more mountain peaks in the wilderness to suggest nature's wildness: Phaedra vows to track down Hippolytus even on the ridges/yokes of snowy hills (233, 614), she weeps like the melting snow on the ridges/yokes of Mt. Taurus (382), and Hippolytus claims that all men who devote themselves to mountain ridges are corrupted by civilization (and eros; 487).

But there are also many yokes that represent control over nature, as the nurse reminds Hippolytus. His very mother, though an Amazon, felt the yoke of Venus (576), as Hippolytus himself stands witness to: the Amazons usually killed their male children. Phaedra hopes to marry Hippolytus and hide her crime under the conjugal yoke (597); and Hippolytus himself likes to dominate animals with yokes, as he does with his chariot horses at line 1002. This is the same yoke that the horses struggle to free themselves from when the monstrous bull summoned up by Theseus' curse emerges from the ocean (1083); that is, Hippolytus is ripped apart because of the yoke and harness that entangle his body as he falls from the chariot and that result in his being dragged through brambles and boulders. Something has gone horribly astray with yoking by the end of the play, as the violence of eros and the violence of nature come together in this deadly yoke that proves Hippolytus' undoing. It is the last time we hear the word *iugum* in the drama.

At the beginning, Hippolytus wanted to chase wild beasts over snowy mountains, and later Phaedra wanted to chase *him* over snowy mountains. Eros the hunter, with his bow and arrow, takes over from Diana as hunter, she too armed with bow and arrow and invoked near the beginning of the play: "Whatever beast grazes in lonely preserves / . . . this beast fears, Diana, your bow," says Hippolytus in praise of the goddess (66–72); later the chorus will sing several times of Amor, whose bow and arrow outdo even Apollo's (192–93, 276–78). Another series of associations links bulls, Hippolytus, passion, and monstrous outcomes; Pasiphae loved a wild unyokeable bull; Hippolytus is "feral" and incapable of love (says the nurse at 240); and of course, the monstrous form that rears out of the sea as an indirect result of Phaedra's passion is strangely bull like (though scaly at the back). As the messenger describes (1033–40):

> The sea rushed onto land
> in the wake of its own monster—fear unnerves my voice.
> What an appearance that massive body had!
> A towering bull with dark-blue neck
> raises a tall mane on his greenish brow;
> his shaggy ears stood up, and his eyes varied their hue,
> now like that of the master of a wild herd,
> now like that of something from the depths.

Phaedra's mother loved "the fierce leader / of a wild herd of cattle" and gave birth to a monster, half-bull, half something else, a prodigy of nature. Misdirected love, that perversion of the natural order, creates other perversions in turn, as the nurse well knows (171–77):

Will you commix the son's bed and the father's,
and breed a hybrid fetus in your wayward womb?
Go on then, set nature on its head with your incestuous fires!
Why do monsters cease to be? Why does your brother's
    labyrinth
lie empty? Will the whole world hear of alien prodigies,
will nature back off from her principles,
every time a Cretan woman loves?

The answer would appear to be yes. Phaedra's half-brother the Minotaur is like the outcome of her passion for her stepson, the hybrid sea-beast, and if Theseus killed the one, he himself produced the other.

What are we to make of all this? At least one point emerges clearly from the collapse of these distinctions between civilization and nature, control and freedom, hunting and being hunted, the ridges of mountains and the yokes of beasts, Diana's bow and Amor's. It is that these realms are never fully separate, and certainly not so in the case of the extremes in which the play deals; the result of striving for the extreme is actually to end up in the muddled and dangerous realm of the middle. The outcome is what the two main protagonists feared most: for Hippolytus, a rape-like violation of his purity when a branch penetrates his groin at the moment of death: "as he's dragged along, at last a tree trunk with burnt stock holds him with an upright stake forced right through his groin" (1098–99); for Phaedra, a reputation in tatters, just like that of her mother, despite her desperate wish to maintain her *pudor*, a chaste respectability. The muddled realm of the middle is a danger beautifully illustrated by the doublespeak in which Phaedra finally engages when Theseus presses her about what happened (891–92):

when tried by prayers I resisted; my soul did not yield
to threats and to the sword; but still my body suffered force.

She did indeed resist the Nurse's pleas; and her soul did not yield to Hippolytus' sword, since she lives yet. Moreover, in ripping her hair and putting the sword to her throat, Hippolytus did do her violence.

But in a play where everyone is at an extreme, no one stops to interrogate words that may hold more than one clear meaning.

Suggested Reading

Boyle, Anthony J., ed. 1983. *Seneca Tragicus: Ramus Essays on Senecan Drama*. Berwick.

———. 1985. "In Nature's Bonds: A Study of Seneca's Phaedra." *ANRW* II 32 (2): 1284–1347.

———. 1987. *Seneca's* Phaedra: *Introduction, Text, Translation and Notes*. Liverpool.

Coffey, Michael, and Roland Mayer. 1990. *Seneca: Phaedra*. Cambridge.

Davis, Peter J. 1983. "Vindicat Omnes Natura Sibi: A Reading of Seneca's *Phaedra*." In Boyle 1983, 114–27.

Grimal, Pierre. 1963. "L'originalité de Sénèque dans la tragédie de Phèdre." *Revue des Études Latines* 41: 297–314.

Littlewood, Cedric A. J. 2004. *Self-Representation and Illusion in Senecan Tragedy*. Oxford.

Mayer, Roland. 2002. *Seneca: A Companion to Phaedra*. London.

Paschalis, Michael. 1994. "The Bull and the Horse: Animal Theme and Imagery in Seneca's 'Phaedra.'" *American Journal of Philology* 115: 105–28.

Segal, Charles. 1984. "Senecan Baroque: The Death of Hippolytus in Seneca, Ovid, Euripides," *TAPA* 114: 311–25.

———. 1986. *Language and Desire in Seneca's Phaedra*. Princeton.

Phaedra

LUCIUS ANNAEUS SENECA

TRANSLATED BY SHADI BARTSCH

DRAMATIS PERSONAE

HIPPOLYTUS, son of Theseus and Antiope, an Amazon
PHAEDRA, wife of Theseus and stepmother of Hippolytus
NURSE of Phaedra
THESEUS, king of Athens
MESSENGER
CHORUS of Athenian citizens

*The drama opens in the countryside near the royal palace at Athens.
The rest of the tragedy takes place outside the palace of King Creon at
Corinth, where Jason and Medea have recently arrived after fleeing
Colchis. Their quarters are adjacent to the palace itself.*

ACT 1

> (*Enter Hippolytus with a group of fellow hunters,
> accompanied by dogs on leashes. Hippolytus sends
> the men out across different locations in Attica.*)

HIPPOLYTUS

Go, sons of Cecrops![1] Encircle the deep-shaded woods,
the highest crests of the mountain;
cross far and wide with hastening step
the fields at the foot of rocky Parnethos[2]
and those lashed by the river's quick flow
as it runs through the valley of Thria;[3]
climb hills always white with chill northern snow.[4]
Come this way, the rest, where the grove
is a-tangle with towering alders,
where meadows stretch out   10

that are softened by Zephyr with dew-bearing breath
and coaxed into spring's verdant seedlings;
where the trickling Ilisos lazily glides
through unnourished fields,[5] and erodes
with its miserly stream the infertile sands.
You, go where Marathon opens to pastures,
along the left path, where the ewes
that have lambed, with their wee flocks
in tow, seek to graze overnight;
you, to where rugged Acharnae
softens its frost under warming south winds.[6]
Let one tread the highlands of honeyed Hymettus,[7]
another the hamlets of tiny Aphidna;[8]
that region where Sunion's protrusion[9]
juts into the shores of the ambient ocean
has too long enjoyed its freedom from man.
If the charm of the woodlands inspires
anyone, Phyle is calling for him:[10]
here is the haunt of the boar, fearsome to farmers,
winning renown by many a wound.
As for you, play out the leashes, but only for hounds
who don't bay on the trail; let the strap pull back eager
    Molossians;[11]
let Crete's fierce greyhounds, chafed
at the neck, strain their thick collars.
But prudently hold down the Spartans by tightly-bound knots;
their kind is audacious and greedy for prey.
A moment will come, when the rocks of the dell will resound
    with their barking.
Now's when the dogs should sniff at the breezes,
lowering their keen-scented noses, and
track down wild lairs with snout to the ground,
while the daylight is dim and the damp earth retains
the marked indentations of paw prints.
Make quick, one of you, to carry the loosely-meshed
nets as a load for your shoulders; let another man

20

30

40

carry the smooth-woven nooses.
Let a string that is hung with vermillion feathers
hem in the beasts with irrational fear.

(*Pointing at different hunters.*)

It's your task to launch an arrow in flight,
and yours to heave with both hands at once
the sturdy oak spear with its broad iron tip.   50
You, lie in wait, and flush deer headlong
with a hullaballoo; and you, when we've won,
use your curved knife to extract the innards.
Unwomanly goddess,[12] appear to your friend,
you for whose rule the most recondite parts
of the earth are reserved,
for whose unerring arrows the wild beasts
provide targets: those who drink the frigid Araxes,[13]
those who frisk on the iced-over Danube.
Your right hand has hunted Gaetulian lions,[14]   60
and in Crete it has hunted the hinds;
now you are shooting the speedy roe deer
with hands less weighted down.[15]
The striated she-tigers dare to confront you,
but shaggy-haired bisons show you their backs
and so do wild oxen with widely spread horns.
Whatever beast grazes in lonely preserves,
whether known to the Arab with exuberant forests,
or to the Libyan devoid of all wealth,
or to Sarmatae who roams empty plains;[16]   71
whether the heights of the cruel Pyrenees   69
or the Caspian groves keep it hidden:[17]   70
this beast fears, Diana, your bow.[18]   72
If a follower pleasing to you has carried
your godhead with him to the groves,
his nets hold the wild beasts entangled,
no hooves can break through the noose:
the cart groans that carries the spoils of the hunt.

The hounds then sport noses red with much blood,
and the rustic assemblage returns to the hamlet
80   in triumphant procession.
Goddess, show me your favor! The shrill hounds
have given the sign: I am called to the woods.
I'll go by this path, this one which shortens
the long expedition.

(*Hippolytus and his companions exit.*)
(*Enter Phaedra, from the palace.*)

PHAEDRA
O Crete! Great island, mistress of the boundless sea,
along whose every coast too many ships to count
have sailed, that sea where Nereus cuts a path[19]
for prows that go as far as Syria,
why do you force me, a hostage given to a hated home,
90   married to an enemy, to pass my life in troubles
and in tears? My husband's far afield and on the run,
as faithful to his wife as you'd expect of Theseus.
He goes, brave soldier for a daring suitor,[20] through the
        profound darkness of the lake of no return,
to steal the wife of Hades' king, and seize her from the throne.
He presses on, this comrade to insanity, and neither fear nor
        shame
has held him back. The father of Hippolytus pursues
adultery and lawless coupling in the depths of Acheron!
But another, greater pain is weighing on me as I grieve.
100   Not the quiet of the night, nor a profound sleep
has released me from my cares. An evil thing is nursed and
        grows
within me; it burns me like the vapor pouring out
of Etna's crevasses. Athena's loom stands idle
and the weighed-out wool tumbles from my hands;
I no longer care to pray at shrines with votive gifts,
nor, at the altars, brandish torches witness to
the silent rite, mingling with a band of Attic girls,

nor approach with spotless prayers or pious act
the goddess who guards this land adjudged to her.[21]
I want to track at a run beasts startled to flight, 110
and hurl stiff hunting spears with a delicate hand.
My mind, where are you heading? Why this mad love for the
    woods?
I see my wretched mother's fatal illness:
our kind of love knows how to sin in forests!
O Mother, I pity you. Gripped by lust too vile
to name, you dared to love the fierce leader
of a wild herd of cattle. Grim-looking and unyokeable,
that lover-bull of yours, the ruler of an untamed herd—
but at least he could love *something*![22] In my misery,
what god, what Daedalus can help my burning? 120
Not even if that man returns, that master over Attic sorcery,[23]
who shut our monster in his labyrinthine home,[24]
could he promise any recourse for my case.
Venus, who hates the children of the hated Sun,
uses me as retribution for the chains that bound her
and her lover Mars,[25] and burdens all of Phoebus' family
with shocking acts of deviance. No daughter of Minos
has ever had an easy love: crime's always her bedmate.

NURSE

Wife of Theseus, famous child of Jupiter,
drive these evil thoughts from your blameless heart at once, 130
put out these flames, don't make yourself an easy mark
for this dreadful hope. Anyone who blocks the path of love
and repels it at the outset, ends up safe and wins the fight;
if you feed the sweet disease by fawning on it,
you'll reject too late the yoke already on you.
It's not that I don't know how stubborn royal pride is,
and intolerant of truth: it hates being bent to the right path
I'll bear whatever outcome fate decides:
proximity to death—and freedom—makes us old folks brave.
Best is to want what's right and not to stumble on the way; 140

second best's the shame to know that you have crossed the line.
Where are you headed, sorry girl? Why aggravate the bad name
of your family and outperform your mother? Incest's worse than
abnormality: incest is due to character—abnormality to fate.
If, because your husband does not see the upper world,
you think your crime is safe and you don't need to fear,
you're wrong. Suppose that Theseus *is* held back, cloaked
by the depths of Lethe, and endures the Styx forever;
what about the one who quells the seas with far-flung rule,
and gives laws to a hundred towns—your father?
Will he allow so great a crime to hide uncaught?
Parents are keen-scented in their care. But let's suppose again
that we can cover up so great a crime with craft and trickery:
what about the one who pours his light upon the world,
the father of your mother? What about the one who shakes the
    Earth
and wields the bolt of Aetna in his flashing hand
the father of the gods? Do you think this can be done,
to hide unseen among all-seeing grandfathers?
But let's suppose the kind support of the divinity
conceals your vile amours, and that your incest
finds a loyalty not granted greater crimes: what about
that ever-present punishment, the knowing fear of the mind,
and a soul replete with guilt and fearful of itself?
Some women's crimes stay hidden, but not with peace of mind.
Suppress the fires of your wayward soul, I beg of you.
An outrage which no barbarous land has ever
carried out, no Getae nomads on their plains,
no hostile Taurian, no scattered Scythian:[26]
expel this vile crime from your modest mind,
recall your mother, shun novel copulation.
Will you commix the son's bed and the father's,
and breed a hybrid fetus in your wayward womb?
Go on then, set nature on its head with your incestuous fires!

(*Rhetorically.*)

Why do monsters cease to be? Why does your brother's
    labyrinth
lie empty? Will the whole world hear of alien prodigies,
will nature back off from her principles,
every time a Cretan woman loves?

PHAEDRA

      Nurse, I know that what you say
is true. But passion forces me to take the path
that's worse. My mind full-knowing takes the plunge,
and tries in vain to trace its steps and aim for sane reflection.   180
Just so a sailor steers a heavy-laden boat when the current
flows abreast; his labor's all in vain, and the ship
is carried off, defeated, on the rapid tide.
What can reason do? Passion's won and rules me,
the potent god is master of my entire soul.
No master of himself, he lords it over all the earth,
this winged one scorching Jupiter with wild flames.
The martial god Gradivus felt those fires,[27]
so has the god who crafts the tri-forked thunderbolt,
the very one who tends the always raging kilns
under Etna's peak—he's aflame as well, from such a tiny spark.   190
Apollo too, who shoots sure arrows with his bow:
this boy can hit *him* with a shaft that's better aimed,
and flies around on land and sea, a plague to all alike.

NURSE

I know that vile lust, which is fond of human fault,
pretends that love's a god, and in order to enjoy more liberty
has bestowed on this passion the false name of divinity.
As if Venus sends off her son to wander[28]
all the lands, and he goes flying through the sky
with mischief-making arrows in his childish hand,   200
and though he's smallest of the gods, holds so great a realm!
Love-mad minds have taken up these empty claims
and invented Venus' power and the weapons of her son.
Whoever gets too spoiled in prosperous times

and is awash in luxury, always looks for something new.
Then excess appetite steals in, that dire companion
of great wealth: the usual dinners don't give pleasure,
nor do normal fabrics,[29] nor cheap wine cups either.
Why does this illness rarely sneak in homes
210   of meager means, preferring fancy houses?
Why does a moral form of love live under humble roofs,
and average folks have feelings that are healthy;
why does what's ordinary hold itself in check? And on the
      other side,
why do the rich and those propped up by kingship
seek more than what is right? A man with too much power
      wants power *beyond*
his power. You know what suits a woman in high place.
Fear and revere your returning husband's rule.

PHAEDRA

It's love whose power I consider greatest over me;
I fear no one's return. Anyone who's ever reached
220   the silent resting place, has never gained again
the vaulted skies, once sunk in endless night.

NURSE

Don't trust in Dis. Even though he's closed his realm
and the dog of Styx defends the gloomy doors,
Theseus alone can find forbidden paths.

PHAEDRA

Maybe he'll give his blessing to my love.

NURSE

He was severe even to a faithful wife:
barbarian Antiope found his hand inhuman.[30]
But let's suppose your angry husband can be bent:
who will bend the young man's stubborn soul?
230   He hates the very name of "woman" and avoids them,
harshly dedicates his youth to celibacy,
steers clear of marriage. You'd recognize his blood as Amazon!

PHAEDRA

This man—I'd follow as he plodded through the peaks
of snowy hills, trod ragged rocks with nimble feet,
through the deepest groves, through mountains.

NURSE

You think *this* man would stop and yield to a caress,
leave a virgin way of life for aberrant forms of sex?
You think for *you* he'll put aside his hate, when perhaps it's
because he hates you, that he condemns them all?

PHAEDRA

But he *can* be bent by prayer!

NURSE

He's feral.   240

PHAEDRA

I've learned that feral creatures can be bent by love.

NURSE

He'll flee from you.

PHAEDRA

I'll follow if he flees across the very seas.

NURSE

Keep in mind your father!

PHAEDRA

I keep in mind my mother too.

NURSE

He shuns our entire gender.

PHAEDRA

No fear he'll take a mistress!

NURSE

Your husband will turn up.

PHAEDRA

Right—the adulterer's best friend.[31]

NURSE

And your father will turn up.

PHAEDRA

A kind father to eloping Ariadne.[32]

NURSE

I beg you. By this bright white hair of my old age,
by my heart worn out from care, and by these breasts
you love, I ask you: stop this madness, help yourself:
part of gaining back your sanity is the will to do so.

PHAEDRA

250   Not every shred of shame has left my highborn soul.
Nurse, I yield to you. Let the love that will not be controlled
be quashed. I'll not allow my good name to be stained.

261   And so: I'll arm my hand as savior of my chastity.[33]
This is the only way, the one escape from evil:
to take my husband's path, and hold off depravity through
            death.

NURSE

My child, calm these urges of a frenzied mind!
Control yourself! That you deserve to live is clear to me
through your claim that you deserve to die.

PHAEDRA

I'm set on death. The only question's *how* to die.
Should I choke off my life with a noose, or fall upon a sword?

260   Should I throw myself headfirst from Athena's citadel?

NURSE

262   Can my old age let you die like this, in
sudden suicide? Stop this crazy impulse![34]

PHAEDRA

No reasoning can stop someone about to die
if his mind's made up and he deserves to die.

NURSE

Mistress, sole comfort for my weary years,
if such a wanton passion presses on your mind,
forget your reputation. It hardly favors truth,

270   is kinder to the less deserving, and less kind to the good.
Let's try our fortune with that grim and stubborn soul.

My job is to approach the feral youth
and bend the hard man's brutal mind.

CHORUS

O goddess born of the ungentle sea,
whom a double Cupid calls mother,[35]
a boy free with his flames and his arrows alike:
that lascivious, smiling young fellow
shoots his missiles from such a sure bow!
Passion goes creeping through all of one's marrow,
secret flames lay waste to one's veins.[36]   280
The wound once inflicted has no widespread front,
but devours its way through the deep-lying marrow.
There's no making peace with that boy. Nimbly
he sprays swarms of shafts through the world.
The shore that beholds the sun as it dawns,
the shore that lies under the sun's western turning,
any shore set beneath the fiery Crab,
any glacial shore of Callisto the Bear,[37]
enduring the tillers who are always nomadic—
they all know these flames. He kindles   290
the violent loves of young men, he calls back to life
the embers of worn out old men,
he strikes virgin hearts with a heat they don't know,
he orders the gods to depart from the sky
and live on the earth in falsified guise.[38]
When Apollo was herding Thessalian livestock
he drove on the cattle with lyre laid aside, for love,
and called bulls with a shepherd's reed pipe.
Even he who created the sky and the clouds—
how often did *he* don inferior forms!   300
As a bird now, he fluttered his snowy white wings
his voice sweeter than swans as they die;
next as a lustful young bull with truculent brow
he lowered his back for the play of young girls,
and through alien realms, the waves of his brother,

with his hooves imitating the slow drag of oars,
he breasted the waters and thus tamed the deep,
a captain who feared for his plunder alone.[39]
The radiant goddess of the murky-dark world[40]
felt this fire and abandoned the night, giving her brother
her luminous coach to be driven awry.
He learned how to whip on the horses of night
and circle an orbit with tighter diameter.
Nor did the nights maintain their own time,
but the day reappeared with the sun rising late,
while the car-axles shook with their heavier load.
The son of Alcmena put down his quiver
and the fearsome hide of the terrible lion,
willing to deck out his fingers with emeralds
and have order imposed on his unruly hair.[41]
He covered his legs in gold-knotted strands, and
confined his feet to slippers of saffron;
in the hand that used to carry a club
he drew out wool thread with the spindle awhirl.
Persia and Lydia, fertile in rich sand,[42]
saw the wild lion's skin tossed to the side;
on the shoulders that once had supported[43]
the realms of the towering sky,
lay a delicate shawl made of Tyrian thread.
This fire's supernatural—trust those whom it's hurt—
and too powerful by far.
Where the earth is embraced by the deep salt sea,
where the bright constellations traverse heaven itself,
the heartless boy here has his realm.
In the depths of the ocean his arrows are felt
by the sky-colored throng of Nereids;[44]
they cannot assuage the flames with the sea.
All the species with wings feel his fire.
Goaded by lust, the audacious bull
takes on warfare for all of his herd;
If they fear for their spouses,

310

320

330

340

the timorous stags call for battle;
by means of their bellows, they make known the signs
of the stirring of passion. Then the
swarthy-skinned Indians fear striped tigers,
then the boar hones his tusks that rip flesh
and foams over all of his snout.
The lions of Carthage shake up their manes
when love has aroused them. The forests then groan
with the murmurs of beasts. The giant of   350
the frothing sea loves, and the elephant too.[45]
Nature claims all as her own.
Nothing's exempt; when Love says the word,
hatred is gone. Old rages yield to his flames. Why sing on?
Love's worries overcome the cruel stepmother.

ACT 2

CHORUS LEADER

Nurse, give us your news: in what state is the queen?
Is there any limit to her fierce flames?

NURSE

There is no hope that such a curse can be assuaged;   360
there'll be no ending for these maddened flames.
She's burning with a silent heat, and though her inner passion
is concealed, it's betrayed upon her face:
fire flashes from her eyes, her tired sight can't stand the light;
she wavers, and the same thing doesn't please her
twice, a pain she cannot pinpoint jolts her every way:
now she flags and falls, her legs give way,
she can hardly hold her head up on her drooping neck;
now she puts herself to bed, but forgets to sleep
and spends the night lamenting; she orders that they lift her up   370
and put her down again, that her hair be now untied
and then re-styled; she cannot stand her state,
which changes constantly. No thought of food or health
crosses her mind. She walks on unsure feet,

abandoned by her strength; her vigor's not the same,
376   nor the ruddy red which used to flush her radiant face.[46]
379   The eyes which used to show the light of Phoebus' torch
380   are not gleaming with nobility, nor with her ancestry.
Tears pour down her face and her cheeks are wet
with endless drops, like when the snows on Taurus' peaks[47]
are struck by tepid showers and melt away.
But look, the lofty palace doors are opening,
and she herself lies on the cushions of a gilded couch
and waves away her usual garb; she isn't of sound mind.

PHAEDRA
Slaves, take away these clothes ornate with purple and
with gold, remove the red of Tyrian dyes, the filaments
that faraway Chinese pluck from their branches.[48]
390   Let a narrow belt hold down my garment's simple folds.
No necklace at my throat, I don't want snowy pearls,
the gift of Indian seas, weighing down my ears;
my hair should not be oiled with Assyrian scent.
Let my curls, tossed carelessly, flow down my neck
and shoulders, and let them bob to my quick pace
and stream upon the wind. My left hand will take a quiver,
my right will wield a spear from Thessaly.
This is just how stern Hippolytus' mother was.[49]
Just as an Amazon from Tanais or Maeotis[50]
400   having left behind the shores of frigid Pontus[51]
treads the Attic soil and drives her troops
and knots her hair, then sets it free, her side
protected by a crescent shield: so too I will hurry to the woods.

(Phaedra disappears within the palace.)

CHORUS LEADER

(To the Nurse.)

Stop your wails: grief doesn't help the wretched;
appease the rustic power of the virgin goddess.

NURSE

O queen of groves, sole one to love the mountains,
sole goddess whom the mountains alone love,
change the dark threats of the omens for the better.
Goddess great of woods and glades,
bright star of sky and jewel of night,   410
through whose phases of moonlight the world's aglow,
triformed Hecate,[52] be present and help with our task.
Tame the stubborn soul of stern Hippolytus
open him to listening; soothe that harsh heart;
let him learn to love and to feel a shared passion,
bind fast his mind: though he's sullen, harsh, and wild,
let him come under the laws of Venus. Direct your force
this way: so may a shining face attend you,
may you go clear-horned through broken clouds,
so may Thessalian spells never work to drag you down   420
as you guide the reins of the nocturnal sky
and may no shepherd boast of glory over you.[53]
You are here, goddess I invoked; now heed my prayer.

(*Hippolytus enters and pauses at Diana's shrine.*)

I see the man himself making holy offering at your shrine,
no companion at his side. Why hesitate? Chance
has conferred time and place. I must use my skills.
Am I fearful? It's not an easy thing, to dare a crime
that's been commanded, but if you fear kings, you must
reject what's right and drive all honor from your mind:
shame's an inept aide to royal power.   430

HIPPOLYTUS

My faithful nurse, why drag here aged steps,
tired as you are, with troubled brow
and sad of face? Surely my father is still safe
and Phaedra's safe, and both of their twin sons?

NURSE

Put aside your fear, the kingdom thrives,

your family is well, and enjoys its good fortune.
But you should relax more these happy days!
You see, concern for you keeps me on edge:
you're cruel to yourself, you curb yourself with over-heavy
    penalties.

440 It makes sense to be wretched if your fate compels you.
But anyone who harms himself spontaneously, and
of his own accord torments himself, should lose the benefits
he ignorantly wastes. Be mindful rather of your age,
and let your mind relax; take up a torch
for night's festivities, let wine alleviate your weighty cares.
Enjoy your youth: it goes by very quickly.
Now's when your heart is light, now's when love is fun.
Let your spirits soar! Why occupy an empty bed?
Shed the glum young man: pick up your pace,[54]
450 throw off the reins, don't let the best days of your life
just drain away. God has marked out due
responsibilities and guides life through its stages:
joy for the young man, a stern brow for the old.
Why constrain yourself and kill your proper disposition?
The crop which as a tender shoot runs wild with
fertile growth, will grant a farmer great return;
the tree no stinting hand has cut or pruned
will dwarf the grove with lofty crown.
Good character wins praise more easily
460 if lively freedom feeds a noble spirit.
You truculent and woodsy fellow, ignorant of life,
will you cultivate a joyless youth, leaving love behind?
Do you think this is the task enjoined on men:
to suffer hardship, to break in horses in their course, and
fight out savage wars in bloody conflict?
The mighty father of the world, when he found
the hands of fate so greedy, took care
to forever make up losses with new births.
Come now, let's suppose that love abandons humankind,
470 love which fills out and restores our worn-out race.

The world will lie rotting in gross neglect,
the sea will stand empty without a single fish,
birds won't populate the sky nor beasts the woods,
only breezes will traverse the upper air.
How varied are the forms of death which drag at
and destroy our mortal throng, sea and steel and treachery!
But suppose these outcomes weren't there: we'd seek out
black Styx voluntarily! Barren youths would smile on
life spent celibate: what you see is all there'd be,
a single generation's throng, soon to topple on itself.   480
So then: take up nature as your guide in life:
go to see the city, be sociable with citizens.

HIPPOLYTUS

No other life is freer and more blameless, and
cares more for ancient rituals, than the one
that leaves behind the city walls and cherishes the woods.
The frenzy of a grasping mind does not inflame a man
who's given his pure soul to mountain heights,
nor the fickle crowd nor the mob disloyal to good men,
nor toxic envy, nor brittle popularity;
he does not kowtow to a king, nor pine to *be* a king   490
while chasing empty honor or fleeting wealth.
He's free of hope and fear; black gnawing malice
doesn't set on *him* with cankered teeth.
He doesn't know the crimes that crowded cities
generate, he doesn't quake in guilt at every outcry,
nor make up explanations; he doesn't try, a wealthy man,
to have a thousand-pillared home, nor insolently plate the
roof-beams with ample gold; floods of gore don't drown
his pious altars; no snow-white oxen in the hundreds
bend their necks when dabbed with sacred grain.   500
He's the empty fields' lord, and roams innocuous
under the open air. He only knows how to contrive
tricky snares for beasts; and when he's tired by hard work,
the stream Ilisos, cold with snow, pampers his flesh.

Now he skirts the banks of quick Alpheus,[55] now
he passes through the thickets of a towering grove,
where the icy Lerna runs pellucid with her pure stream,
and avoids the sun;[56] here fretful birds are quarreling,
and the branches and the ancient beeches tremble,[57]
shaken gently by the breeze. It's nice to rest one's length along
a twisting brooklet's banks, to take untroubled naps
on open turf, whether by a wide spring gushing rapid
waters, or while a sweet sound murmurs from a stream
that flows through budding flowers.
Apples shaken from the trees appease his hunger,
berries plucked from bushes growing low
provide him easy meals. His instinct is to keep afar
from royal luxury. Great men drain gold cups
with dread; how nice to scoop up running water
with bare hands! A sounder sleep refreshes him
as he rests carefree limbs on an unyielding bed.
He's no villain plotting intrigues in seclusion
or in a secret room, who hides himself in fear inside
a labyrinth-like house; he seeks the open air and light,
and lives beneath the watchful sky.
                    This is the way I think
they lived—those mortals mingled with the gods
whom the primal age produced. No blind lust for
gold was theirs, no sacred stone on land marked off
the fields as arbiter of land for men;
ships did not yet credulously cross the deep:
we only knew our native seas. Cities had not ringed their sides
with massive walls and staggered towers,
no soldier picked up savage weapons in his hands,
no wound-up catapult broke bolted gates
with heavy stones, nor was the earth compelled to bear
a master, enduring bondage under oxen teams:
instead the fields, fruitful of themselves, fed people
making no demands; the forests and the shaded caves

510

520

530

provided nature's wealth and nature's homes.
This pact was broken by a wicked lust for lucre,   540
by headlong rage and forms of greed which goad
the inflamed mind. A bloody thirst for power
swept in, the weaker were the stronger's prey,
and might was right. The first time that these humans
fought, they had no spears in hand, but turned
the rocks and simple branches into weapons. There was no
light cornel-shaft tipped with tapered iron, no long-edged
sword strapped at one's side, no helmets flashing from afar
their crests: anger forged the armaments.
The God of War brought in new skills and a thousand   550
forms of death. From here streams of butchery
dyed every land and turned the sea to crimson.
Then limits were abolished, crimes entered
every home, no outrage lacked a precedent.
Brother fell to brother, father to his son's right hand,
a husband lies dead by his spouse's sword,
and godless mothers kill their very children.
I'm mute on stepmothers: not one is kinder than a beast.
But woman is the leader in all evil: this mastermind of crime
besets our souls. Thanks to a slut's adulteries,   560
so many cities smoke in ruin, nations wage so many wars,
and kingdoms torn up by the roots afflict so many people.
No need to mention others: just Aegeus' wife,
Medea,[58] will render womankind a plague.

NURSE

Why make the misdeeds of a few the fault of all?

HIPPOLYTUS

I hate them all, I dread, run from, and curse them.
Let it be reason, nature or a dire madness:
I've resolved to hate them. You'll sooner mix water
with fire; the shifting Syrtes sooner offer
friendly shoals to ships;[59] western Tethys raise   570

the sunlit day up from the farthest bay,[60]
and wolves bestow on does fond glances,
than I'll give in and be gentle to a woman.

NURSE

Love has often bridled stubborn men
and transformed their hate. Look at your mother's realms:
those fierce women feel the yoke of Venus;
you're proof of this, sole male child of the race.

HIPPOLYTUS

I consider this the only solace of my mother's death,
that now I can despise all women.

NURSE

580   Just like a rocky crag, on every side unyielding,
that fights the waves and flings far back
the gnawing tide, he spurns my words.
But Phaedra's rushing up, impatient with delay.
How will her luck turn out? What outcome will her frenzy find?
Suddenly, her fainting body crumbles to the ground
and a corpse-like pallor veils her face.
Raise your head, cast off what stops your speech:
Look, your own Hippolytus is holding you, my child.

PHAEDRA

Who returns me to my grief, restores the painful surges
590   of my mind? How good it felt to be rid of myself!

HIPPOLYTUS

Why reject the pleasant gift of being restored to life?

PHAEDRA

(*Aside.*)

Dare it, try it, do what you decided to, my mind:
let your words be firm and fearless. Asking timidly
is asking for rejection. A huge part of my crime
was long ago complete. Shame's too late for me:
I've started the unspeakable. If I follow what's begun,
perhaps I'll hide my sins behind the marriage torch:

a successful end makes certain crimes respectable.
Come on, my mind, begin!—

(*To Hippolytus.*)

      Hear me out a moment, please,
in private. If there's a servant with you, have him leave.   600

HIPPOLYTUS

See, the place is empty, and free of any witness.

PHAEDRA

My mouth won't grant a passage to the speech I've started:
a great force makes me speak, a greater holds me back.
I call all of you to witness, gods: I don't want
the thing I want.

HIPPOLYTUS

You desire to say something but aren't able?

PHAEDRA

Small worries find expression, huge ones are stricken dumb.

HIPPOLYTUS

Trust your worries to my ears, Mother.

PHAEDRA

Mother's a very lofty term and far too grandiose.
A humbler term is fitting for my feelings: 610
Either call me sister, or call me slave, Hippolytus—
and slave is better. I'll suffer any servitude.
If you should order me to cross deep-lying snows
on Mount Pindus' icy peaks,[61] I'd not complain;
nor if you had me to walk through fires and hostile ranks
would I pause to bare my chest to waiting swords.
Receive the scepter of the regent, take me as your slave;
it's right for you to rule the kingdom, me to act on orders.
It's not a woman's job, protecting rule over the cities.
You, thriving in the youngest bloom of youth,   620
you should rule the citizens, strong in your father's power.[62]
Hold me in your arms, protect your suppliant and slave;
pity me without a husband.

HIPPOLYTUS

May the greatest god avert that omen!
Father will arrive here safely any moment.

PHAEDRA

The ruler of that realm of no escape and of the silent Styx
has made no path that goes back to the beings above:
will he release the man who stole his very wife?
Unless Pluto too indulges love while he rules Dis?

HIPPOLYTUS

The just divinities will grant to *him* a safe return.
But while god holds our prayers in the balance,
I'll love my dear brothers with due loyalty
making sure you don't feel widowed;
I'll fill my father's place for you myself.

PHAEDRA

(Aside.)

O foolish hope of lovers, O deceitful love!
Perhaps I've said enough? I'll continue pressing prayers.

(To Hippolytus.)

Have pity on me, hear the prayers of my silent mind.
It pleases me to speak, and it disgusts me.

HIPPOLYTUS

What on earth's this trouble?

PHAEDRA

One you'd hardly think could suit a stepmother.[63]

HIPPOLYTUS

You're blurting ambiguities in a speech made up of riddles:
speak openly.

PHAEDRA

Heat and passion scorch
my maddened heart.[64] A fierce fire wanders
that hides deep within my inmost guts and my veins,
just as quick flames run through lofty trees.

HIPPOLYTUS

You're enflamed, no doubt, by pure love for Theseus?

PHAEDRA

Hippolytus, here's how it is. I love the face of Theseus,
the prior one, which he once had as a boy,
when hairs first stubbled his smooth jaws
and he saw the Cretan monster's labyrinth
and took back up the long thread on its twisty path.   650
How luminous he was then! Bands tied back his hair,
a tawny modesty tinged his youthful face;
there were strong muscles in those soft-fleshed arms
and the face of your Phoebe or my Phoebus,
or rather yours—he was like you, like you when
he pleased his enemy;[65] he carried his head high like you.
In you an artless splendor shines out more:
all your father's in you, and yet some part
of your fierce mother contributes beauty equally.
In your Greek face a Scythian rigor can be seen.   660
If you'd entered Cretan straits together with your father,
my sister would have rather spun her thread for you.[66]
You, you, sister: in whatever section of the starry sky
you gleam, I call on you in a case like yours:
a single family has ruined two sisters,
the father you, but me the son. Look, fallen at your knees
sprawls the suppliant daughter of a royal house.
Spattered by no stain, untouched and innocent
I've changed for you alone. I've resolved to lower myself
to beg. This day will put an end to pain—or life.   670
Have pity on my love.

HIPPOLYTUS

(Her meaning dawning on him.)

O great ruler of the gods,
can you hear this outrage and be so slow to act? *See* it, and be
    slow?
When will you hurl the lightning from your brutal hand,

if now the skies are calm? Let all the upper air be smashed
to ruin and bury the day in pitch-black clouds,
let the stars turn back, and twisting run their course
askew. And you, lord of stars, ray-giving
Sun, do you see the outrage by your offspring?
Drown your radiance and flee to shadow.
680   Why is your right hand empty, lord of gods and men,
why does the world not catch afire from your triple torch?
Throw your thunderbolt at *me*, impale me, let swift lightning
stab me and cremate me: I'm guilty, I deserve to die:
my stepmother fell for me. —Am *I* fit choice for adultery?
Did I alone seem to you easy matter for such
a crime? Is this my severity's reward?
O you who outdo all of womankind in crime, O you who's
    dared
an outrage greater than your monster-birthing mother,
you're worse than she who bore you! She at least defiled
690   herself alone with her adultery; her offspring with its
hybrid form revealed the crime so long concealed
and the malformed baby gave away the mother's crime
with its feral face. That womb bore *you*!
O thrice and four times given to a happy fate
were those whom hate and guile drained dry of blood,
destroyed, and did to death! Father, I begrudge you:
this evil's worse than a stepmother from Colchis—worse![67]

PHAEDRA

I too recognize my lineage's fate: we pursue
the acts we ought to shun. But I can't control myself.
700   I'll even follow you through flames and maddened sea,
over cliffs and rivers driven by a raging flood.
Wherever you direct your steps, I'll be insanely driven.
Once again I grovel at your knees, proud man.

HIPPOLYTUS

Get away! Remove your filthy touch from my
chaste flesh! What's this, she's desperate to hold me?

Out with my sword: let it demand the death that she deserves.
Look: I've grabbed her twisted hair in my left hand
and forced her shameless head back: never more justly
has blood been offered at your hearth, goddess of the bow.

PHAEDRA

Hippolytus, now you've fulfilled my wish, you cure me   710
as I rave. This is more than I had hoped for:
to die thanks to your hands, but with my honor safe.

HIPPOLYTUS

Go! Better you should live than get the thing you pray for.
Let me unstrap this impure sword from my chaste side.
What Danube's stream will wipe me clean, what Maeotis[68]
flushing barbarous waters into the Pontic sea?
Not even the Great Father of the Gods himself, using all
the ocean, could purge this massive crime. O woods, O wild
    animals!

(*Exit Hippolytus.*)

NURSE

Her guilt has been discovered! My mind, why be dazed and
    slow to act?
Let's rebound the blame on him and take the lead in charging   720
    him
with unfilial lust. Crime must be veiled by crime.
The safest moment to attack is when you're scared.
Did we dare the outrage first, or did we suffer it—since
the crime took place in isolation, what witness will know?
Over here, Athenians! Loyal band of servants,
bring help! Hippolytus is trying to rape—it's horrible!—
he's forcing her, attacking her, she fears for her life,
he threatens the chaste girl at sword-point! —Look, he's taken
to his heels! Panicking, he left his sword as he ran off in fear.
We have proof of his guilt! But first help this poor girl   730
recover. The strands he tore, the bits and pieces of her hair,
should stay just as they are, tokens of his awful crime.
Announce it in the city! —Mistress, come to your senses now.

Why tear at yourself, avoiding meeting all our eyes?
It's intention that makes an adulteress, not what's happened to
    her.

CHORUS
He rushed away like an unstable storm-wind,
faster than Corus that gathers the clouds,[69]
faster than flame that devours its path
when a shooting star driven by winds trails
ribbons of fire.
Let Fame that admires past generations
compare to you all ancient glory:
your form shines out fairer by far,
just as rose-colored Phoebe more brightly gleams
when her sphere is full and her horns come full circle
and she joins her fires, and from her quick carriage
all through the night she reveals her face
and smaller stars can't keep their own.
The evening star Hesperus looks like you too, when he
    ushers in
the twilight; and that herald of night, when just now
washed in the waves, when the darkness is banished
once more, is known as Lucifer too.
You, Liber, from India, the country of the thyrsus,
a youth with hair that's always unshorn
guiding your tigers with ivy-tipped spear[70]
and binding your head with its horns in a turban:
you'll never surpass the unguent-less hair
of Hippolytus. Don't be too proud of your face:
the story has spread through all nations,
whom the sister of Phaedra picked over Bromius.[71]
Beauty, you double-edged gift for mankind,
a short gift for a small span of time,
how swiftly you pass on your hastening feet!
Not so fast does the heat of a burning hot summer
plunder meadows green at first spring,

740

750

760

when noontime seethes at the solstice
and the nights speed by in short orbits.
Just as lilies with pale petals droop,
and roses festooning our heads fade away,[72]
and the glow that shines from young cheeks   770
is gone in a flash; no day has not stolen
its share from a beautiful body.
Beauty lasts for a moment: what wise man would put trust
in a good he can lose? Use it while you can.
Time is eroding you silently, and each hour
upon you is worse than the last.
Why head for the wilds? Beauty's no safer
in unfrequented spots: in a faraway grove,
those naughty Naïads, a lascivious crowd with a habit
of catching cute boys in springs, will surround you   780
when the sun has brought in the midday,
and the frisky grove-goddesses
will lay traps as you sleep,
or the Pans who wander the mountains.
Or else gazing at you from the start-studded sky,
the moon-star that followed the ancient Arcadians
won't be able to steer her luminous carriage.
Just now she shone reddish, and no darkening cloud
blocked her bright gleam. We were alarmed
at the goddess's distress, and thought   790
she was pulled by Thessalian spells;
we set up a jingling of brass: but *you* were her problem,
you the cause of delay; it was while gazing at you
that the goddess of night held back her swift course.
May cold frosts more rarely bite at this face,
may this face more sparingly turn to the sun:
its hue will be clearer than Parian marble.
How pleasing a face that is virile and fierce,
and the serious weight of an older man's scowl!
You could match your own splendid neck with Apollo's.   800
His full head of hair is never tied back, and

flows down to adorn and to cover his shoulders;
a shaggier hairline is fitting for you, shorter hair
that falls as it will. You could dare to defeat even
fierce and bellicose gods with your strength
and the massive expanse of your body;
as a young man you're equal to Hercules' muscles,
your chest wider than that of the warmonger Mars.
If you wanted to ride on the back of a horse,
810   you could put through his paces the Spartan Cyllaros,[73]
your hand on the reins more pliant than Castor's.[74]
Ply the strap for the spear with your prior-most fingers
and hurl it with all of your strength:
the Cretans well-taught in shooting the bow
do not fire their slender reed arrows as far.
And if you decide to send showers of shafts
into the sky in the Parthian way, not one will come down
with a bird unattached, but wedged in warm guts
they'll fetch your prey from the midst of the clouds.
820   Rarely has beauty in men gone unpunished
—look at past times. May a kindlier god
pass over you and leave you unharmed, may your
noble good looks show the features of ugly old age.

ACT 3

CHORUS

What will this woman's reckless frenzy leave undared?
She's preparing awful charges against the guiltless boy!
Just see her wickedness! To be believable, she looks to her torn
    hair,
messes all the beauty of her face, wets her cheeks:
the trick's prepared with every form of female fraud.
But who's this man whose face reveals a regal dignity
830   and who holds his head at such a lofty height?
How much his face resembles the young Theseus,

if his cheeks weren't wan with tired pallor
and unlovely filth did not stiffen his hair.
—Look, it's Theseus himself, brought back to the world!

THESEUS

At last I have escaped the region of eternal night
the pole that keeps the dead souls shaded in their far-flung jail;
and my eyes can hardly bear the light I longed for.
Now Eleusis reaps the fourth crop of Triptolemus,[75]
and Libra for the fourth time makes day equal to night,
while the confusing labor of my unknown fate   840
has held me back between the ills of life and death.
Though I was dead, one part of life remained to me,
a sense of my misfortune. Hercules made it end;
absconding with the dog he stole from Tartarus,
he brought me likewise to the upper realms.
But my courage is worn out and lacks its former strength,
and my footsteps stagger. Ah me, how hard it was
to seek the distant sky from lowest Phlegethon,[76]
both in fleeing death and keeping pace with Hercules!
What sounds of sobbing have struck my ears?   850
Someone should explain. Mourning, tears and sorrow,
sad lamentation at the very threshold—it's
hospitality that wholly fits a guest from hell.

NURSE

Phaedra won't give up her stubborn plan to die;
on the verge of suicide, she spurns my tears.

THESEUS

What's the reason for this death? Why die when your husband
    has returned?

NURSE

This very cause has brought her ill-timed death.

THESEUS

Your cryptic words hide something serious.
Tell me openly what grief weighs on her mind.

NURSE

She shares it with no one: sad, she hides her secret;
she's resolved to take her cause of death with her to the grave.
Come now, come, I beg of you: there's need for haste.

THESEUS

Unlock the closed doors of the royal palace.
O sharer of my marriage bed, do you greet thus the coming
of your spouse, the husband's face you longed for?
Why not drop the sword from your right hand, restore to me
my peace of mind, and tell me what is driving you
from life?

PHAEDRA

Unhappy me! Great-hearted Theseus, I beg you
by the scepter of your rule, by the promise of our sons,
by your return, and by my future ashes,
let me die.

THESEUS

What cause demands your death?

PHAEDRA

If the cause of death is told, its benefit is lost.

THESEUS

No one else will hear it, except for me alone.

PHAEDRA

A chaste wife fears her husband's ears alone.

THESEUS

Tell me: I'll hide the secret in my loyal heart.

PHAEDRA

What you want another person not to spill, don't spill first.

THESEUS

No chance for suicide will come your way.

PHAEDRA

For one who wants to die, death is never far away.

THESEUS

Reveal the crime for which your death is expiation.

PHAEDRA

That I'm alive.   880

THESEUS

Don't my tears move you?

PHAEDRA

The best death is while loved ones will still mourn you.

THESEUS

(Aside.)

She persists in silence.

(To all.)

The old nurse will divulge what she declines
to say—when whipped and bound by chains!
Throw her in irons, and let the force of lashes dredge out
the secrets of her mind.

PHAEDRA

Wait! I myself will tell you.

THESEUS

Why do you turn aside your mournful face, and pull your cloak
    over
your cheeks to hide the tears that all at once spill down your
    cheeks?

PHAEDRA

I call on you as witness, you, father of the gods,
and you, gleaming splendor of celestial light,
from whose rising my own lineage is drawn: 890
when tried by prayers I resisted; my soul did not yield
to threats and to the sword; but still my body suffered force.
My blood will wash away this stain upon my purity.

THESEUS

Out with it! Who overthrew my honor?

PHAEDRA

Whom you'd least expect.

THESEUS

  I must hear his identity.

PHAEDRA

  This sword will tell you, which the rapist left behind,
  scared off by the outcry, and worried that the citizens would
   come.

THESEUS

  Unhappy me, what is this crime that I discern? What unholy
   sight is this?
  Royal ivory engraved with minute symbols gleams upon
  the hilt—the honorific seal of our Aegean line!⁷⁷
  But the man himself—where did he escape to?

PHAEDRA

   These slaves saw him
  running off in fear, going at a rapid clip.

THESEUS

  O holy Piety, O ruler of the sky, and you
  who agitate the second kingdom with your waves,
  where did this foulness in our line come from?
  Did a Greek land raise this boy, or Taurus in Scythia
  and Colchian Phasis?⁷⁸ The breed reverts to its first founders,
  polluted blood recalls its primal stock.
  This corresponds entirely to the madness of that warrior tribe,
  to hate the pacts of Venus, and then to prostitute
  one's long-chaste flesh among the crowd. You disgusting race,
  you've never been restrained by the laws of better lands!
  Even wild animals avoid unnatural intercourse,
  and instinctive shame upholds the laws of parturition.
  What of that visage, and the man's fake dignity,
  the rugged look that aimed at the old-fashioned,
  his old-man strictness of morality and his solemn airs?
  A life spent in deceit! You harbor hidden feelings
  and you put a pretty face on your rotten character!
  Shame conceals the lack of shame, calm conceals audacity,
  duty what's unspeakable: dissemblers praise the truth

and sybarites feign strictness. So, Mr. Forest-Dweller,
wild-natured, pure, untouched, unpolished,
were you holding back for *me*? Did you decide to usher in
your manhood first in *my* bed, and with such a crime?
Now, *now* I'm grateful to the powers above
that Antiope fell stricken by my hand, and that
I didn't go down to Styx's caves while leaving you
your mother. Flee far away through unknown
peoples as an exile! Even if some distant land at   930
earth's far edge parted us by Ocean's realms,
even if you occupied the planet's other side,
even if you hid away in some deep abscess,
having crossed the northern pole's ice-laden lands,
even if you pass the reach of winter and hoary snow
and leave behind cold Boreas' howling threats[79]
raging at your back, you'll be punished for your crimes.
As you flee through every lair I'll follow you inexorably;
the two of us will tread far distant lands—hidden, without
    access,
diverse and pathless; there's no place will impede us: 940
you know where I return from. Where weapons can't be sent,
I'll send my curses. My father, ocean-dweller,
let me make three wishes he would grant,
and he ratified this present by calling on the Styx.
So fulfill your dismal gift, ruler of the seas!
Let Hippolytus no more see the shining day,
let him join while young the shades his father angered.
My parent, give now your son this hateful help.
I would never use this supreme gift of your divinity
if overwhelming ills did not oppress me: 950
in the midst of deepest Tartarus and horrid Dis
and the looming threats of the infernal king,
I refrained from pleas. Now keep the pledge you made.
Father, are you waiting? Why are the waves still calm?
Bring on night with winds that drive dark clouds,
snatch away the constellations and the sky,

spill forth the sea, call up the throngs of marine life
and as you swell, call on the very Ocean's floods.

(*They exit into the palace.*)

CHORUS
　　O nature, great parent of gods,
960　and you, king of fiery Olympus,
　　who hasten the stars that are spangling
　　the quick-wheeling sky and the wandering paths
　　of the planets, and who rotate the poles on swift hinges:
　　why do you take such great care to stir up
　　the paths of the uppermost ether,
　　so that now the frosts of white winter
　　strip bare the forests, and now the shadows return
　　to the grove, now the stars of the[80]
　　summertime's Lion ripen the crops
970　with seething hot air,
　　and then the year tempers its force?
　　And why—a ruler yourself of so much,
　　under whose sway the weights of the infinite
　　universe are balanced and complete their orbits—
　　why are you absent, too neglectful of men,
　　not concerned to assist the ones who are good
　　and do harm to the wicked?
　　Fortune is queen over human affairs
　　with no logic, and tosses out gifts
980　with an unseeing hand, and favors the worse:
　　awful lust overwhelms pious men,
　　fraud reigns in the loftiest court.
　　The people enjoy the transfer of power
　　to someone who's base, it flatters and hates him.
　　Strict virtue reaps inverse rewards for what's right:
　　painful poverty follows the chaste, the adulterer gains
　　　　strength
　　through his vice and holds sway.
　　O meaningless shame, and deceitful decorum!

ACT 4

CHORUS LEADER

But what's the news this envoy brings with hasty step
while he wets his mournful face with tears of sorrow?   990

(Enter messenger.)

MESSENGER

O what a hard and bitter fate, o slavery, harsh to bear,
why call on *me* to announce the dreadful news?

THESEUS

Don't be scared to speak of cruel misfortunes bravely;
I have a heart that's scarcely unprepared for hardship.

MESSENGER

My tongue won't grant my grief its painful words.

THESEUS

Tell us the fate that presses heavy on our shaken house.

MESSENGER

Hippolytus—ah me!—has died a tragic death.

THESEUS

I his father long since knew my son was dead;
now the rapist's died. Tell us how his end came.

MESSENGER

When he left the city as an exile, angrily,   1000
unfolding his quick path with hasty steps,
he set his horses under their high yoke at once
and curbed their mouths, and pulled the bridle tight.
Then speaking to himself at length, he cursed
his native land and often called upon his father,
and used the lash urgently, letting the reins go slack:
when suddenly the vast sea thundered from its depths
and rose up to the stars. There's no wind blowing
on the brine, no quarter of the calm sky makes a noise,
but a self-made storm riles up the placid water.   1010
The southeast wind is not as strong as this, when it roils the straits

129 | PHAEDRA

of Sicily, nor does Ionia's gulf surge with waves so violent
when the northwest wind is lord, when crags shake at the
    tide-pull
and white foam strikes Leucate's highest part.[81]
The vast sea surges up into a massive column, and the water,
swollen with some monstrous thing, crashes on the shore.
This huge destructive force isn't formed to damage ships:
it's the land it threatens. The flood sweeps forward
with no light force: the pregnant water carries something
in its burdened breast. What land is showing to the stars
its new-born head? Is a new Cycladic island rising up?
The cliffs famed for the godhead of Asclepius are hid,[82]
so are the rocks of Sciron famed for crime,[83]
and the land that two straits press on either side.
While we stare at this in stupefaction, look! the whole sea
roars, and all around the crags send clamor back:
the highest peak is wet with thrown-up spray,
and foams and vomits back the sea alternately
like when a giant whale swims through the Ocean's depths
flushing out the water from his mouth.
The shaken globe of water shivered
and collapsed and carried to the shore an evil
greater than fear itself. The sea rushed onto land
in the wake of its own monster—fear unnerves my voice.
What an appearance that massive body had!
A towering bull with dark-blue neck
raises a tall mane on his greenish brow;
his shaggy ears stood up, and his eyes varied their hue,
now like that of the master of a wild herd,
now like that of something from the depths: now they spew
out flame, now they gleam remarkably with green.
His fleshy neck bulges with huge muscles and
the gaping nostrils roar with flared intakes of air.
The dewlap and the chest are green with sticking algae.
the long flanks mottled with red lichen;
then at the back, the last part of his body ends

in a monstrosity, and the huge and scaly beast
drags along this massive part. He's like a sea-monster
who in the farthest seas sucks in quick ships, or shatters them.
The lands quaked, and the frightened herds fled helter-skelter   1050
through the fields; trailing his flock fell from the cowherd's
mind; the wild beasts all fled from their groves,
every hunter froze and paled with icy dread. Hippolytus alone
was free from fear; he held his horses back
with tightened reins, and roused the frightened animals
with the urging of his well-known voice.
There's a high path to the fields between the broken hills,
adjacent to the lands that border on the sea below.
Here that leviathan sharpens himself and hones his rage.
When he'd roused his energy, testing himself sufficiently   1060
and practicing his rage, he took off at a headlong run.
He barely touched the surface of the ground in his rapid rush,
and then came, ferocious, to a stop before the frightened horses.
Your son rose up to face him, with menace in his fierce look.
He didn't change expression, but thundered at him loudly:
"This empty terror doesn't break my spirit:
it was my father's work to conquer bulls."[84]
But the horses, disobedient to the reins, at once bolted
with the chariot; now they've left behind the path and run
wherever frenzied terror takes them in their madness,   1070
and they dash themselves against the cliffs.
But like a helmsman who controls his boat in stormy
seas, and doesn't let it turn its side to face the waves
and cheats the current with his skill, just so he guides
the rapid chariot: now he pulls their heads back, held
by tightened reins, now he drives them on with frequent
lashings of their backs—but their constant partner follows on,
now covering equal ground, now moving from his path
to block them, and everywhere he incites fear.
Then they could escape no more: that bristling, horned   1080
creature of the sea charged full-on to meet them.
Then in truth the horses, spooked by fearful minds,

threw off control, fighting to free their bodies from
the yoke; rearing they throw their burden to the ground.
Flung out headlong on his face, he tangles up his body as he
    falls
in the tenacious reins, and the more he fights against them
so much the more the clinging knots grow tight.
The horses realize what they've done; with lightened chariot
and no one in control, they dash where fear bids them.
Just so his horse-team threw out Phaethon in a far-flung
region of the sky; they did not recognize their load, and were
indignant that the day was trusted to a phony Sun.
The fields are bloody far and wide; his smashed-in head
bounds off the rocks, thickets shred his hair, and
hard stones devastate his handsome face;
his unlucky looks are ruined by many wounds.
The swift wheels spin his dying limbs around;
as he's dragged along, at last a tree trunk with burnt stock
holds him with an upright stake forced right through his
    groin,
and for a while the chariot stops because its master's stuck.
The team is held back by this wound—then they cut short
delay and master both. After this the bushes rip apart the
half-dead man; brambles rough with sharp-edged thorns
and every tree trunk take a section of the body.
A band of servants sadly wander through the fields,
through the places which Hippolytus, all torn apart,
marked out his lengthy path with bloody signs;
his downcast dogs sniff out the pieces of their master.
But his grieving servants' careful labor hasn't managed yet
to make a body from the pieces.

(Looking at the remnants.)

Is *this* the beauty of his form?
The man who just now was a famed companion of his father's
    throne,
just now shone as certain heir, as if he were a star,

is being gathered here and there for the final pyre
and being assembled for his funeral.

THESEUS

O nature, all too powerful,
you hold us parents in such a bond of blood,
how we honor you even against our will!
When he was guilty, I wanted him to die; now he's gone, I weep
for him.

MESSENGER

No one can rightly weep at the outcome that he wanted.

THESEUS

Yet I consider this the greatest height of evils,
if fortune makes us hope for what we hate. 1120

MESSENGER

If you hate him still, why is your face sodden with tears?

THESEUS

I weep because I've killed,[85] not because I am bereaved.

CHORUS

Ah, how great is the chance that whirls human affairs!
Fortune's rage is less forceful against minor folk,
god strikes trifling lives but triflingly.
Undistinguished leisure keeps people peaceful,
and a cottage provides for secure old age.
Peaks that are close to ethereal homes
admit the east wind and the south,
the menace of insane Boreas 1130
and rain-bringing Corus.
It's rare that damp valleys feel strikes
from the lightning,
but towering Caucasus trembles
at the weapon of high-thundering Jove,
as does the Phrygian forest of mother Cybele.
Jupiter fears for high heaven and
attacks what's close by.
The commoner's house with its low-lying roof

never feels great commotions; thunder strikes around thrones.

The slippery hour flies by on wavering

wings, and swift Fortune stays steady

for none. He who finally saw

the stars of the world and the luminous day,

having left death behind, laments[86]

his cheerless return, and finds

the hospitality of his paternal home

more lamentable than hell itself.[87]

Pallas Athena, revered by Athenians,

though your Theseus looks on the sky and its gods,

and has fled the swamps of the Styx,

you owe nothing, chaste goddess, to your grasping uncle:

the number of dead hasn't changed for the underworld's tyrant.

ACT 5

(*Phaedra appears in front of the palace, holding Hippolytus' sword.*)

CHORUS LEADER

What grieving voice sounds from the inmost section of the
house?

And what is maddened Phaedra planning with that naked
sword?

THESEUS

What frenzy goads you, roused with grief,

what sword is that, and what can your outcry

and lament mean, over a hated corpse?

PHAEDRA

Me, attack me, savage ruler of the profound depths,

and send your monster of the sea-blue sea to fall on *me*,

and add whatever far-flung Tethys rears in her inmost

bays, and whatever Ocean covers with his furthest

floods, embracing it within his nomad waves.

O Theseus, always too harsh: you are never restored to your
family

without some harm. Your son and father paid for your

homecoming with death; you always ruin your house,
hurting it because you love your wives—or hate them.
Hippolytus, is *this* how I see your face,
is this what I did to it? What savage robber Sinis,[88]
what Procrustes tore apart your limbs,[89] what Cretan bull,   1170
filling Daedalus' labyrinth with his deafening bellow,
a ferocious biform beast with horns upon his head?
Ah me, where did your beauty flee,
the eyes that were my stars? Do you lie dead?
Stay here for just a short while: hear my words.
I'm saying nothing shameful: I'll avenge you
with this hand, and plunge the sword into my evil chest,
I'll free Phaedra from her life and from her crime together,
I'll trail you frenzied through the waves and lakes
of Tartarus, through the Styx and streams of fire.   1180
Let me appease the shades.

(*Cuts off a lock of hair and places it on Hippolytus.*)

Accept these spoils from my head,
take the hair I've torn off from my battered scalp.
We couldn't join our lives, but we can surely
join our deaths.

(*To herself.*)

If you are pure, die for your husband;
if impure, for love. Should I reclaim my husband's bed
when it's stained by such a crime? This would be the final straw,
that I should wallow as if chaste in a bed of vengeance.
O death, sole comfort for unsanctioned love,
O death, tainted honor's greatest glory,
in you I seek refuge: take me in your arms, placated.   1190
Hear me, you of Athens, hear me, Father worse than
a deadly stepmother: what I said was false, a crime; I lied,
in madness I made up the very outrage I enjoyed
in my unhinged heart. You punished, as a father, a nonexistent
    crime,

and a pure young man lies dead on an impure charge,
innocent and harmless.

(*To Hippolytus.*)

Take back now your integrity.

(*She stabs herself with his sword.*)

My incestuous heart's exposed by this just sword,
my blood performs the funeral rites for a pious man.
Learn from a stepmother what you should do as father
1200   when your son's been taken: bury yourself in Acheron.

THESEUS

O jaws of pale Avernus, and you, Taenarus' cave,[90]
Lethe's streams that soothe the stricken, and you, sluggish
    lagoons:
Seize this unloving father, keep him plunged in eternal pain.
Now appear, savage monsters of the deep, now appear, O
    boundless sea,
and what Proteus hides in his furthest watery bays:
drown me in deep eddies for glorying in such a crime—
and you too, Father, always ready to accommodate my anger.
I don't deserve an easy death. I spread my son's torn body
    through the fields
in newfangled murder, and while I chased fictitious crime
1210   as a pitiless avenger, I stumbled into real criminality.
I've filled the heavens, underworld, and oceans with my crime.
No other region was allotted: all three kingdoms know me.
Did I return for this? Did a pathway open to the light
so I could see a double death, twin funerals,
and burn as one the final pyres of my son and wife
with but one torch, bereft of spouse and child?
Hercules, who granted me this darkened light,
return to Dis your gift: restore to me the ghosts
you stole from me. Impiously, in vain, I call upon
1220   the death I left behind. O you savage architect of death,

deviser of a penalty both barbarous and bizarre,
now exact just punishment from your very self.
Should two pine trees, with their tops forced down to earth,
hoist me in the air and split me between their trunks,
or should I throw myself headfirst down Sciron's rocks?
I've seen worse things, which Phlegethon, that girds
the guilty and confines them with its fiery river, bids them bear.
I know what punishments, what final home's in store for me:
make way, you guilty shades, and let the rock that's been
eternal toil for ancient Sisyphus be placed upon *these* shoulders,   1230
these, and be a burden for my weary hands;
let the stream that bypasses one's nearby mouth, mock *me*,
let the feral vulture fly to *me*, and abandon Tityus,[91]
let my liver constantly regrow for punishment.
And you, father of my Pirithous,[92] take rest:
Let the wheel that never stops carry this body
in its rapid whirling as its circle turns around.
Earth, gape open; dire Chaos, take me in,
take me in; this pathway to the shades is better justified:
I'm following my son. Have no fear, you who rule the shades: 1240
we do not come with lust. Take me in; I will not leave this
    home
for all eternity. —My prayers do not move the gods;
but if I prayed for evil, how ready they would be!

CHORUS LEADER

Theseus, time unlimited remains for your laments.
Pay now the due rites for your son and quickly hide
the limbs gruesomely scattered by a savage mangling.

THESEUS

Here, here bring the remnants of that dear body,
give me that mass, the limbs heaped up at random.
Is this Hippolytus? I recognize the crime as mine:
it was I who ruined you. And lest I should be guilty just once   1250
or by myself, as a parent ready to dare crime
I called upon my father. See how I enjoy paternal favor!

Bereavement is a grim misfortune for my weakened years.
Embrace the limbs, you wretched man, and as you kneel over
    your son,
hold close to your grieving heart whatever's left.
As his father, set aright the mangled body's
severed limbs, restore the straying parts to their
location. Here's the place his brave right hand goes;
here you must put the left hand taught to wield
1260   the reins; I recognize the signs of his left torso.
How great a part is still not present for my tears!
Endure, my shaking hands, for this dismal duty,
and eyes, be dry, check your floods of tears,
while the father portions out his offspring's limbs
and reconstructs his body. What's this nasty lump
without a shape, truncated all around by many wounds?
I don't know what part of you it is, but it's a part of you.
Here, put it here, not the right place but an empty one.
Is this that face that gleamed with fire like the stars
1270   and looked around with lively eyes?[93] Has his beauty come to
    this?
O cruel fates, O savage favor of the gods!
Is this how a son returns, when a parent prays for him?
Here, accept your father's final gifts. You'll need this ritual
many times: in the meantime, let the pyre take these things.

                                        (*To the servants.*)

Open up my house, made bitter by this tragic death:
may all of Athens ring with loud cries of lament.[94]
You men prepare the flames to light the royal pyre;
but you, go scour the countryside for vagrant body parts.
—As for *her*: let earth press down upon her buried body,
1280   and may the soil weigh heavy on her incestuous head.

The Trojan Women

Seneca's *Trojan Women* begins with Hecuba's lament. Queen of the fallen city of Troy, widowed wife of Priam, she mourns the reversal of fortune that has placed her amid the titular chorus of captive women. The women join in, and the first act of the play ends as a testament, unique in Seneca's work, of collective grief. Next appears Pyrrhus, the sadistic son of Achilles. He demands that Agamemnon, the leader of the Greeks, sacrifice Polyxena in a blood wedding to Pyrrhus' father Achilles. Agamemnon attempts to dissuade him by appealing to the novel basis of human rights (334), but this interesting mix of epic etiquette and Senecan Stoicism proves ineffective.

The apparition of Achilles, belched from the earth and frothing for his son to impale Polyxena, provides a basis for Pyrrhus' act. The prophet whom Agamemnon summons to resolve the dispute ratifies the grisly bidding of specter and son. Referring to Agamemnon's prewar sacrifice of his daughter, Iphigenia, Calchas reports that "The fates grant the Greeks a path at the usual price" (360); then adds, "The son of Hector, Priam's son, must meet his death. / Then the thousand sails of the fleet may fill the straits" (369–70).

Back among the chorus of the Trojan women, Andromache anticipates some final ruthlessness against her son, Astyanax. She contrives a desperate trick to hide him, concealing him in the tomb of his father, Hector. But then Ulysses, the master strategist of the Greeks, arrives. More rational than any prophet, he claims that the murder of Hector's son Astyanax is a political necessity. When the boy grows up, he'll revisit a war of Trojan proportions on the Greeks. With threats of torture and the dismemberment of Hector's funeral site, Ulysses pries the truth from Andromache.

For her part, Helen, cunning but less effective than Ulysses, tries to convince the captive women that Polyxena will be married to Pyrrhus, not his still-bloodthirsty father beyond the grave. After the women see through the trick and demand the truth, the play ends with the willful deaths of the two youths: Astyanax hurls himself from the last remnant of Troy, and Polyxena marches to her murder with fierce dignity in the play's self-conscious climax, set in "a valley [that] seals the inner space with a slight incline / and rises as though a theater" (1125).

Introduction

ALEX DRESSLER

Seneca's play the *Trojan Women* is a study in the experience of women and children in the aftermath of war. Though bookended by scenes of the aged and disgraced queen of the fallen city, it is an ensemble piece, distinguished not only by the fair distribution of speeches and notable actions to the *dramatis personae* but also by the latter's diversity. On the side of the Trojans, Andromache and Hecuba represent two different perspectives on the suffering of female survivors. The grief of the first is focused on the past loss of her husband, "the pillar of our country, the delayer of our doom" (124), and the impending loss of her young son, Astyanax. Tightening her focus even more, she confronts the events of the play as a choice between the past and the future, even as she cannot tell them apart (659): "Hector's on both sides." The grief of the matriarch, Hecuba, is, in contrast, diffuse (1061): "Each person is crushed by her crisis, but I'm crushed by everyone's." Filling out this catalogue of women, on the side of the conqueror, is Helen: the selfish beauty comes on the scene to trick the last surviving child of Hecuba, Polyxena, into a sacrificial marriage, lamenting her own fate ("*I* suffered worse," 907) and eventually gloating over the distribution of the captives as concubines ("You'll envy her more, as soon as you learn your lot," 972).

The play, which begins with Hecuba leading the lament for the father and grandfather of Astyanax, consists mostly of Andromache's attempt, through a feckless trick, to postpone his slaughter. With minimal action, driven by hardly a human agent, there is little moral decision and a lot of delay. The word for the latter (*mora*) occurs twelve times in the play.[1] In contrast with Seneca's other plays, whose tragic events convince the characters that history is ending,[2] in this play history won't stop. The epic event par excellence, the Trojan War, is over. The winners want to leave, and the survivors want to die. But something won't let them.

Aim, Date, and Strategy

Why did Seneca write the *Trojan Women*? When we approach his plays of tyrants run amok and aristocratic ladies behaving badly, such as the *Thyestes* or *Phaedra*, we remember Seneca's role at the court of Nero and the representation of the ravening Julio-Claudians such as Tiberius and Caligula in his work *On Anger*, and we indulge explanations of authorial decision so fantastical that they have a chance of being true. We may even feel compelled to *date* the plays (an insuperable enigma, which *communis opinio* follows Fitch in settling only relatively) on the basis of their internal representations. Surely Seneca, a recent biographer writes, offered the *Thyestes* as a cri de coeur about the impossibility of ruling others or even oneself without corruption after years of disenchantment at the court of Nero.[3] Speaking in philosophical tones about temptation, surely Atreus represents Seneca himself on the brink. Likewise, did Seneca need to look further for models for Medea than his own employer, Nero's, mother, Agrippina?

Such can be no more than speculation. With how little we know about the context of Senecan drama and how much we know about the conventionality, indeed "generic composition" of Roman poetry, it raises questions of the order of art and life. What if, as is *probably* true of our play, *every* play was written before the death of Claudius and the accession of Nero in the early 50s? Was *Nero* then impersonating *Seneca's* Thyestes, himself an imitation of Caligula, who was himself impersonating the Thyestes of earlier Roman tragedy? The possibility that life imitates art, and that tragedy presents a model for reality, is implicit in the most intriguing datum submitted for dating the *Trojan Woman*, which one of the play's several editors explains is equivocal. If the coincidence between the lament that opens the *Trojan Women* and Seneca's comic sketch on the *Pumpkinification of the Emperor Claudius* provides any clue, then perhaps the play was written around 54 CE.[4] If so, *perhaps* the poet was thinking of his recent lessons to the next in line: "the pedagogic purpose of the Agamemnon-Pyrrhus scene corresponds with this phase of Nero's education . . . Whereas we meet tyrannous kings (Atreus, Creon,

Lycus) in the other plays, Agamemnon acts as a model king with his moderate views."[5] These include "A young man's weakness: poor impulse control"; "The more power you have, the more you should put up with"; and "No one ever kept power long with violence; / with moderation, it lasts (*moderata durant*)" (250, 254, 258–59).

A model king with moderate views, including even the word "moderation." But as the lines proceed, the lesson does not so much continue as turn inward, and the "model king" reflects on his own experience and gives us reason to doubt either the sincerity of his new lesson or the likelihood that anyone confronted with such a lesson, in word alone, will heed it (276–84):

> I will even admit (let me say this with your leave, Argos)
> that making the Phrygians suffer and be defeated
> was something I wanted; but as for wreckage and leveling,
> if only I had forbidden it! Still, one can't
> put reins on anger, on a burning sword, and on a victory
> won at night. What one would have thought
> indecent or inhuman—it was committed
> by darkness and resentment, through which madness incites
> itself, and by the lucky sword.

The ambivalence of the king's thematic *volta* is instructive: is it evidence of psychological introspection, a depth of character that makes Agamemnon "realistic," or is it simply the result of superficial piling on, of theme and variation of the kind that makes Roman poetry of the period sometimes stifling? At any rate, it is not *obvious* that such a "lesson" is likely to persuade the impetuous tyrant-to-be.

The tension between the drama's self-conscious references to the world outside the play and the apparent sincerity and suffering of so many of its characters provides much of the interpretive interest of this play. Addressing her son before his death at the hands of the conquerors, Andromache says (774–79):

> You will not touch little weapons with tender hands.
> You will not pursue beasts scattered in far-flung
> groves in your boldness or, on the day fixed for the *lustra*,

revive the sacred rite of the Trojan games
and lead the speeding squadrons, noble child.

At the height of a list of activities that death will take from Astyanax, which includes "powerfully wield / Ilium's scepter," "give laws for the people," and "bring / defeated races under your yoke" (771–73), it is surprising to find a reference to a horse-riding display for elite Roman youths with toy swords and shields.

The explanation is complex and multiple, superficial and revealing. In Andromache's speech, the reverse crescendo from war to its festal imitation brings her closer to the present moment, the actual youth, and pathetic smallness, of her young child. Here the movement of Andromache's speech *discloses*—again, it is appropriate to use a rhetoric of depth—the actual inner workings of Andromache's mind. At the same time, as we saw with Agamemnon's speech, it provides further evidence of superficial, circumstantial, and even artificial composition. After all, as Keulen (2001, 9) writes, in 47 CE, at the age of ten, Nero himself participated in Rome's "Trojan Games," the propagandistic festivity that linked Rome to Greek mythology through the great losers (and, in Rome, next ascendants) of the Trojan War. With this reference, including the conspicuous reference to the Roman religious denomination of time, *lustra*, Seneca situates the play in Roman sensibilities. Whether or not this violates any ancient sense of propriety, it brings the moment home, not to the character of Andromache as a product of a verisimilar poetics, but to the Roman audience at the moment of their reading or watching the play. It does so by putting before "Andromache's" mind, not a scene of personal, domestic intimacy, but an experience of a spectacle, a game *or a play*. The Latin word *lusus* in the phrase "Trojan games" means both. The same metapoetic strategy strengthens—or does it weaken?—the conspicuously theatrical death of Polyxena in the valley "as though a theater."[6]

In contrast, the character whom the most affecting speaker, Andromache, paints in the most sinister colors, the "architect of deception and craftsman of crimes" (750), Ulysses, proves uncharacteristically sincere (762–65):

> Ah would that it were
> permitted to pity you! Still the one thing permitted
> to give, the time of delay, I will. Take your fill
> of crying as you like. Tears lighten toil.

The reason for Ulysses' apparent sincerity is that he is the most businesslike about fate. The unwilling "executor" (524) views all sides with equal compassion—mothers of Greece and the grief of Andromache (725–28)—or with no compassion, depending on one's interpretation (522–23): "with an untrustworthy . . . expression," Andromache says and then adds, "he weaves shrewd tricks in his heart." The latter is, however, an interpretation, as are so many of her lines, including especially when she looks at her son and sees only his father (464–65): "This was the look / my Hector had." Suggesting the mediated, even fabricated character of the most visceral feeling, Seneca presents her words here as an imitation of Vergil.[7]

Ulysses and Andromache represent two approaches to one's own feelings, and Seneca does not make us choose. The reason is that *the choice is yours.* The figure of this choice for the reader, as for the audience, is, again, the scene that closes the play, *as a scene,* with Polyxena's death march (1125–30):

> The teeming throng
> filled all the shore: some think the delay of their fleet
> will be undone by this death, some just enjoy
> their enemies being uprooted. Much of the fickle
> crowd can't bear the crime but watches it. No fewer
> Trojans attend this, their funeral.

With such lines, the very aesthetics of the genre, the image of theatrical space, present the multiple possible psychological, ethical, and aesthetic responses to a "tragedy." Should one, like Helen, gloat on the scene of destruction? Should one, like Andromache, see oneself or one's loved ones in it? Should one, like Ulysses, do what "needs" to be done? Or should one keep watching, or reading, even if one thinks that the "play" is abhorrent?

More to the point, is it possible to read the play and *not* be affected by the events that it describes, when they are so terribly common and "real?" Again, I suspect that *Seneca's* answer to this question is "yes": it is both possible and ethical. After Calchas ratifies Pyrrhus' claim to Polyxena and adds the sacrifice of Astyanax to mix, the chorus declares, in another sudden and estranging contrast (371–72): "Is it true, or a story to deceive the timid, / that shadows live apart from the bodies we buried?" The chorus interrupts this story with the acknowledgement that fear of death may be itself a response to a story. In its last appearance in the play, the chorus is almost heartless (1013–17):

Always, ah always uncharitable is grief.
It rejoices when its fate is dispensed to many
and is not satisfied to be punished alone.
Suffering the lot that everyone does is something
no one refuses.

While not exactly blaming the victim, the chorus suggests some complicity with horror on her part. How "realistic" is such a message in the mouths of mourning women? More importantly, how should we react to it being delivered to people at the height of victimhood?

It is easy, and maybe justified, to conclude that Senecan Stoicism is inhumane. But as soon as one draws this conclusion, which the play certainly permits,[8] one has to confront one's own complicity as a reader. One can, on the other hand, seek the refuge of historicism: easy for the winner of world history, the Roman elite of the early empire, to write such things; easy for a beneficiary of patriarchy to do a poetic experiment on the suffering of women and children. In the peculiar mix of relativism and positivism of our time, historicism has much to recommend it. Nevertheless, it raises again the question of why Seneca chose to write such a play in the first place, not so much in view of his commitments as a Stoic, but as someone as close to the historical center of imperialism as he was.

I would suggest that this is precisely Stoic poetry, poetry that does not renounce emotion but rather puts it at a distance, even "in quotation marks."[9] Its relevance to the present tragedy, in contrast with the others, is the very normality, "reality," and ubiquity of the events it describes. Rare is the parent who eats his children, the mother who murders them, or the stepmother who lusts for them. All too common is the torture, murder, and trafficking of the women and children who survive a war. In the *Trojan Women*, Seneca subjects even this population to the estranging test of Stoic poetics. In other words, it is *because* of his Stoicism, "inhumane" or otherwise, that Seneca wrote such a play. In a patriarchal and imperialist society, only those who try to put themselves at a distance from *themselves*, as Stoics do, would take an interest in the suffering of the truly other. Whether or not such an interest, in the end, is enough—enough to get the playwright off the hook, enough to exempt the interested parties from the brutal system, enough to make a difference to the suffering of others—is not a question that concerns the poet.

Suggested Reading

Benton, Cindy. 2002. "Split Vision: The Politics of the Gaze in Seneca's *Troades*." In *The Roman Gaze: Vision, Power, and the Body*, edited by D. Frederick, 31–56. Baltimore.

Boyle, Anthony J. 1994. *Seneca's* Troades: *Introduction, Text, Translation and Commentary*. Leeds.

Fantham, Elaine. 1983. *Seneca's* Troades: *A Literary Introduction, with Text, Interpretation, and Commentary*. Princeton.

Keulen, Atze J. 2001. *L. Annaeus Seneca:* Troades. Brill.

McAuley, Mairead. 2015. *Reproducing Rome: Motherhood in Virgil, Ovid, Seneca, and Statius*. Oxford.

Romm, James. 2014. *Dying Every Day: Seneca at the Court of Nero*. New York.

Trinacty, Christopher. 2014. *Senecan Tragedy and the Reception of Augustan Poetry*. Oxford.

Troades

LUCIUS ANNAEUS SENECA

TRANSLATED BY ALEX DRESSLER

DRAMATIS PERSONAE

HECUBA, widow of Priam, the former king of Troy

TALTHYBIUS, herald of the Greek army

PYRRHUS, son of Achilles

AGAMEMNON, king of Mycenae and victorious commander
   over Troy

CALCHAS, Greek seer

ULYSSES, king of Ithaca

ANDROMACHE, widow of Hector, Priam's son

OLD MAN, attendant of Andromache

ASTYANAX, young son of Andromache

POLYXENA, daughter of Hecuba

HELEN, wife of Menelaus and cause of the Trojan War

MESSENGER

CHORUS of Trojan Women

*The drama is set in the open area between the ruins of Troy and the shore-
line studded with Greek ships. Act 3 takes place at Hector's tomb.*

ACT 1

HECUBA

Whoever puts his faith in sovereignty and rules great halls
with power, whoever has no fear of fickle gods
and credulously yields his mind to prosperous times,
should take a look at me and you, Troy. Fortune has never
offered greater proof of how fragile the foundation is
on which the haughty stand. Overthrown and toppled is
the pillar of powerful Asia, that eminent labor of the gods![1]

Many came to its defense: he who drinks
the cold Tanais that opens seven mouths,[2]
and he who salutes the day's rebirth and mixes
warm Tigris with the ruddy sea,[3] and she who sees
nomadic Scyths nearby and with unmarried hordes
pounds on hoof the Black Sea shore.[4] Now Troy
is cut down with the sword; Pergamum's fallen on itself.
The soaring beauties of the walls—look! They lie in piles,
the homes are burnt; fires stalk the royal palace,
and Assaracus' house is all in smoke from end to end.
The flames do not restrain the conqueror's greedy hands:
Troy is plundered as she burns. The sky is veiled
by billows of smoke. As if clad in thick cloud
the day is foul and black with Ilium's ashes.
The conqueror is greedy for anger. He measures hard-won
        Ilium
with his eyes and, savage after ten long years, he still
does not forgive her; he's astounded at her downfall
and, although he sees her conquered, barely believes his eyes
that conquering was possible. The plunderer seizes
the spoils of Troy; a thousand ships can't hold her riches.
I call as witnesses the gods, though they oppose me;
I call as witnesses the ashes of my country, and you, king of
        Phrygia,[5]
whose grave lies under Troy, covered by all your kingdom
and Hector, your ghost too I call—when you stood, Ilium
        stood—
and I call you, my children in your great numbers,
all lesser shadows: whatever ill has happened to me now,
whatever evils Phoebus' raving girl with frenzied speech
predicted and the god kept us from believing,
I, Hecuba, saw first, and, in my pregnancy, did not forebear
to tell my fears;[6] I was a useless prophet before Cassandra.
The cunning Ithacan was not the one who scattered[7]
night-time torches on you, nor his friend,[8] nor the liar Sinon.[9]
Those flames are mine, my brands set you on fire.

But why do you, a living image of old age, groan at the wreck
of a city overthrown? Look back, unhappy, to these
most recent griefs! The fall of Troy is an ancient sorrow.
I saw atrocity—unspeakable: the king being killed
and, at the very altars, a greater crime committed
than the outrage that Ajax did,[10] when with a savage hand
Pyrrhus[11] pulled back the king's head by its twisted hair
and plunged the wicked iron deeply in the wound;
after his chest welcomed the driven edge,
the iron exited, still dry, from the throat so aged.   50
Who could not have been deterred from savage murder
by one treading the last threshold of his mortal life,
by the gods on high as witnesses of the crime, by the respect
    due
a fallen kingdom? Priam, the father of so many kings,
is lacking a tomb and wants for cremation while
Troy burns. But this was not enough for the gods on high.
Look—lots are tossed for possession of the virgins and brides
of the house of Priam. Here I follow, one poor prize.
One of them lays his claim to Hector's wife.
One of them wants Helenus' bride, and one wants Antenor's.   60
Someone even wants to sleep with you, Cassandra.
My lot scares them. I am the Greeks' one fear.
Is the wailing dying down? Come, my crowd of captives,
beat your chests with your hands and raise your lamentations
and give Troy its due. Doomed Mount Ida ought
to be echoing by now, the haunt of that accursed judge.[12]

CHORUS

We are not a crowd without experience, nor new to tears,
whom you ask to weep.
We have been doing this for years without cease
from the moment the Phrygian guest first reached[13]   70
Greek Amyclae and the sacred pine of Cybele
cut through the straits.
Ten times now Ida has gone white with snow,

and ten times stripped for our pyres;
ten times in the Sigean fields, the plowman has
trembled fearfully as he harvested his crops,
so that no day has lacked its share of sadness,
but some new reason offers anguish.
Women, go to grieving;
80   raise your hands in sorrow, queen.
We will follow our mistress, a crowd, and we
are not unversed in weeping.

HECUBA

Faithful companions of my downfall,
loosen your locks now.
Let the hair you dirtied with the still warm ashes
of Troy spill down your necks in mourning.
102   Fill up your hands.
103   This alone is what we take from Troy.
87   Let the crowd offer up its exposed arms.
Unloose your clothes and tie their folds,
and let your bodies be naked to the womb.
90   For what marriage do you veil these chests, modest captives?
Tie cloaks around your loosened clothes,
let frenzied hands be free to beat frequent lament.
This pose is pleasing, pleasing. I recognize
a Trojan throng.[14]
Let your former keening return once more,
but surpass your usual norms in weeping. We
are crying for *Hector*.

CHORUS

All of us have loosened our locks, which were torn
at many a funeral.
100   Our hair has been released, freed from its knot,
101   and the ashes, hot, are sprinkled on our faces.
104   Our garments fall from our shoulders and leave them naked,
just pulled up and tied to cover our hips.
Our naked breasts call for our fists.

Now, now, express your power, Pain!
Let the Rhoetean shores resound with our pounding,[15]
and let Echo, who lives in the hollow mountains,
abandon her usual terseness and return   110
just our last words:
let her pay back to Troy its full due of grief.
Let the sea and the sky hear it all.
Be savage, hands, and hit our chests with ravaging blows.
I am not satisfied with the usual sound. We
are crying for Hector.

HECUBA

For you my right fist strikes my upper arms
and strikes my shoulders bloody, for you.
For you my fist is striking my head.
For you my breasts are torn   120
by a mother's hands.
Let flow, and with copious blood let stream
whatever jagged scars I made
at your funeral. The pillar of our country, the delayer of our doom
is what you were, protector of the exhausted
Trojans. You were our wall. On your shoulders stood
that city, supported for ten years until
she fell with you. The final day for Hector
was the same as that for his country. Women,
direct anew your pounding grief: 130
pour forth your tears for Priam. Hector has enough.

CHORUS

King of Phrygia, accept these sounds of our fists.
Accept our weeping, old man captured twice.
Troy suffered nothing just once in your reign:
two times with Greek iron the Dardan walls
have been struck,
two times they have suffered the arrows of Hercules.[16]
After Hecuba's children were buried, and a crowd of kings,
you, father, finally end the funeral line,

and, slaughtered as sacrifice to great Jupiter,[17]
you lie on the Sigean shore,[18] a headless trunk.

HECUBA

Direct anew your lamentation, women.
No more must you pity my Priam's
death, women of Ilium, but
"Happy is Priam!" let everybody say.
He has been freed to go to the shades below,
and will never carry the Greek yoke on a conquered neck—
he does not see the two sons of Atreus,
does not see deceitful Ulysses.
He will not, as plunder of the Argive triumph,
bear their trophies on his bent shoulders.
The hands that were used to holding the scepter will not
be bound behind his back as he follows the chariot of
    Agamemnon,
bearing golden shackles on his hands,
transformed into wide Mycenae's celebration.

CHORUS

"Happy is Priam," every one of us says:
He took his kingdom with him as he died.
Now in the woods of Elysium among the safe
shades he wanders and among the dutiful souls[19]
he is happy, as he looks for Hector:
Priam is happy.
Happy is he who died in battle and took
the world in ruins with him as he went.

ACT 2

TALTHYBIUS

O long the delay for the Greeks, forever in harbor,
whether they want to fight or just go home![20]

CHORUS

Tell us the cause of delay for the Greeks and their ships
and the name of the god who bars their journey back.

140

150

160

TALTHYBIUS

My mind is afraid. A terrible shudder shakes my frame.
Omens too big to be true, which you'd scarcely believe—
I've seen them, I've seen them myself. The sun was brushing the   170
    tops
of the mountains, just up, day finished nighttime off,
when suddenly the earth was groaning with a mysterious
    lowing
and, shaken to the core, dragged all her innards from the deep.
Woods shook their heads, tall stretches of forest thundered
with a huge crash. So did the Sacred Grove.
The boulders of Ida showered down shattered crags,
and the earth was not alone in shaking: the sea,
feeling its own Achilles close by,[21] rolled waves.
Then, with a rip, a chasm opens on endless caverns.
A mouth of the underworld offers a road to the world above   180
through broken ground and eases the weight on the mound.
The enormous shade of Thessaly's leader sprang
up as when he defeated the weapons of Thrace[22]
as practice for your fate, Troy; or when
he laid low Neptune's white-plumed son;[23]
or raged with violent Mars between battle lines
and clogged the rivers with corpses, as Xanthus slowed
and wandered and looked for a path for its current of blood;[24]
or when he stood on his arrogant chariot, victor,
driving the reins, with Hector and Troy dragged behind.   190
The shore was filled with the sound of his fury:
"Go, go, lazy people! Take the honors
you owe my ghost, and launch your ungrateful ships
to voyage through my ocean! The wrath of Achilles
has cost Greece more than a little; it will still cost a lot:
Polyxena is betrothed to my ashes;[25] let Pyrrhus'
hand ritually slay her and soak my grave."
So he said; then he cleft the day with a thick darkness,
and plunging down sought the Kingdom of Death; as he went,
he sealed the huge hollow with fused earth. Motionless   200

lay ocean's stillness, the wind quit threatening,
and the calm sea sighed with a soft flow. From the depths,
a chorus of Tritons sang wedding songs.[26]

(*Enter Pyrrhus and Agamemnon.*)

PYRRHUS

When you were happily setting sail for home,
did Achilles slip your mind? It was by his hand alone
that Troy was stricken, and in the delay that followed his death,
it stood wondering where to fall. Even if
you could hurry to give him what he wanted,
you're still too late. All your leaders already took
their prize. What smaller gift can be awarded
210   for such bravery? Or did he merit nothing special
when, ordered to flee battle and live sedentary
in long senescence, and surpass the age
of the old man of Pylos,[27] he stripped off his false dress—
his mother's trick—and confessed himself man with his
      weapons?[28]
When reckless Telephus in his desolate realm[29]
barred him access to the wild land of Mysia,
he stained Achilles' untried hand in royal blood
and knew that hand could be both harsh and gentle.
Thebes fell; defeated Eetion saw his kingdom
220   seized.[30] In similar disaster fell
little Lyrnesos that capped a lofty mountain;[31]
and the lands renowned for the capture of Briseis.
Chryse too, cause of the conflict of kings, is fallen;[32]
and famous Tenedos and the fertile place that feeds
the Thracian flocks with its fruitful fields,[33]
Scyros,[34] and Lesbos that cuts the Aegean sea,[35]
and Cilla,[36] dear to Phoebus—and what of the places
washed by Caycus,[37] swelling its stream with spring rain?
Such slaughter of the races of men, such terror,
230   so many cities scattered as by a huge hurricane

would be another's fame and crowning glory.
For Achilles, it was a journey. That's how my father traveled,
raising battles like that on the way to battle.
To say nothing of his other merits, would not
Hector alone have been enough? My father conquered
Ilium, you people only wrecked it. I like to list
my great forebear's famed acts and famous praises:
Hector lay dead before his father's eyes,
Memnon before his uncle's; because of her grief,
his mother bore that bleak day with pale face.[38]   240
Achilles, who beat him, was scared by the lesson of his
       achievement[39]
and learned that the sons of goddesses also die.
Then the last fear, that savage Amazon, fell.[40]
You owe Achilles, if you assess his merits rightly
and he should demand it, a Mycenean or Argive girl as well.[41]
Are you hesitating? Do you suddenly reject approved procedure
and think it brutish to sacrifice the daughter of Priam
to Peleus' son? And yet, as a father, you slaughtered your
       daughter
for Helen! By now, my demands have a precedent.

AGAMEMNON

A young man's weakness:[42] poor impulse control.   250
Others this fever first seizes as a matter of age.
For Pyrrhus it's paternal. I endured Aeacus' pompous
       grandson's[43]
threats and sullen disposition with patience, once.
The more power you have, the more you should put up with.
But why spatter with dreadful bloodshed
the noble shade of that great leader? You should know this first:
what the victor ought to do and the vanquished suffer.
No one ever kept power long with violence;
with moderation, it lasts. To the extent that Fortune
has elevated and raised a person's capacities,   260

it's right for him to restrain himself and his happiness,
dreading changing circumstances and scared
of gods who prove too kind. A moment crushes
greatness, as I have learned from conquering. Does Troy
    make us
too proud and fierce? We Greeks stand in the place
from which it fell. I admit, at one point, proud
with power, I lacked control and held my head too high;
but Fortune's favor, which would have given others
reason for insolence, broke it in me. Do you make me
arrogant, Priam? You also make me scared.
Could *I* think sovereignty anything but a name
wrapped in vain shining and a head of hair
decked with false crown? These things, a moment can take;
not even, perhaps, a thousand ships and a decade:
Fortune does not menace everyone in slow-motion.
I will even admit (let me say this with your leave, Argos)
that making the Phrygians suffer and be defeated
was something I wanted; but as for wreckage and leveling,
if only I had forbidden it! Still, one can't
put reins on anger, on a burning sword, and on a victory
won at night. What one would have thought
indecent or inhuman—it was committed
by darkness and resentment, through which madness
    incites
itself, and by the lucky sword. Bloodied even once,
its lust for slaughter is senseless. If anything of toppled
Troy is left, let it remain. It paid
the price enough and more. To slay a royal
girl as a gift for the grave and to wet her ashes,
to call an inhuman act of slaughter a wedding,
I will not tolerate. Collective guilt comes home to me.
He who can prevent a crime but does not, orders it.

PYRRHUS
Then Achilles' ghost will have no reward?

270

280

290

AGAMEMNON

It will. Humanity will sing his praise
and lands unknown will hear his great name.
But if his ashes are consoled by the flow of blood,
let them slaughter fat-necked Phrygian flocks and let
the blood-flow make no mother weep. What sort
of custom is that? When is a person spent as
a person's offerings? Keep hatred and resentment
from your father. You order him honored via vengeance.   300

PYRRHUS

How inflated you are when good fortune
has raised your spirits, how fearful when terror creaks,
O tyrant of kings! Do you carry a heart inflamed
again with the heat of love and some new lust?[44]
Of all of us, will you alone take spoils so often?
I'll give Achilles his victim with this right hand,
and if you refuse and hold her back, I'll give
a greater victim, worthy of Pyrrhus. Now much
too long has my hand refrained from the slaughter of kings.
Priam demands an equal.

AGAMEMNON

       I'll hardly deny   310
that Pyrrhus' greatest glory in war is this:
with a brutal sword, he dispatched Priam,
his father's suppliant.[45]

PYRRHUS

       My father's suppliants were
his enemies too, I know. But Priam begged
in person, while you trembled in great fear, too
scared to beg, and sent your requests through the Ithacan
and Ajax, quaking at your enemy in seclusion.[46]

AGAMEMNON

Then your father was not afraid, I admit;
during the slaughter of the Greeks and the burning of the
    ships,

he lay idle, unconcerned with battle and weapons,
plucking his sonorous lyre with a little pick.

PYRRHUS

At that point, great Hector despised your weapons
but feared Achilles' song. And amid great fear, there was deep
peace, at least where his Thessalian ships were docked.

AGAMEMNON

And amid those same Thessalian docks of yours,
there was deep peace later for the father of Hector.

PYRRHUS

That's what high kings do: they spare kings' lives.

AGAMEMNON

Why then did *you* rip out the king's life?

PYRRHUS

Often the compassionate man grants death instead of life.

AGAMEMNON

And now in compassion do you look for a girl for the tomb?

PYRRHUS

So you think virgin sacrifice an atrocity *now*?

AGAMEMNON

Country over children is the king's right view.

PYRRHUS

No law spares captives or impedes their punishment.

AGAMEMNON

What the law does not forbid is forbidden by decency.

PYRRHUS

Whatever he wants, the conqueror is permitted.

AGAMEMNON

The man permitted the most should want the least.

PYRRHUS

This is what you throw at those whom your ten-year kingship
crushed till Pyrrhus freed them from your yoke?

AGAMEMNON

The arrogant spirit of Scyrus[47]—

PYRRHUS

    —has no share of your cousin's crimes.[48]

AGAMEMNON

Confined by the waves—

PYRRHUS

    —of my family's sea.   340
I know the noble house of Atreus and Thyestes.[49]

AGAMEMNON

You, conceived from a virgin's secret rape
and sired by Achilles, not yet a man.[50]

PYRRHUS

By Achilles, yes, who embraces the universe with his lineage,
spread through all the kingdom of the gods: he holds
through Thetis the ocean,[51] through Aeacus the shadows,[52] and
    the sky through Jove.

AGAMEMNON

That Achilles, yes, who is dead by the hand of Paris—

PYRRHUS

    —but whom the gods were afraid to test in hand-to-
    hand combat.

AGAMEMNON

If I wanted, I could curb those words and discipline
your daring with pain. But *my* sword knows how   350
to spare even captives. Better let the gods' interpreter,
Calchas,[53] be called in. If fate asks it, I will give her.
You who loosed the chains of Pelasgian ships
and delays of war, who unlock the sky with your skill,
for whom the secrets of entrails and the flash of
the firmament and the comet dragging its path with a fiery tail
reveal the signs of fate—and you whose mouth
has cost me dearly:[54] say what the god
is ordering, Calchas; direct us with your counsel.

CALCHAS

The fates grant the Greeks a path at the usual price: 360
the girl must be sacrificed on the Thessalian leader's grave,

but ornamented as Thessalian brides are usually married,
or Ionian and Mycenean ones.
Let Pyrrhus present his father with his bride.
Thus, it will be done right. Still, this is not
the only thing that holds our ships. Blood
nobler, Polyxena, than your blood is owed.
The one sought by the fates must fall from the top
of the tower: the son of Hector, Priam's son, must meet his
        death.
370   Then the thousand sails of the fleet may fill the straits.

CHORUS
Is it true, or a story to deceive the timid,
that shadows live apart from the bodies we buried,
after the wife has placed her hand on one's eyes
and the final day obstructed the rays of the sun
and the grim urn has closed up the ashes?
Is it no use to yield the soul to burial?
Are the wretched forced to live still longer?
Or do we wholly die and afterward no part
of us persists when, with a fugitive breath,
380   the spirit has mixed with the clouds and entered the
        atmosphere
and the torch placed underneath has touched the naked side?
Whatever the sun knows when it rises, whatever it knows when
        it sets,
whatever Ocean with its cerulean tides
washes as twice it ebbs and twice it floods,
will be swept away by time with its Pegasus-like stride.[55]
At the rate the twice six constellations are rushing in the
        whirlwind,
at the rate the lord of the stars[56] hastens to roll
the centuries along, in the way that Hecate[57]
is hastening to run on sideways tracks:
390   so we all pursue our fate, and he who has touched the river
by which the gods on high swear oaths, exists

no more. As smoke that rises from hot fires
vanishes, filthy for a little span,
or like clouds we just saw sodden, when
a gust of northern Boreas scatters them:
just so this breath that steers us will flow off.
After death, there is nothing, and death itself is nothing—
the final turning post of a quick-run course.
Let the greedy give up hope; let the anxious give up fear:
greedy time devours us, as does emptiness.   400
Death admits of no division: harmful to the body,
it also does not spare the soul. Taenara and the royal
threshold under its harsh master,[58] Cerberus the guard
lying in wait at the impassable gate[59]—
are empty talk and pointless words,
a story like an anxious dream.
You ask where you will lie when life is done?
With things that are unborn.

ACT 3

ANDROMACHE

Why, bleak crowd of Phrygia, do you tear your hair
and beat your wretched chests and wet your cheeks   410
with streams of tears? Light was what we bore before
if we have to weep for what we suffer. Your Ilium just fell,
but mine fell long ago, when, with its speeding chariot
that savage Pelian axle snatched away the corpse rightfully
    mine,
and groaning deeply trembled with Hector's weight.
Crushed already then and overwhelmed, I endure whatever
    happens,
dumb to misfortune, petrified, and senseless.
Escaped from these Greeks by now, I'd follow my husband
if this one

(She points to Astyanax.)

didn't hold me.[60] He tames my pride
and does not let me die. He forces me even now to beg
the gods for something and stretches out my suffering.
He's robbed me of misfortune's greatest fruit—
the fear of nothing. Every place for happiness is snatched
away, but the door to hardship still lies open.
Fear is most wretched when you have no hope.

OLD MAN

What sudden terror stirred you in your ruin?

ANDROMACHE

From this great evil, a greater one is coming.
The fate of Troy is suspended in its fall.

OLD MAN

What crises could god find, assuming that he wanted to?

ANDROMACHE

The prisons of deep Styx and the lurid caves
are opening and, to keep no fear from the fallen,
our buried enemies return from the depths of Dis;[61]
do only Greeks get an easy journey back?
Surely death is impartial. That collective fear
panics the Phrygians and unnerves them. Uniquely fearful
to *my* mind is this dream from a terrifying night.

OLD MAN

Convey what you saw and share your fear publicly.

ANDROMACHE

Hardly had passed two thirds of gentle night
and turned the seven stars their carriage bright,
at last a strange calm came on me in my ruin
and brief sleep suddenly stole over my tired eyes
(if the numbness of a stricken mind is sleep)—
when suddenly Hector stood before my eyes,
not as he was when he carried forward war against the Argives
and hunted Greek ships with the torches of Ida,
nor as when, mad with copious slaughter of Greeks,
he stripped true weapons from counterfeit Achilles:[62]

he did not have that look that glanced a fiery radience,
but was tired and depressed and heavy with a weeping
similar to mine, his hair matted with filth.   450
I'm glad I saw him still. Then he shook his head
and said, "Shake off this sleep and grab your son,
my loyal wife! Let him hide: he's your one hope.
Stop crying! Do you mourn that Troy has fallen?
Would that it were wholly leveled. Hurry
and take our house's tiny offspring where you can!"
Cold terror and a shudder shook out my sleep,
and, turning my eyes here and there, afraid and wretched,
I forgot my son in my search for Hector. His
deceptive shadow vanished in my embrace.   460
O my child, true child of a great father,
one and only hope of the Phrygians and our ruined house
and too renowned descendent of old blood
and too much like your father! This was the look
my Hector had, and this was how he walked
and held himself, and he had brave hands like this
and was tall in his shoulders like this, threatened with fierce
     face
like this, spreading unbound hair with a toss of his neck!⁶³
O my child, born too late for the Phrygians and too early
for your mother, will the happy moment of that day   470
ever come when, defending avenger of Trojan earth,
you set up a second Pergamum and return
her exile-scattered people, restoring their name
to the Phrygians and their nation? I remember my fate
and fear my own great wish. This is enough
for captives: let us live. Unhappy me: what place
will keep faith with my fear? Where should I hide you?
That citadel, strong with resources and walls of the gods,⁶⁴
famous to all races and a bane to envy,
is now deep piles of dust. All is strewn with flames,   480
and out of that vast city, not enough remains
to hide a baby. What place should I choose for my deceit?

There is the great mound, my husband's sacred grave,
revered by his enemy, which his father built[65]
with a massive heap and great expenditure. Not cheap in his
    grief,
that king. Best to entrust him to his father[66]—
but a cold sweat covers my whole frame! Wretched,
488   I shudder at the omen of the gloomy place.

OLD MAN

497   Let the wretched seek protection first. Let the carefree choose.

ANDOMACHE

But what of this?: He can't hide without an awful fear
of somebody's betrayal.

OLD MAN

492   Have no witnesses to your plot.

ANDROMACHE

And if the enemy comes looking?

OLD MAN

493   He died in the toppled city.
489   This one cause has saved many from death:
they were believed to be dead.

ANDROMACHE

490   No hope is left.
491   He's crushed by the weight of his status and rank. What's the
    point
490   of hiding just to return to the enemy's hands?

OLD MAN

The conqueror's impulse is only fierce at first.

ANDROMACHE

What area, what separate place and pathless,
will keep you safe? Who will bring the timid aid?
500   Who will protect them? Guard your own even now,
as you always did, Hector. Keep safe the theft of your pious
wife; take him up to find life in your faithful ashes.
Go up to the tomb, child. —Why do you recoil?

Do you disdain base hiding places? I recognize
your character. Fear embarrasses you. Banish your arrogance
and habitual nature. Take the one disaster has assigned.
Look at the crowd of us who remain: a tomb,
a child, a captive woman. You must give in to suffering.
Come, dare to enter a buried parent's sacred
seat. If fate helps the wretched,   510
you have your safety. If fate denies you life,
you have your grave.

OLD MAN

      The enclosure holds him
in trust; just don't let your fear broadcast him.
Get out of here and keep yourself far off.

ANDROMACHE

She fears less who fears nearby, but if
it seems a good idea, then we'll retreat.

OLD MAN

Hold your tongue a while, and check your complaints: the
    Cephallenian leader[67]
approaches us with ill-intentioned steps.

ANDROMACHE

Earth, open, and you, my husband, split the ground
apart to its remotest cavern. In a deep   520
hollow of Styx, keep my deposit safe.
Ulysses is here—and with an untrustworthy gait
and expression. He weaves shrewd tricks in his heart.

(*Enter Ulysses.*)

ULYSSES

As executor of a difficult lot,[68] I ask this first,
that you believe that these words, though they come
from my mouth, are not my own: all the Greeks and all their
    leaders
are making this speech, I mean the men whom the child of
    Hector

is keeping from seeking their homes this late. It is fate who
    seeks him.
Anxious belief in an uncertain peace will always keep
530   a grip on us Greeks; fear will always force us to look behind
our backs, and it will not let us put our weapons aside
as long as the toppled Phrygians take courage from that son
of yours, Andromache. Calchas the prophet declares these things
and, if Calchas the prophet were silent about them, nevertheless
Hector said it too, and I fear even his offspring.
Superior seed rises to the level of its ancestry—
just like that small companion of the enormous herd,
whose first horns do not yet split its skin,
but, suddenly tall at the shoulder and high of forehead,
540   it leads its father's flock and commands the cattle;
just like the tender sprig that has sprung from a fresh cut trunk
soars, the size of its mother, in a little time
and casts a shadow over the earth and raises its leaves to the sky;
just like an ember from a great fire carelessly left behind
renews its force. Pain, it is true, is a biased appraiser
of any situation. Nevertheless, if you reflect on it,
I think you'll forgive us that after ten snows and as many
    harvests,
the soldier is an old man now, wary of battle, of
the renewal of other disasters, and of Troy, which is never
550   sufficiently fallen. A great thing moves the Danaans:
a coming Hector. Free the Greeks from fear.
This is the only thing that keeps our ships beached,
that stalls our fleet. Don't think me cruel because
I'm the one ordered by lot to demand Hector's son.
I would have demanded Orestes.[69] Endure what the victor has
    borne.[70]

ANDROMACHE
O child, would that you were in your mother's arms
and that I knew what disaster snatched and held you away
from me, or else what place. Not even if my chest

were pierced with enemy spears and my hands restrained
by slicing chains, and not if my sides were hemmed   560
by raging fires, would I ever give up a mother's
loyalty. O my child, what region, what fortune
is holding you now? In pathless wandering,
do you stray through lands in exile? Did the conflagration
of our country destroy your body? Did the crazy
conqueror play in your blood? Or do you feed
the birds of Ida, caught in the maw of a big wild beast?

ULYSSES

Stop with the made-up stories. It isn't easy for you
to fool Ulysses. I have outdone the tricks of mothers
before, even goddesses. So quit your silly plots.   570
Where is your son?

ANDROMACHE

       Where's Hector and all the Phrygians?
Where's Priam? You seek one; I seek them all.

ULYSSES

Under pressure you'll say what you refuse to freely admit:
it's foolish devotion to hide what you'll soon confess.   587

ANDROMACHE

Safe is she who can perish—and should, and wants to.   574

ULYSSES

Death shakes out big talk as it comes near.

ANDROMACHE

If you want to coerce Andromache with fear, Ulysses,
threaten with life. For now death is my wish.

ULYSSES

With whips and fire, death and torture, pain will force
you, even unwilling, to say what you conceal
and will extract the secrets deeply hidden in your heart.   580
Necessity tends to be more effective than love.

ANDROMACHE

Bring out the fire, the wounds, and the dreadful techniques
of wicked pain, the hunger and fierce thirst

and varied tortures on all sides and iron pressed into
my scorched innards and vermin in a dark cell and[71]
whatever the conqueror dares in his anger and fear:[72]

588   a mother with courage does not submit to terror.

ULYSSES

This very love in which you persist in your intransigence
590   reminds the Greeks to think of our little children:
after so long with weapons and ten years, I'd fear
the terrors that Calchas raises less if I feared
it for myself, but you're readying war for Telemachus.[73]

ANDROMACHE

Unwillingly, Ulysses, will I give joy to Greeks,
but give it I must. Pain, admit the grief you suppress.
Take joy, sons of Atreus, and you, bring happy news
to Pelasgians as you usually do: Hector's son is dead.

ULYSSES

And what proof do you offer to show the Greeks this is true?

ANDROMACHE

Let the worst the conqueror can threaten befall
600   and let fate free me with an end that is
easy and timely and bury me in my country
and let our homeland weigh on Hector light—
I swear he quit this life: he lies among the lifeless,
he is entombed and had his final rites.

ULYSSES

Fate is fulfilled, Hector's offspring is uprooted!
That the peace is secure, I'll report to Greeks in good spirits—
but what are you doing, Ulysses? The Greeks will trust you.
        Whom
do *you* trust? A parent? Would a parent make this up
without fearing the omen of a horrible death?
610   But people fear omens only when there's nothing worse to fear.
She pledged her faith with an oath—but if she lies,
is there anything worse for her to dread?

Now, soul, be cunning, bring tricks and deceptions and plots;
bring the whole Ulysses. Truth never perishes.
Scrutinize the mother: she cries, she groans, she grieves,
she turns her nervous paces here and there,
and listens for every noise with an anxious ear—
she's more afraid than grieving. This is a job for your talents.

(*To Andromache.*)

It's right to console other parents when they mourn,
but you, poor woman, ought to be congratulated for losing   620
    your son.
A terrible death was waiting for him—tossed from the one
tower that remains of the toppled walls.

ANDROMACHE

My mind deserts my limbs—they shake, they buckle;
my blood stops, stiffened in an icy chill.

ULYSSES

That really shook her. That's it, the tack to take.
Terror exposed the mother. I'll double the fear.

(*To the soldiers.*)

Go, men, be quick! The enemy has been hidden
by his mother's trick—the final plague of the Pelasgian
name, wherever he's lurking, dig him up and show him to us.
That's good. I've got her. Hurry, rush, and get him.   630

(*To Andromache.*)

Why look around and tremble? He's surely dead.

ANDROMACHE

I wish I *were* scared! But fear is an old habit.
The mind is slow to unlearn what it learned for so long.

ULYSSES

Since the boy has cheated the sacrifice owed
to the walls and can't obey the prophet now that he's escaped

to a better fate, Calchas says that the one
way to expiate the return of our ships
is if the ashes of scattered Hector appease the waves
and his whole tomb is leveled with the earth.
640 Now since that one escaped the death he owed,
our hands will have to attack the hallowed place.

ANDROMACHE
What can I do? Twin terror rends my mind—
here is my son and there my dear husband's dust:
which side will win? Be my witnesses, you cruel
gods and you true god, my husband's ghost:
there is no source of pleasure in my son
except you, Hector; let him live so that he can mirror
your looks. Will your dust be dug from the tomb
and sunk? Will I let your scattered bones be strewn on
650 the vast waves? Better to let him die[74]—
but, as mother, can you see him given to criminal
slaughter, spun headlong from the lofty rooftops
downward? I can. I will. I'll suffer it just
as long as the conqueror's hand, after death, doesn't throw
my Hector away. This one who's here can still feel
his punishment; death stations the other someplace safe.
Why do you waver? Decide: which will you save
from punishment? You hesitate, ingrate? Your Hector's there—
you're mistaken: Hector's on both sides. Here living feeling,
660 a coming avenger of his dead father perhaps. . . .
You can't save both. What will you do? Between
the two, my mind, save the one the Greeks still fear.

ULYSSES
I'll accomplish the oracle. I'll dig up the tomb.

ANDROMACHE
The one you granted for ransom?[75]

ULYSSES
I go to tear down
the grave from the top of the mound.

ANDROMACHE

    To the gods on high
and Achilles' promise I appeal. Pyrrhus, protect
the gift of your father!

ULYSSES

    The funeral tomb will soon
be strewn across the entire field.

ANDROMACHE

    This was the one atrocity
the Greeks had not dared. You defiled temples,
even of favorable gods. Your madness passed graves by.   670
I'll fight back. I'll face armed men with bare hands.
Anger will give me strength. As when the wild
Amazon routed Greek battalions or when a Maenad
stricken by god runs at inhuman pace; armed with the thyrsus,
she terrifies the woods, and beside herself, she wounds
others, but felt no wounds: I'll run in the midst
and die as an ally defending a pile of dust.

ULYSSES

                                    (*To the soldiers.*)

Are you men stopping? Does the tearful shout and empty
fury of a woman move you? Hurry
and follow your orders.

ANDROMACHE

    Kill me, kill me with your swords   680
here first. They push me back. I'm lost! Release death
from its delay. Hector, burst the earth. To crush Ulysses,
even the shadow of you is enough. He wields
arms in his hand, hurls fire. Greeks, do you see
Hector, or is it just me?

ULYSSES

    I'll dig it all up.

ANDROMACHE

What are you doing? A mother, in one wreck
you level son and husband. Perhaps you can soften

the Greeks with begging. The enormous weight of the
    tomb
will crush its contents at once. Let the wretched boy
690   die anywhere else before the father should bury
the son and son ruin father. I fall to your knees, Ulysses,
in supplication, and with this hand that no feet
have felt, I now reach out to touch your feet.
Pity a mother; accept devoted prayers
with gentle tolerance. The higher the gods
have lifted you, the more lightly oppress the fallen;
whatever you give to the wretched you give to fortune.
This way, may the bed of your holy wife
see you again and, until he welcomes you, may
700   Laertes live longer still; may your child accept you
and outdo your expectations with good character,[76]
besting grandfather in age and father in genius.
Pity a mother. To me, in my ruin, this
alone consoles me.

ULYSSES

       Show us your son, then ask.

ANDROMACHE

Come out, come out from your concealment,
tearful theft of a mother in wretchedness.
Here he is, here is the fear, Ulysses,
of a thousand ships.
Up with your arms and, on the ground,
worship the master's feet with suppliant hand
710   and do not suppose that what Fortune
commands the wretched is disgraceful.
Put out of your mind your forefather kings,
the laws of the magnificent old man
renowned in all lands; let Hector fall from
your mind. Play the part of the captive on bended knee,
and if you still don't feel your doom,
imitate your mother's weeping.

Troy from before also saw a boy-king's
tears, and it was a little Priam
who bent the threats of terrible Hercules.   720
Fierce was he, fierce was he. To his massive
strength all wild beasts gave way,
and after he broke through Hades' threshold,
he opened a lightless journey back;
when the tears of a little enemy conquered him,
"King, take up the reins," he said;
"sit tall in your ancestors' seat but
wield your rule with better faith."[77]
That was the way that that conqueror captured.
Learn from Hercules' peaceable fury—   730
or is it just Hercules' weapons you like?[78]
No less of a suppliant than that one then
lies at your feet and asks for his life.
Let Fortune carry the kingdom of Troy
wherever she will.

ULYSSES

Of course, the pain of a stricken mother affects me.
I am, nevertheless, more affected by the mothers of Greece,
as that son of yours is growing to their great grief.

ANDROMACHE

Will this boy rouse these—these ruins of the city, reduced
to dust? These hands of his, will they raise Troy?   740
Troy has no hope now, if its hopes are such.
We Trojans lie so low we could not frighten
anyone. Does his father inspire him?
But he was a dragged corpse. With the fall of Troy, his father
    himself
would have surrendered the pride great suffering breaks.
If retributions are demanded (and what worse retributions can
    there be?),
let him take up the yoke of the slave on his noble neck.
Permit him servitude. To a king is this refused?

ULYSSES

It isn't Ulysses but Calchas who refuses.

ANDROMACHE

750 O architect of deception and craftsman of crimes,
whose courage in war never killed anyone!
Through the treachery and cleverness of your evil-working
mind
even Greeks lie low.[79] Are guiltless gods and the prophet
your pretexts? This crime is from your heart.
You—a soldier at night, a hero in killing a boy[80]—
dare now to act on your own in the light of day.

ULYSSES

The courage of Ulysses is known well enough to the Greeks
and too well to you Phrygians. As for the day, there isn't time
to waste it in pointless words. The ships weigh anchor.

ANDROMACHE

760 Give a little delay for a parent to do her last
duty to her child; with a final embrace,
let me satisfy greedy sorrow.

ULYSSES

Ah would that it were
permitted to pity you! Still the one thing permitted
to give, time and delay, I will. Take your fill
of crying as you like. Tears lighten distress.

ANDROMACHE

O sweet love-pledge, O glory of a fallen house and crowning
loss of Troy,
O fear of the Greeks, O futile hope of your mother! Out of my
mind,
I prayed you'd have your father's praise in battle—better,[81]
770 your grandfather's age. These wishes the god has forsaken.
In the royal hall, you will not powerfully wield
Ilium's scepter nor give laws to the people nor bring
defeated races under your yoke and hack
Greek in flight. You will not drag Achilles' son.

You will not touch little weapons with tender hands.
You will not pursue beasts scattered in far flung
groves in your boldness or, on the day fixed for the *lustra*,[82]
revive the sacred rite of the Trojan games
and lead the speeding squadrons, noble child.
No, among the altars, quick with a nimble foot,   780
as the curved horn resounds sped measures, you
won't honor our foreign temple in ancient dance.[83]
O type of destruction bleaker than dreadful death!
A thing to weep for more than Hector's murder
is what our walls will see.

ULYSSES
            Stop weeping, Mother.
Great sorrow never comes to an end by itself.

ANDROMACHE
Grant me a tear or two, Ulysses (how little
is the delay I seek!), so I can close
the eyes of the living with my hand. You're small to die,
but feared already . . . Your Troy awaits you. Go,   790
be free, and go see the Trojans who are free.

ASTYANAX
Mother, pity me!

ANDROMACHE
            Why do you cling to my breast
and why seize the empty protection of mother's hand?
Just so, when the tender calf hears the roar of the lion
and timidly cowers into his mother's side, but the lion
gets the mother out of the way, then, in his savagery,
crushes his tiny prey with his huge jaws
and breaks him and drags him away—just like that, the enemy
will snatch you from my breast. My tears and my kisses
and my torn hair, child—accept them. Go, full of me,   800
to meet your father. But bring a word or two
of maternal grievance also: "If ghosts still care
about what came before, if love doesn't die in the fire,

then are you allowing Andromache to slave for some Greek,
unfeeling Hector? Do you lie unresponsive and slow?—
Achilles came back!" Take my hair
a second time and my tears and whatever remains
from my wretched husband's funeral. Take kisses to give
to your father.[84] As a solace, only leave
810   this garment. It was touched by my tomb
and my own, dear ghost.[85] If any of his ashes
are left, I'll track them down with my lips.

ULYSSES

    Her tears have no limit.
Quick, get rid of this delay of our Argive ships.

CHORUS

    What home calls us captives to dwell within it?
Mountains of Thessaly,[86] shadowy valley of Tempe,[87]
819   or Iolcos who rules the enormous sea?[88]
821   Is it tiny Gyrtone? Or is it barren Tricce?
822   Or Mothone that teems with its leaping waterways?[89]
816   Or is it the soil that's better at making men
to be soldiers, Phthia,[90] or the better producer
818   of strong cattle, Trachis,[91] full of rocks,
823   which, out of its hiding places and Oetan forests,
sent dangerous arrows to Troy's downfall
not once only?[92]
Or Olenos where they dwell in sparse houses?[93]
Pleuron, which is hateful to the maiden goddess?[94]
Troezen,[95] with winding coast on a wide sea?
Or Pelion,[96] arrogant kingdom of Prothous,[97] three
830   steps from heaven? Here it was that, relaxing
in the cave of a carved out mountain, sprawling
Chiron,[98] the instructor of that already fierce child
was striking with his pick the ringing strings
and honing that already outsize anger then
singing him war songs.
Or is it Carystos with dappled stone for produce[99]

or the shore that presses the restless sea,
Chalcis with its constantly hastening strait?[100]
Or Calydnean islands,[101] with easy access to any wind,
or never-windless Gonoessa[102] and   840
Enispe trembling at north wind, Boreas?[103]
Is it sprawling Crete with its one hundred cities,   820
or Peparethos dangling from Attic coast[104]   842
or Eleusis rejoicing in silent mysteries?
Surely not Salamis, home of the real Ajax,[105]
or Calydon,[106] famous home of the savage boar,   844
or the lands that Titaressos soaks
with sluggish ripples on the way to the sea?[107]
Bessa and Scarphe and old-man Pylos,[108]
Pharis or Jupiter's Pisa or Elis
renowned for its garlands?[109]   850
Let this grim hurricane send us wherever you lie
in our wretchedness and give us to any land,
as long as Sparta which produced that great pestilence[110]
for the Trojans and the Greeks is far, and far
are Argos and Mycenae, home of savage Pelops,[111]
and Neritos, smaller than little Zacynthus[112] and
Ithaca that harms with its treacherous rocks!
What fate awaits you, what master will take you,
Hecuba, to what country for display?
In whose kingdom will you die?   860

ACT 4

HELEN

Any wedding that's grim and seems like a funeral,
with laments and slaughter, bloodshed and groans,
should have Helen as witness. I'm being forced
to harm the Phrygians even in their defeat. Under orders,
I make up stories about Pyrrhus' wedding and bring
Greek raiment and decoration. With my skill and deceit
Paris' sister will be captured and be killed.

Let her be tricked. I think it's better for her like this.
To die a death without fear of death is something to wish . . .
870   Why do you pause in following orders? Blame for a crime
committed under duress returns to the author.

(To Polyxena.)

High-born girl
of Dardan house! A better god has begun to look
out for the ruined and prepares to give you
a happy marriage. A Troy still safe and Priam
couldn't have given you such a partnership!
The greatest glory of the Pelasgian race,
878   the one who commands wide realms of Thessalian fields,
877   seeks you for the holy pact of his wedding bed.
Great Tethys and many goddesses of the sea
880   and Thetis, kind power of the swollen deep, will call
you theirs. Married to Pyrrhus, as father-in-law
Peleus will call you daughter and so will Nereus.
Take off your dirty clothing. Dress in festive
attire. Unlearn the captive part. Smooth down
your messy hair, let your locks be plaited by an expert hand.
Perhaps this catastrophe will put you back
on a loftier throne. Being captured has helped many.

ANDROMACHE
The defeated Phrygians were free of this one sorrow—
celebration. Razed Pergamum is burning
890   on all sides. Time for a wedding! Who would dare
deny it? Would anyone hesitate to head to the marriage
recommended by Helen? Plague, death, devastation
of both populations! Do you see these funeral mounds
of our leaders, the naked bones that lie unburied
in all the fields? Your wedding scattered these.
For you the blood of Asia and Europe flowed, flowed,
as you stolidly surveyed the contending men and could
not make up your mind. Go, prepare the wedding!

What need for lights and ritual torches? What need
for fire? Troy lights the way to this strange union.   900
Celebrate Pyrrhus' wedding, Trojan women!
Celebrate it right: let it sound with flagellation and lament.

HELEN

Although great grief lacks reason and cannot
be deflected and sometimes even hates
its own companions, still I can
defend my case before a hostile judge.
I once suffered worse: Andromache mourns for Hector,
and Hecuba mourns for Priam; only Helen
must mourn for Paris in secret. Is it hateful and hard and
    oppressive
to put up with slavery? A captive, I suffered that yoke   910
for ten years. Has Ilium been overthrown
and its homes toppled? It's hard to lose your homeland
but harder to fear it. So many companions in sorrow
lighten your load. The victor and the vanquished rage at me.
Each man has pondered, with uncertain outcome, which
slave-girl he should take. My master took me
instantly,[113] without drawing lots. Was I
the cause of war and so much slaughter for the Trojans?
    Consider
that true if a *Spartan* ship sailed your straits, but if
I was the prize that was plundered by Phrygian oars,   920
and the goddess who won the contest gave me as a gift
to the judge,[114] then forgive Paris.[115] My case is about to get
an angry arbiter: that decision awaits
Menelaus. For now let go of your grief for a little,
Andromache, persuade that girl[116]—I can't
hold back my tears.

ANDROMACHE

        How great is any sorrow that Helen weeps!
But why does she weep? Confess the crimes and the traps
that the Ithacan weaves! Is the girl to be tossed from the cliffs

of Ida or thrown from a jutting rock on
930   the lofty citadel? Surely she's not to be hurled
into the vast sea over these crags that tall
sharp-sided Sigeum raises with bay full of shoals?
Speak, confess what you hide with your treacherous face!
Any evil is easier than having Priam and Hecuba's
son-in-law be Pyrrhus. Confess, disclose the punishment
you prepare and remove this one thing from our downfall—
deception. The women you see are ready for death.

HELEN

Would that the gods' interpreter[117] also ordered me
to break off my stay in hated daylight
940   with the sword or die before Achilles' pyre
by the furious hand of Pyrrhus, companion of your fate,
O pitiful Polyxena! Achilles has bidden
you to be given to him and sacrificed in front of his dust
so he can get married in the field of Elysium!

ANDROMACHE

See how her mighty spirit hears death with joy!
She reaches for the beauteous raiment of royal dress
and deigns to let a hand arrange her tresses.
She thought that marriage was death. *This* she thinks is
        marriage.
But her mother, the wretch, is dazed by the grievous message;
950   her tottering mind has collapsed—rise up and lift
your spirits, wretch, and steel your failing courage!

(*Aside.*)

How her frail life-force hangs on a fine-spun chain:
the littlest thing could make Hecuba happy—but
she breathes and comes to life. Death flees the wretched first.

HECUBA

Does Achilles still live for the punishment of Phrygians?
Does he still renew combat? O Paris, your hand was weak!
Even his grave and his dust thirst for our blood.

Just now, a plenteous crowd surrounded me;
I got tired dividing my motherhood into so many kisses
in such a throng! Now this girl alone is left as   960
my desire, companion, relief, and rest to my affliction.[118]
She's Hecuba's whole offspring. By this voice alone
am I called mother now. Come, stubborn, unhappy
life, and slip away. Release me at least
from this one funeral. Tears wet her cheeks
and a sudden shower falls from her conquered face.
Be happy, rejoice, child. How Cassandra and
Andromache would wish a wedding like yours!

ANDROMACHE

It's us, Hecuba, it's us, it's us, who must be
mourned for, Hecuba, whom the fleet as it casts off will scatter   970
everywhere. Her parents' dear land will cover her.

HELEN

You'll envy her more, when you learn your own lot.

ANDROMACHE

Am I unaware of any part of my punishment?

HELEN

The shaken urn gave all the captives masters.

ANDROMACHE

Whose slave-woman am I? Say it! Whom do I call master?

HELEN

The young man from Scyros took you at the first lot.[119]

ANDROMACHE

Happy Cassandra, whom madness and Phoebus exempt
from distribution!

HELEN

The greatest king of kings gets her.[120]

HECUBA

Does anyone want to lay his claim to Hecuba?

HELEN

A short-lived prize, you fell to the unwilling Ithacan.   980

HECUBA

What caster of unfair lots, so rash, hardhearted,
and savage, has given royal to royal?
What god so perverse has distributed captives?
What arbiter, cruel and oppressive to the wretched,
does not know how to choose masters, and with a brutal
hand gives unjust fates to the wretched? Who matches
the mother of Hector with Achilles' weapons?[121] I'm called
to Ulysses! Now even to myself I look conquered
and captive, beset by all catastrophes: I'm ashamed of my
    master,

990 not my slavery. [Will he carry the spoils of Hector
who carried those of Achilles?][122] That barren land
closed in by savage straits cannot hold my grave.
Lead on, lead on, Ulysses, I don't delay. I follow
my master. My fate will follow me—no calm peace
will come to the sea, the ocean will rage with the wind[123]—
and war and fire and my sorrows and also Priam's;
and until these come, this is your interim punishment:
I take my lot in advance and steal your prize.
But Pyrrhus is running over in haste, and with fierce

1000 face. Pyrrhus, why pause? Come on, open
my chest with iron and unite your dear Achilles'
in-laws. Come on, butcher of old men. This
blood is right for you. He seizes me and drags me off.[124]
Spatter the gods on high with calamitous slaughter.
Spatter the spirits—what should I pray for you? I pray
for seas equal to this abomination; may there
befall the whole Greek fleet and the thousand ships
the same outcome that I'll ask for my ship when I sail.

CHORUS

Sweet is a group of mourners to someone who grieves.
1010 Sweet are populations noisy with weeping.
The tears and the lamentation that teem from a crowd
of people weeping the same way stings more gently.

Always, ah always uncharitable is grief.
It rejoices when its fate is dispensed to many
and is not satisfied to be punished alone.
Suffering a fate common to all is something
no one refuses.
No one will believe that he's wretched, even if he is—
Just get rid of the happy; take away those affluent in
gold, and take away the people who   1020
plow rich fields with a hundred oxen—
the dejected minds of the poor will soar, for
no one is wretched except by comparison.
Sweet it is to the person who stands amid unmeasured ruins
that no one else has a happy face.
That person laments and complains about his fate
who has cut the waves with a single ship
and turns up penniless at the port he sought.
He bears the catastrophe and storms better
if he sees that a thousand ships sink in the ocean   1030
together and sees the shore littered with shipwrecked
planks while Corus, the northwest wind, won't let
the sea ebb as it piles on the waves.
Phrixus lamented that Helle had fallen
when the lord of the flock with his radiant fleece
carried brother and sister together on
his golden back and jettisoned her in
mid-ocean,[125] but Pyrrha and her husband[126] checked
their laments when they saw the ocean
and saw nothing beyond the ocean, left   1040
alone on the earth, the last of the human race.
This gathering and these tears of ours will be
broken up and scattered here and there by the driven fleet,[127]
and the sailors, bidden by the horn to spread the canvas
with their oars racing along with the wind
will seize the deep and abandon the strand.
What will the state of mind of the wretched be
when all the earth will shrink and the sea will expand

and tall Ida will start to hide a long way off?

1050 Son to mother and mother to child then will
gesture to the region where Troy extends
and say, as they trace it from afar with their finger,
"Ilium's there, where the pillar of smoke and the foul
clouds are winding high in the sky." The Trojans
will recognize their homeland by this sign.

ACT 5

MESSENGER

O hard fate—savage, wretched, hair-raising! What crime
did the god of war ever see so fierce, so bleak
these twice five years? Whose news should I lament first—

(*To Andromache, then Hecuba.*)

your griefs or yours, old woman?

HECUBA

1060 Whatever griefs you'll weep, you'll weep my own.
Each person is crushed by her own crisis, but I'm crushed by
everyone's.
I have lost all. Whoever is wretched is wretched for Hecuba.

MESSENGER

The maiden was sacrificed. The boy was hurled from the tower.
But both of them bore their doom with a noble attitude.

ANDROMACHE

Relay the sequence of death and follow through
the double atrocity. Great grief rejoices to handle
all its wounds. So tell all. Speak.

MESSENGER

There is one tower left of massive Troy,
the haunt of Priam. From its peak and lofty
1070 parapets, arbiter of the war he sat,
directing the lines. In this tower, in his kind
lap he'd hold his grandson as Hector put the Greeks

to flight, retreating in fear, with iron and fire,
and the old man traced father's battles to the boy.
This tower, once upon a time the badge and glory
of the wall, is now a brutal crag, surrounded on all
sides by crowds of kings and commons. The whole mob
leaves their ships behind and converges. For some,
a distant hill gives a clear sight-line to the open
space. For others, a rock-formation: on its height,   1080
the straining crowd is poised on the tips of its toes.
A pine holds one man, a laurel another, one
a beech: the whole wood shakes with people draped.
One goes for the edge of a jagged cliff. One puts
his weight on a burnt-out house or the hanging rock
of the fallen wall, and one inhuman onlooker—
atrocity!—sits on the funeral mound of Hector.
Through vast and thronged expanses, with high steps,
approaches the Ithacan, dragging in his right hand
Priam's tiny grandson. The boy with no slow step   1090
heads to the high walls. When he stood at the top
of the tower, he turned his sharp-eyed look now here
and there, and his mind was fearless. Just like the small
and tender offspring of some great beast, not yet
able to rage with its teeth, still threatens and takes
empty bites and swells with anger—like that,
that child, taken in the enemy's hand,
was lordly and contumacious. He moved the mob,
its leaders, and even Ulysses. Of all the crowd,
he only, for whom they wept, wept not. While Ulysses   1100
    declaimed
the words and prayers of the fate-dealing prophet and summoned
the savage gods to the rites, of his own accord
the boy leapt into Priam's kingdom.[128]

ANDROMACHE
What person from Colchis, what Scyth of impermanent home
did this? What race that borders the Caspian

sea and knows no law dared it?[129] Not even inhuman
Busiris' altars were spattered with blood from boys[130]
and not even Diomedes served little limbs
to his horses to eat.[131] Who'll wrap your body and give
it to the tomb?

MESSENGER

What body could that steep space
leave intact? Bones scattered and shattered from the weight
of the fall. The traces of the famous body,
a face, and those noble features of his father—
as his weight hit the far ground, it mangled everything.
His neck broke from the impact of the rock. The head
was shattered with brains dashed from within—he lies
a shapeless mass.

ANDROMACHE

Like this he is his father's likeness, too.

MESSENGER

As the boy fell headlong from high walls and the crowd
of Achaeans wept at the atrocity it committed,
the very same people went back for another crime
at the funeral mound of Achilles. Its furthest side
the Rhoetean shallow laps with a gentle wave.
On the near side, a field surrounds it and a valley
seals the inner space with a slight incline
and rises as though a theater. The teeming throng
filled all the shore: some think the delay of their fleet
will be undone by this death, some just enjoy
their enemies being uprooted. Much of the fickle
crowd can't bear the crime but watches it. No fewer
Trojans attend this, their funeral. Shaking with fear,
they see the final piece of Troy fall down:
Suddenly, as if in a wedding, torches light
the way for Helen, bridesmaid, sad with head
bowed. "May Hermione marry like this, may
vile Helen be returned so to her husband,"

the Phrygians pray. Terror grips both stricken
populations. Polyxena herself walks with
her eyes cast down in modesty—her face shines still,
and beauty at its end beams more than usual,
like the light of Phoebus that tends to be sweeter when   1140
he's all but setting, when the stars take their turn,
and night, approaching, closes on faltering day.
The entire crowd goes numb: [all tend to praise that which
is soon to die.][132] Some respond to her bodily beauty, some
to her tender age, and some to life's vagaries.
All respond to her mind brave facing death.
[She walks before Pyrrhus. All their spirits quake.]
They feel awe and pity. When she reached
the height of his steep mountain and the young man stood
on the prominent peak of his father's tomb,   1150
the fearless girl did not step back. Wild with
fierce face, she stands turned toward the blow.
So brave a spirit strikes the minds of all,
and strange to see is Pyrrhus slow to kill.
When he buried deep the driven iron with his right hand,
then drew back the deadly blade, sudden blood shot from her
gaping wound, but on the verge of death, she didn't
lose her spirit: as if to make the earth weigh hard
on Achilles, she fell head-forward with angry momentum.
Both sides wept—the Phrygians emitted timid   1160
groans; the victor groaned more eminently.
That was the course of the rite. The spilled blood did not pool
or flow across the ground. The savage mound
swallowed it instantly—drank the gore all down.

HECUBA

Go, go, Danaans, seek your homes in safety now.
Care-free, the fleet can cut the sought-for sea
with sails spread. A girl and boy are dead.
The war is done. But where will I bring my tears?
Where can this old woman get rid of death's delay?

Should I weep for my daughter or grandson, my husband or
        homeland?
    For all of them, or just myself? My only wish is death.
    With violence you come to babies and virgins.[133] Savage,
    you hurry everywhere. Only me do you fear
    and avoid. Amid swords and spears and torches,
    sought all night long, you flee me although I desire you.
    No enemy or falling ruins, no fire
    consumed my limbs. I stood so close to Priam!

MESSENGER
    Captives, hurry to seek the sea.
    The boat already unfurls its sails. The ships are departing.

Octavia

This drama occupies three days in 62 CE, in which the Emperor Nero divorces the emperor Claudius' daughter Octavia and marries his mistress Poppaea. In the long opening dialogue, Octavia and her nurse explain the prehistory of the emperor Claudius' marriages and the successive unnatural deaths of Claudius, his son Britannicus, and his widow Agrippina. The nurse urges Octavia to put up with Nero, but she finds him too repugnant. On cue, the chorus sings of how Nero even murdered his mother Agrippina. Next, the philosopher and imperial advisor Seneca appears and expresses regret that he came back from exile. Nero comes in to tell Seneca that the people must obey his will and that he will divorce Octavia in order to marry Poppaea, who is bearing his child. He ignores Seneca's warning that this will not go down well with the people and rejects the idea that a good ruler is a merciful one.

This is followed by three detached scenes. The ghost of Agrippina appears to denounce Nero's treachery, then leaves without any contact with Octavia, who is shown leaving the palace of her father Claudius, her family home. Next Poppaea rushes from the bridal chamber to report an ominous dream to her nurse, and they leave to perform a propitiatory sacrifice. In the following episode the citizens riot against Nero's marriage, attacking the palace and demolishing Poppaea's statues. An apparently different chorus, sympathetic to Poppaea, sings of the power of Love. Nero enters giving orders for the suppression of the riot and execution of its leaders, including Octavia, whom he orders into exile. In the last scene Octavia is escorted by a chorus of supporters to the ship that will take her to exile and death.

Introduction

ELAINE FANTHAM

Octavia and Senecan Tragedy

The *Octavia* survived the centuries between Rome's pagan empire and the rebirth of humanism in the thirteenth century through a fortunate misunderstanding. Because it so resembled Senecan tragedy in its verse technique and dramatic devices, it was mistaken for Seneca's (much more skillful) compositions and included with the corpus of Senecan tragedies in one of the two main manuscript traditions (A). But for all its Senecan mannerisms, the *Octavia* cannot be the work of the philosopher-dramatist, all the more because—uniquely in ancient Greek and Roman drama—its supposed author, Seneca, is himself one of the *dramatis personae*. He figures prominently in an unsuccessful dispute with Nero, who claims that as emperor he is above the law. As a political fact, Seneca, originally invited by Nero's mother Agrippina to be the young man's adviser, may have still tried to advise the emperor during the period represented in the dramatic text, but Tacitus reports that Seneca's power had already been crushed (*Annals* 14.52 and 14.57) by the death of his colleague Burrus before Octavia's fall.

Besides featuring the supposed author in his own drama, the script of this play includes another anomaly. Its action is set in 62 CE, but the prophecies or curses expressed by Agrippina and other characters show knowledge of events leading up to Nero's death in 68 CE, three years after Seneca's own enforced suicide. The playwright, a less capable poet than his model, must have written the drama after 68, either in the immediate aftermath of Nero's death, during the "year of the four emperors" (69 CE) or at least early in Vespasian's principate when there was not yet any need to pay explicit homage to the new Flavian dynasty. The dynastic intrigue of *Octavia* could not have been written without knowledge and deliberate imitation of Seneca's tragedies, any more than Seneca himself could have written his *Oedipus* or *Medea* without knowledge of the most important Attic tragedies, but Seneca wrote under the influence of another genre—the great epics of Virgil and Ovid—and created his own dramatic intrigues independently of both earlier tragedy and more recent epic. Certainly he adapts some episodes from Greek tragedy, but his dialogue and dramaturgy is original.

This play is often referred to as *Octavia praetexta* and treated as a deviation from the early Republican pageant plays or *praetextae* composed to celebrate the victories of Roman generals or civic action of magistrates, whose official dress was the purple bordered toga or *praetexta*. Little as we know about those plays from a few brief quotations and later discussion by Roman critics, there is enough evidence to encourage refining our ideas of the genre. As Harriet Flower shows in her definitive discussion, one or two early *praetextae* were written to honor Rome's founders (e.g., Naevius' *Romulus*) or celebrated contemporary generals (e.g., Naevius' *Clastidium*, which was performed either at Marcellus' funeral or perhaps at his dedication of a temple), but a number of others honor aristocratic patrons by representing the heroic deeds of their ancestors, as Accius' play *Brutus* glorifies the action of L. Junius Brutus in expelling the Tarquins after the rape of Lucretia. The relatively long excerpts from this play given by Cicero (*On Divination* 1.44) show Tarquin preoccupied with a dream that has troubled him, which is interpreted for him by compliant soothsayers—a scene comparable to that of Poppaea and her nurse in *Octavia* (712–55), which also presents a false interpretation. Dreams and portents are predominant in Roman historiography (e.g., in the work of the historian of the Hannibalic war Caelius Antipater), as they are in the much later *Octavia*, but we should remember the limitation on female space; only exceptional women such as the foreign Medea or Phaedra, in her husband's absence, could determine dramatic action. Even imperial women belonged to the interior and could only make known their desires and emotionally significant experiences through dreams reported in private to (female) subordinates and confidantes. It is characteristic of plays centered on heroines that, unlike Aristotle's ideal drama, the protagonist may be confined and limited to confrontations within her family; she has no power of decision and cannot control the action, which, as in *Octavia* or Seneca's *Trojan Women*, is simply a study in defeat; all of which is offset only by the moral victory of endurance (Seneca's Stoic virtue of *constantia*).

Not enough excerpts of the lost Roman pageant plays survive to determine whether this genre of national historical drama echoed the five act structure of Greek classical tragedy and used a chorus (often of Roman citizens), but by their nature these plays contained no tragic reversal and ended in a literal or moral triumph, even when celebrating a commander's sacrificial death (e.g., the *devotio* of Decius at the battle of Sentinum in Accius' *Aeneadae* [see Warmington's *Remains of Old Latin* 2.552–559]). The action of *Praetextae* in no way resembled the downfall of Octavia as depicted in our play; it was largely public and often centered on two related (and positive) events: a battle and the triumph earned by Roman victory. In fact it is difficult to imagine any relevant additional episodes to fill out five acts. Instead, *Octavia* begins and ends as a personal or dynastic tragedy with the triumph of evil over the emperor Claudius' surviving family.

Besides creating the material of its dialogue and choruses from Roman, indeed dynastic, memories, the *Octavia* also borrows from Greek tragedy several of its features and themes, such as Octavia's second monody (57–71) contrasting her fate with the monody of Sophocles' *Electra*, released from imprisonment by the return of her brother. Likewise in *Octavia's* final scene, the chorus supporting her as she goes to her death evokes the mythical rescue of Iphigenia from sacrifice at Aulis (973–76), but the action itself as she is escorted from the city to what will be her death, echoes the last chorus of Sophocles' *Antigone*. The protagonist, Octavia, is essentially a victim of repeated injustice: when Nero first appears in the play ordering the execution of innocent descendants to Augustus (seen as possible claimants to the throne) and when in his second appearance he takes the crucial decision that Octavia must die. As he overrides in the first scene all opposition from his adviser Seneca (437–592), so he far more easily overrides the military Prefect: both yield to his power (see 870–76) and both, recognizing defeat, disappear from the action of the play. This scene type occurring in the second act, imitates the futile dissuasion of the protagonist by nurses and henchmen in the second acts of Seneca's *Phaedra*, *Medea*, and *Thyestes*.

Is there a recurring theme, as opposed to events, emphasized through the play? Yes: within the scheming of this dynasty marriage—which was by this period always made for political or partisan motives—is an unremitting evil, and the most often repeated phrase in the author's repetitious text is "through the crime of his/her partner" (*coniunx*). It recurs constantly, used of more than one husband or wife in the doomed family. As we shall see below, it is the secular symbol behind the successive calamities that destroy the house of Claudius. We should note that the play avoids literal naming, relying on kinship terms instead. The sheer density of these terms dominates the text, and serves two functions—it serves as a kind of rejection and as the way of projecting the blame for the various murders onto kinship by birth or adoption. Outsiders like the chorus or messengers freely name the chief imperial figures, but one noticeable anomaly is that while Octavia lays stress on her unwelcome double role as sister (by adoption) and wife of Nero (46–47), others, including the messenger, name her as Claudius' child (her birth is her claim to public loyalty). Only once is she called by her second name, Octavia (786), seemingly for variation.

Octavia and History

This play would have been all too familiar to its intended elite Roman audience, but to understand the constraints which brought Octavia to her doom we must go back to the man who became Augustus and set in motion the Julio-Claudian dynasty. This dynasty, with its ensuing series of personal tragedies, arose from the unprecedented circumstance that a single leader (Octavian, who then renamed himself Augustus) ruled Rome as commander-in-chief and first citizen for forty-four years, sustained by his defeat of Antony and the goodwill given to his own authority from 30 BCE to his death in 14 CE. Augustus cast the best possible light on his own actions in his *Res Gestae* (a brief list of his accomplishments as princeps), but this official narrative is exposed as mere propaganda in the *Octavia*, where the dialogue between Seneca and Nero (*Octavia* 498–533) offsets Seneca's orthodox Augustan narrative with Nero's reply—a far more cynical narrative of the young Octavian's ruthless exploitation of power during the triumviral years 43–31 CE.

Due to the deaths of his blood heirs, Augustus had to reluctantly adopt Tiberius, his wife Livia's son by her prior marriage, to Tiberius Claudius Nero. When he did so late in life in 4 CE, he shared his administration with Tiberius on the condition that Tiberius himself would adopt as his son Germanicus, husband to Augustus' granddaughter, Agrippina the elder, and father to her three sons and three daughters. This was a power couple whom Tiberius saw as a continuing threat. But Germanicus' mysterious death away in Syria in 19 CE had a disastrous effect on relationships within the dynasty, which deteriorated further with the death of Tiberius' own son Drusus Gemellus in 23. From that time there was increasing ill will between Tiberius and Agrippina, since her sons were potential candidates for the succession. Their feud was intensified by the fact that descent from Augustus was now almost a prerequisite for succession, and the endogamy that generated rivals for succession also led to technical incest. When Tiberius died in 37 CE, he was over 70, with no living son. Agrippina's youngest child, the unstable Gaius (Caligula), briefly took his place but was soon assassinated.

We come now to Octavia's father and mother: Claudius was the first emperor to have no inheritance of Augustus' blood, which made him more vulnerable to challenge. At the time he was chosen as emperor, his third wife, Valeria Messalina, descended from Augustus' sister Octavia on both her maternal and paternal side, named her daughter Claudia Octavia, reinforcing the proud name of the Claudian clan with that of her imperial great-great-grandmother, Augustus' sister. This is our heroine. Confirmed as emperor by the senate (41 CE), Claudius had two children by Messalina: Octavia, born soon after 39 CE, and her brother, given the honorific Britannicus to commemorate his father's (partial) conquest of Britain. But Messalina's blatant promiscuity and a public act of marriage with her lover Silius brought on her divorce and enforced suicide in 49. As Octavia tells the nurse and her audience at the opening of our play, her mother's folly brought the downfall of the Claudian house (10ff.); it exposed Claudius to the schemes of Agrippina the younger. Agrippina was now unmarried, and might have chosen a consort she could raise to imperial power: instead she schemed to marry the widowed Claudius in order to wield power through her son. Because Claudius was her uncle, there had to be a dispensation from incest before they could marry. Next she persuaded Claudius to adopt her son Domitius under the new name Tiberius Claudius Nero and to put him in the public eye, at the expense of Claudius' own young son by Messalina, Britannicus. After Claudius' death, however, when Nero as emperor began to feud with his mother, she threatened to change her backing and sponsor Britannicus as Claudius' successor. This was fatal to herself and to the guileless boy. As he approached his fourteenth birthday, when he would assume the toga of manhood, he was mysteriously poisoned.

All this Octavia tells in her opening monody, but in riddling terms that prefer to speak of relationships rather than proper names. For a woman proud of her noble, indeed imperial, birth, she suffered further damage. To contrive her marriage with Nero, now adopted as her brother, the imperial advisors had to arrange Octavia's adoption out of her own family; hence her repeated complaints about being deprived of her own *penates* and her Claudian home. She was doubly dishonored and married to a hostile overbearing young thug—but the horror of their marriage was outdone when Nero fell in love with another man's wife, Poppaea, and in order to rid himself of the emperor's daughter contrived accusations of adultery against Octavia. Divorce and retreat from public life would have been welcome to her, but her popularity meant that he could not let her survive; hence the popular uprising after Nero's new marriage that forms the crisis of the play and precipitates his desire to have her permanently out of the way—first exiled, then murdered.

Mythological, Literary, and Theatrical Motifs

Somewhat incongruously, it is the nurse who revives the old Hesiodic myth of man's injustice driving out Piety (repeated more appropriately by Seneca in 397f.) and the entrance of Erinys, the spirit of Vengeance for kin-murder, into the household. That motif occurs four times (23, 161, 263, and 619, usually with references to Stygian darkness). The more "positive" myth of Jupiter's infidelities and Juno's long suffering is taken over from the nurse by the chorus as an analogy (201–21, Juno, like Octavia, is sister and wife) and interwoven with praises of Amor/Cupid by Nero (554f.). Somewhere between cosmology, mythology, and anthropology is the negative portrait of human evolution produced by Seneca in his long meditation grafting the Hesiodic "Ages of Man" (375–25) onto the theme of modern corruption within the family echoing well known passages of Aratus, Catullus 64, *Georgics* 1, and Ovid's *Metamorphoses* 1. But these are swift and superficial, even disorganized.

As we have noted, Greek mythology is supplemented by Roman legends, from the Livian heroes of the republic to the Augustan narrative, but the legends demonstrate human and civic, not divine, power and wisdom. More stimulating is the author's use of the supernatural; the omens, dreams, ghosts, and prophecies of this play are not, as far as we know, taken over from a historical source, but Roman historiography from Caelius Antipater onward delighted in the dreams and vision and portents we associate with poetry. Both Octavia (115–22) and Poppaea dream (712–739), and we have seen that dream interpretation was a welcome feature in Accius' *Praetexta, Brutus*. Seneca opens the *Agamemnon* with the shade/ghost of Thyestes, and the *Thyestes* with the shade of their ancestor Tantalus. In his *Trojan Women*, Achilles' ghost is confined to a messenger speech, and Hector's ghost is only a hallucination of Andromache, as is the ghost of Medea's brother Absyrtus. But a hallucination is almost as powerful in atmosphere as a stage ghost. One element that is real in Seneca, ritual (as in the diabolical ritual of Atreus), is barely represented in *Octavia*. The household gods are revered, and a marriage is celebrated, but there is no ritual. Is this a tragedy of godless evil

(Octavia claims "there are no gods") or are the author and his society godless? It is most un-Roman. But evil predominates as a theme in post-Augustan poetry.

What about purely literary features? The author operates with only two modes (the basic iambic senarius of dialogue and the anapaestic dimeters and tetrameters of choral verse and monody), but meter is relatively smooth. The most positive element in the text is the author's careful use of repetition in patterning and ring composition, recalling key themes to frame beginning and ending (e.g., Octavia's invocation of her parents; 10 and 34; the invocation is named at 270–72) and of thematic recall, not only of themes like criminal marriage and the crimes of a bride mentioned above but, for example, the death of Agrippina sung in the first long choral ode (309–76) in anticipation of her own first person account. But the author is better at ideas than their expression; his protests, antitheses, paradoxes, and extravagant *adunata* may already be rhetorical clichés but they are vivid; where he fails is as a poet or versifier, with too poor a vocabulary and too limited a command of syntax. He was obviously educated and had been in the audience of many texts, but the play reads as though it was his own first attempt at verse: it would be unpleasant for a translation to replicate features of his Latin, but I have tried to convey his limitations by translating some of the most overused and superfluous epithets with similar repetitions in English.

Suggested Reading

Boyle, Anthony J., trans. 2008. *Octavia*. Oxford.

Dupont, Florence. 1995. *Les monstres de Sénèque*. Paris.

Ferri, Roland. 2003a. "Octavia and the Roman Dramatic Tradition." In Wilson 2003, 89–111.

———., ed. 2003b. Octavia: *A Play Attributed to Seneca*. Cambridge.

Flower, Harriet. 1995. "*Fabulae Praetextae* in Context: When Were Plays on Contemporary Subjects Performed in Republican Rome?" *Classical Quarterly* 45: 170–90

Kragelund, Patrick. 2002. "Historical Drama in Ancient Rome: Republican Flourishing and Imperial Decline?" *Symbolae Osloenses* 77: 5–51.

Marshall, Christopher W. 2006. *The Stagecraft and Performance of Roman Comedy*. Cambridge.

Wilson, Marcus, ed. 2003. *The Tragedy of Nero's Wife: Studies on the Octavia Praetexta*. Auckland.

Wiseman, Peter. 1998. *Roman Drama and Roman History*. Exeter.

Octavia

ATTRIBUTED TO SENECA

TRANSLATED BY ELAINE FANTHAM

DRAMATIS PERSONAE

OCTAVIA, wife of Nero, daughter of the emperor Claudius
NURSE of Octavia
SENECA, Nero's advisor
NERO, the emperor
PREFECT of the guard
NURSE of Poppaea
POPPAEA
GHOST of Agrippina
CHORUS of Roman citizens, supportive of Octavia
CHORUS of supporters of Poppaea

The action of the play takes place over three days. Most of the events take place within Nero's palace, especially the imperial bedchamber, though some scenes are outside and the final scene appears to be at a dock.

DAY 1

OCTAVIA
Now gleaming dawn drives from the heavens
the wandering stars,
Titan arises with glittering locks
and brings back bright day to the world.
Come now,[1] you who are burdened with such vast woes
renew your now accustomed laments
and outdo the sea-borne halcyons,
outdo Pandion's swift-winged daughters,[2]
since your fate is yet worse than theirs.
I must bewail my mother forever,   10

Mother, first cause of my misfortunes,[3]
listen to your daughter's sad laments
if any feeling persists among the shades.
If only aged Clotho's hand had snapped
my life's thread before I lived
to see in grief your wounds and features
spattered with defiling blood!
O daylight that will always be my doom!
From that time on
daylight has been more loathsome to me than the dark.
I endured the orders of a cruel stepmother,
her hostile feeling and grim countenance.
She, she, harsh Erinys,[4] carried in
the Stygian torches for my bridal bed,
and took your life, lamented father,
whom all the world so recently obeyed,
to whom the Britons beyond Ocean,[5]
unknown as yet to our commanders
and independent,
turned their backs in flight.
Ah me, Father; by your wife's treachery[6]
you lie destroyed, your house and children,
captives enslaved to the tyrant.[7]

NURSE

(Entering but turned away from her mistress.)

Whoever is dazzled and stunned by the first flash
and brittle benefits of the deceitful court:
Look! Let him see the house just now all-powerful
and Claudius' children, laid low by the sudden attack
of lurking Fortune! To his power the world was subject,
and Ocean, left free for so long, obeyed him,
and unwillingly took in his ships.
See! He who first set yoke upon the Britons
covering straits unknown with such vast fleets,

he who went unharmed amid barbarian tribes
and savage seas, was killed by his wife's crime,
as she was by her son's. That son's brother lies dead
from poison, that son's unhappy sister-bride
laments, without strength to hide her painful grief,[8]
though compelled by her cruel husband's anger.
Constantly she seeks seclusion, and the married pair
burn with equal loathing and a mutual flame.   50
In vain my loyalty and devotion soothes
her grieving mind. Merciless sorrow
defeats my advice, and her mind's noble passion
cannot be controlled but takes strength from misfortune.
Ah, how vicious a crime our fear foresees!
If only the god's power would avert this deed.

OCTAVIA

O my ill-fortune, beyond compare with evils,
even though I recall
your mourning, Electra:[9]
When you were grieving, you were able   60
to bewail your murdered father, to avenge
the crime with your brother as champion,
whom your loyalty snatched from the enemy
and your devotion sheltered.
But fear forbids me to mourn my parents
snatched away by cruel fate, or to lament
my brother's murder, he who had been
my only hope, a short-lived comfort
for so many misfortunes.
Now surviving just to mourn my family   70
I am the shadow of a mighty name.[10]

NURSE

Ah! the voice of my sad nursling
has struck my ears.[11]
Shall my old age be slow to enter her bedchamber?

OCTAVIA

Receive my tears, nurse,
loyal witness of my grief.

NURSE

What day will release you
from such cares, piteous girl?

OCTAVIA

The day that will send me to the shades of Styx

NURSE

80   Keep such omens far from away, I beg you.

OCTAVIA

It is fate that rules my destiny,
not your prayers.

NURSE

God will be mild and grant your sorrow
better times.
Only beguile your man
with sweet obedience.

OCTAVIA

Sooner shall I soothe savage lions and grim-faced tigers
than the fierce breast of that savage tyrant.
He hates those born of noble blood,
90   despises gods and men alike, and does not know
his own good fortune, given by his loathsome mother
through a monstrous crime.
Though the ingrate is ashamed
to have seized this power by his mother's gift,
though he may repay so great a gift by death,
the woman will bear this credit always,
after her decease, through the long ages.

NURSE

Hold back the words of a frenzied mind!
Stifle your voice so rashly set loose.

OCTAVIA

Though what I suffer has to be borne, my misfortunes   100
can never have an end, except by my death.
With my mother slain, my father taken by crime,
bereft of my brother, overwhelmed by misfortunes,
burdened by grief, loathed by my husband,
a slave to my own menial,[12] I find the light of day unwanted.
My heart is always trembling, fearing not death but evil-doing.
Just let villainy be absent from my fate:
I shall rejoice to die. For it is punishment worse than death
for me to see—oh, horrible!—the tyrant's grim and bloated
features, to share kisses with my enemy,   110
to fear his decisions—a man my grief could not obey
after my brother's death, his life cut short
by crime. His lawful power the instigator[13]
of his death now holds, rejoicing to usurp his lot.
How often my brother's sad shade comes before me
when rest releases my limbs and sleep overwhelms
my eyes weary with weeping. At times he takes black torches
into his feeble hands and aims in hatred
at his brother's eyes and mouth. At times my brother flees
trembling into my bed; and even as he clings to me   120
his violent enemy chases him and thrusts the sword into my
    breast.
Then shivers and huge terror drive away my dream
reviving grief and dread in my unhappy being.
Add to these horrors the arrogant shameless whore[14]
glittering with our family's spoils: as her wedding gift,
the son embarked his mother on the Stygian boat;[15]
after the dread shipwreck, when she survived the sea,
her son, more savage than the currents of the deep,
slew her with the sword. What hope of safety then,
after so great an evil, did I have?   130
Victorious, my enemy menaces my bed,
and ablaze with hate for me she asks

of my husband, as price of fornication,
his lawful spouse's head. Rise from the shades,
Father, to bring your daughter aid, who appeals to you:
or open up the Stygian caves, breaking wide
the earth, so I can fall in headlong.

NURSE

Poor girl, in vain you call upon your father's
shades, since no love for his children survives among the dead.
140   He could put another's brat before his son; delirious,
he took his brother's daughter as his wife—with
a wedding torch to weep for and a polluted bridal bed.
This caused the sequence of wrongdoing: murder, treachery,
lust for domination, thirst for accursed blood.
The son-in-law fell slaughtered,[16] a victim of
your father's marriage, lest your wedding bring him power;
O monstrous deed! Silanus was a service rendered
to a woman, and he fouled with blood his own
ancestral gods, indicted on a trumped-up charge.
150   The enemy—ah me!—breached the palace captured by
the wiles of your stepmother; he is now the emperor's son
and son-in-law, that youth of evil nature, ready for
all kinds of crime. His dreadful mother lit the bridal torch
and married you to him, against your will, in terror.
Victorious,[17] made fierce through so huge a triumph,
she dared to strive after rule of our sacred world.
Who could recall so many forms of evil,
the woman's dreadful hopes and wheedling tricks,
seeking the throne through mounting steps of crime?
160   Then holy Piety turned her trembling steps away,[18]
the savage Erinys with deadly foot entered
the empty court, and with the Stygian torch
polluted the ancestral gods and in her fury snapped
the laws of nature and everything that's right. The wife
brewed savage poisons for her man, then quickly died herself
by her own son's crime. You too lie murdered,[19]

to my eternal grief, unhappy boy, just now the world's
bright star, prop of Augustus' dynasty,
Britannicus, now merely fluttering ash and a grim shade,
     ah me,
even your savage stepmother shed tears for you   170
when she gave your body to be burned
upon the pyre,[20] and that face, those limbs so like those
of flying Cupid, were stolen by the raging flame.

OCTAVIA

Let Nero kill me too, to shun death by my own hand!

NURSE

Nature did not grant you the strength for that.

OCTAVIA

Pain, anger, grief, and wretchedness will grant it.

NURSE

Rather by obedience win over your ruthless man.

OCTAVIA

So he can bring me back the brother his crime took?

NURSE

So you can be unharmed, and by your progeny
restore your father's tottering house someday.   180

OCTAVIA

The ruler's house awaits a different child;
The dread fate of my wretched brother dooms me.[21]

NURSE

May your citizens' great loyalty strengthen your heart.[22]

OCTAVIA

That comforts but does not relieve my woes.

NURSE

The people's power is great.

OCTAVIA

          The ruler's is still greater.

NURSE

He himself will esteem his wife.

OCTAVIA

His whore prohibits him.

NURSE

A woman surely loathed by all?

OCTAVIA

But to her husband dear.

NURSE

She is not yet his wife.

OCTAVIA

She will be soon and mother too.

NURSE

A youthful passion rages at first onslaught
but subsides with ease and does not last for long
in shameful lechery, like the fickle smoke of fire;
the love of a chaste wife is everlasting.
She who first dared to violate your couch
and though a menial held her master's heart,
she fears already—that he'll prefer another.
Now she is timid, diffident, has even built a monument
as witness to her fear, since she's been cheated on.[23]
The fickle, lying god, winged Cupid,
will abandon her; though she be fair of face
and proud with wealth, her joy will be short-lived.
Such were the kinds of pain
borne by the gods' own queen,[24]
when the lord of heaven and father of the god
changed himself into all different forms,
taking now the plumes of a swan,
now the horns of a Sidonian bull,
and likewise flowed in a shower of gold.
The stars of Leda shine in the sky,[25]
Bacchus is installed in his father's Olympus,
Alcides made god is master of Hebe,
fearing no more the anger of Juno:
her one-time enemy is now her son in law.

Still the wise obedience and stifled anguish
of Jove's lofty wife prevailed.
Great Juno alone holds the Thunderer
secure in her heavenly bed;
no longer snared by human beauty
does Jove desert his lofty court.
You too, a second Juno on earth,
sister and wife of Augustus,[26] overcome   220
your heavy sorrows.

OCTAVIA

Sooner will savage seas be yoked to stars,
fire to water, and heaven to grim Tartarus,
nourishing light with darkness, day with dewy night,
than my mind, remembering always my dead brother,
will be yoked to the impious mind of my evil spouse.[27]
Would that the ruler of gods were now preparing
to engulf the vile head of the dread emperor with fire,
that god who often shakes the lands with hostile thunder
and terrifies our minds with sacred fires   230
and strange monsters. We have seen a flash in heaven,
burning to spread its comet,[28] a hostile torch,
where slow Boötes with night's alternation
steers his wagon, freezing with northern frost.
See! Heaven itself is polluted with the dread breath
of the savage leader, and the stars foretell
new disasters for the nations ruled by our impious
leader. Our parent, Earth, did not previously
give birth in anger to so fierce a monster,
Typhon,[29] when she broke faith with Jupiter.
This plague is worse than that. This enemy of gods   240
and men has driven deities from their temples
and citizens from their country. He took his brother's life,
and drained his mother's blood, yet sees the light
and savors life, drawing his poisonous breath.
Shame, mighty father,[30] why do you hurl your "invincible" bolts

so often in vain, at random, with your regal arm?
Why does your right hand fail against such a criminal?
Would that he might atone for his offences,
that intruder Nero, born from his father Domitius,[31]
tyrant of a world that he oppresses by his shameful yoke,
staining Augustus' name by his vicious ways.

NURSE

I admit he is unworthy of your bed,
But I bet you yield to fate and your own fortune,
my child, do not stir up the anger
of your violent husband. Perhaps some divine champion
will arise, and a glad day will come.

OCTAVIA

The gods have long since weighed our family down
with heavy anger; Venus was first to burden it, made cruel
by my poor mother's frenzy, who, though married,
madly remarried with an impure torch,[32]
forgetting me, indifferent to her husband and the laws.
The avenging Erinys, letting loose her hair
girded with serpents, came to her Stygian bed
and quenched with gore the torches stolen from her couch;
she inflamed the emperor's chest with fierce anger
for dreadful slaughter, and my unhappy mother,
ah me, met death by the sword, burying me in grief for ever
and dragging first her husband, then his son
down to the shades, she betrayed the fallen house.

NURSE

Cease to renew in tears your loyal mourning,
and troubled though you are, do not importune your mother's
  shade.
She paid a heavy penalty for her frenzy.

(*Both exit into palace.*)

CHORUS

What rumor came just now to our ears?
Would that it were falsely held,

spread in vain, and loses credibility!
May a new bride never enter
our emperor's bed, may Claudius' child
keep her home as wedded wife:
may she give birth to pledges of peace,[33]
so that the world can enjoy this in tranquility   280
and Rome retain its glory ever more.
The mighty Juno keeps her allotted
union with her brother:
Why is Augustus' sister,[34] his partner in marriage,
driven from her father's palace?
Ah, what avails her pure devotion
and divine father?
What her virginity and chastity?
We too forget our leader since his death,
betraying his children, in an age that brings fear.   290
Once real Roman virtue was alive[35]
in our forefathers; the real stock
and blood of Mars was in those men.
They drove from this city
the kings in all their arrogance
and avenged your shade well,
O maiden killed by your father's hand
for fear you might endure grim slavery,
and awful lust bear off in triumph wicked prizes.
You too precipitated a grim war   300
Lucretius' daughter, sacrificed,
poor woman, by your own hand
when you endured the savage tyrant's rape.
Along with Tarquin his wife Tullia
paid the penalty for abominable crime,
she who wickedly drove her savage chariot
over her murdered father's corpse. His own daughter,
violent woman, denied burial to the broken old man.
These ages too beheld a mighty evil,
the deed of a son,[36]   310

when the emperor sent off his mother,
duped by his guile, on a death-dealing boat
in the Tyrrhenian sea.
The sailors hasten to leave the calm harbor
as they were bidden; the waters resound
with the splashes of oars; the boat's swept out to sea,
and falling apart as its timbers are loosed,
it gapes wide under pressure and swallows in sea.
A mighty shout rises to the stars
320 mingled with women's wailing.
Dread death hovers before their eyes.
Each man seeks escape for himself,
some cling to the planks of the torn-apart deck
and naked cut through the breakers.
Others swim for the shore, and
many the Fates drown in the deep.
Agrippina rends her garments apart
and tears at her hair,
and soaks her cheeks with tears of anguish.
330 Once there is no hope of rescue
burning with rage and now beaten by evils
"*These* are your gifts of thanks," she cries
"for such a benefit, son?
I confess I deserved such a shipwreck
for bearing you, giving you life
and empire, and the title of Caesar,
fool that I was.
Husband, lift up from Acheron
your gaze, and feed on my punishment,
340 I, cause of your murder, pitiable man
and architect of the death of your son,
see, I shall now be borne, as I deserve, to your shade
without a burial,[37]
drowned in the sea's savage waves."
The breakers beat on her mouth as she speaks;[38]
she sinks into the sea and rises again

buoyed by the water.
Impelled by fear, she splashes the surface,
but gives up, weary with effort.
Loyalty remains in silent breasts   350
contemptuous of grim death;
many dare to aid their mistress,
her strength shattered by the deep;
as she drags her sluggish arms
they encourage her with words and support her with hands.
But what use was it for you
to survive the savage sea's waters?
You are doomed to die by your son's steel,
a man whose crime posterity will scarcely believe
and the ages always be slow to credit.   360
Impious man, he rages at her rescue from the deep
and grieves that she still lives,
and doubles the monstrous evil,
rushing to doom his unhappy mother,
allowing nothing to postpone his crime.
The henchman is dispatched and carries out his orders,
opening his mistress' breast with steel.
As she dies, unhappy woman,
she begs the agent of her death
to plunge his sword into her womb.   370
"This, this, is what you must stab with the steel," she cries,
"which bore such a monster."
After this appeal
uttered with her final groan
she at last gave up her sad spirit
through brutal wounds.

SENECA

Why, unruly fortune,[39] smiling on me with deceitful
expression, when I was content with my own lot,
did you raise me up high, so that, welcomed into the high
    citadel

I would fall more heavily, foreseeing so many fears?
I was happier when I hid far from envy's malice,
distant amid the crags of Corsica's sea
where my mind, at liberty and under its own control,
was always at leisure as I took up my studies.
O what a joy, greater than any that nature,
our mother gave birth to, designer of this vast work,
to gaze upon the sky, the sun's holy orbits,
motions of the universe, night's changing cycles,[40]
and Phoebe's sphere, surrounded by wandering stars,
the far-shining glory of the mighty heavens.
If it should age, great as it is, and once again fall
into dark chaos, that final day has come for the world,
to bury that impious race in heaven's collapse,[41]
so a better universe can be born again and produce
new offspring, as once it did when young,
when Saturn ruled the kingdom of the world.[42]
The maiden then,[43] goddess with great deity,
Justice, descending from heaven with holy Faith
reigned mildly over the human race on earth.
The nations knew no wars, nor grim trumpets blaring
nor warfare; it was not their wont to ring
their cities with walls; travel was open to all,
and there was common enjoyment of all things.
Earth herself gladly and freely opened
her fertile lap, happy and safe as parent
of such devout nurslings. But another progeny appeared
less mild: a third race was born, ingenious
to devise new arts, reverential at first
but soon restless, daring to chase wild creatures[44]
at a run, to dredge with heavy nets
or catch with light reeds fish sheltered by waves, to trick
wandering birds by wickerwork traps or by snares
holding them fast, to burden fierce bulls tamed by the yoke
and to furrow the earth once exempt from the plough:

once she was hurt, she hid all her produce in her holy depths.
But then there came a viler race that penetrated
its mother's body, digging out heavy iron and gold,
which soon took up weapons with savage hands; it separated
kingdoms, establishing bounds, and raised up
new cities. It defended its homes, or attacked those of others   420
with spears, intent on plunder. Astraea then,
the maiden, the glory of the stars, fled
the earth, spurned; fled the savage ways of men,
their hands polluted with the blood of slaughter.
Throughout the world, the lust for war increased
and greed for gold; luxury,[45] worst of evils, arose,
insidious plague to which long time and harmful folly
gave strength and power. Vices long accumulated
for so long, for so many ages, overflow upon us;
we are burdened   430
by a grim era: where crimes prevail, where impiety
savagely rages, where lust is in power, prevailing
by sexual turpitude; victorious luxury has long been stealing
the world's vast wealth with greedy hands—to waste it.
But look: Nero approaches with excited step
and grim expression. I shudder at his intentions.

NERO
Carry out my orders, send a squad to bring me
the severed heads of Plautus and of Sulla.

PREFECT
I'll not delay your command but go to the camp at once.

(*Exit Prefect.*)

SENECA
It is wrong to make rash decisions about kin.   440

NERO
It is easy for fearless hearts to act with justice.[46]

SENECA
But mercy is a mighty antidote for fear.

NERO

A leader's greatest virtue is to extinguish enemies.

SENECA

Greater, that a nation's father preserves his citizens.

NERO

A mild old fellow should be teaching boys.

SENECA

Hotheaded youth is more in need of guidance.

NERO

I judge this age of mine has wisdom enough.

SENECA

So the gods should always give your deeds approval?

NERO

I'd be a fool to fear the gods whom I create.

SENECA

450   Rather be wary of your unlimited power.

NERO

My fortune allows me to do everything I want.

SENECA

Trust in her goodwill more cautiously: she is a fickle deity.

NERO

It is a weakling's fault not to know his power.

SENECA

It does you credit to act rightly, not with power.

NERO

The mob tramples those at their feet.

SENECA

But crushes whom it loathes.

NERO

The sword will guard the emperor.

SENECA

Loyalty is stronger.

NERO

Men should fear Caesar.

SENECA

Better if men love him.

NERO

No, they must dread him.

SENECA

All compulsion is hateful.

NERO

Let them obey my orders.

SENECA

Then order justly.

NERO

It is I who will decide.

SENECA

What unanimity confirms.   460

NERO

A drawn sword will achieve it.

SENECA

May we avoid this evil!

NERO

Shall I continue letting them seek my blood,
so as to be overthrown, despised and unavenged?
Though remotely banished, their exiles did not break
Plautus and Sulla, whose obstinate frenzy
arms criminal agents for my murder,
while huge support persists in our city
even in their absence, fostering the exiles' hopes.
Let my suspected enemies be destroyed by the sword,
let my detested wife die, let her follow   470
her dearest brother: let all that is lofty fall.

SENECA

It is fine to be prominent among distinguished men,
to take counsel for your country, spare the downtrodden,

refrain from slaughter, give your anger pause,
and rest to the world, peace to your generation.
This is the highest excellence, the pathway to the heavens.
Just so Augustus, first of the nation's fathers,
embraced the stars, adored god-like in temples.
In his case, however, fortune long jolted him
on land and sea in the harsh vicissitudes of war,
until he crushed his father's enemies.
For *you*, she bowed her divinity without bloodshed,
granting the reins of empire with easy hand,
subjecting lands and seas to your authority.
Grim envy, overcome by loyal unanimity
gave way; the favor of senate and knights was kindled.
By the people's vows and the fathers' judgment,
you are the source of peace, chosen as judge
of the human race; you with sacred inspiration rule the world
as the nation's father. Rome begs that you preserve
this title and commends her citizens to you.

NERO

It comes as the gods' gift that Rome herself
and her senate serve me, and that she extorts petitions
and humble cries from the unwilling through fear of me.
What madness is it to preserve citizens who are
harmful to emperor and people,[47] swollen with noble birth
when one can order death to suspected traitors
with a single word? Brutus took up arms
to slay the leader who had spared his life;
master of nations, unbeaten in battle, matched with Jove,
often rising through high ranks of office, Caesar died
through the abominable crime of citizens.
How great a flood Rome witnessed of her blood
so often assailed! How many noblemen, young and old,
did godlike Augustus, whose valor and piety
earned him a place in heaven, annihilate?
They were scattered across the world, since from fear of death

480
490
500

they fled from their own homes and from the steel
of the Board of Three, the Triumviri
who marked on boards those destined for grim death.[48]
Senators seeing the victims' heads displayed   510
upon the public platform were forbidden to weep for kin
or groan for the Forum polluted by putrescence,
as hideous gore dripped from those rotting features.
This did not put an end to bloodshed or slaughter.
Grim Philippi long fed birds and savage beasts; the seas[49]
around Sicily swallowed fleets and men oft slaying their kin.
The world was shattered by the leaders' mighty forces:
the loser in battle sought the Nile with his ships
prepared for flight, though he too would soon die.   520
Again foul Egypt drained the blood of
a Roman general; now she covers their insubstantial
        shades.[50]
It is there the civil war is buried, waged impiously
for so long. At last the weary victor sheathed his swords,
blunted by savage blows, and fear maintained his empire.
He was kept safe by arms, and the soldiers' loyalty,
granted divinity by his son's unique devotion,[51]
worshipped in death and added to the temples.
Me too the stars will await, if I strike first   530
with savage blade whatever stands against me,
and base my dynasty on worthy progeny.[52]

SENECA

Your court will soon be filled with heavenly stock
by the god's daughter, glory of the Claudian house,
who holds like Juno her brother's wedding couch.

NERO

Her impure mother destroys trust in her descent,
and her unwifely temper never allied with me.

SENECA

Loyalty is never obvious in early years
when love conceals its flame abashed by modesty.

NERO

540   Indeed I vainly believed this for too long,
    though obvious signs from her estranged heart
    and expression betrayed her loathing for me,
    which my burning pain has finally decided to avenge.
    I've found a bride in birth and beauty worthy of my bed
    to whom the goddesses, Venus and Jove's wife
    and the fierce goddess of war, will yield in defeat.[53]

SENECA

    The virtue and loyalty of a wife, her behavior
    and modesty, should please her husband; only the good
    qualities of mind and spirit abide forever and are subject to
        none,
550   but each day passing withers beauty's flower.

NERO

    God has conferred all merits on one woman.
    The fates have willed her birth to favor me.

SENECA

    Love will leave you—do not trust it carelessly.[54]

NERO

    Love—whom the lord of thunder cannot avert,
    master of the skies, who delves the savage seas
    and realms of Dis, dragging down the gods on high!

SENECA

    Human folly fashions the merciless god as winged
    and arms his sacred hands with arrows and bow,
560   equips him with a savage torch and thinks him Venus' child
    begotten by Vulcan. Love is a powerful force in the mind,
    and a seductive heat in the heart; born of youth, it feeds on
    lust and leisure, among the joyous gifts of Fortune.
    But if you cease to cherish it and feed it, it fails
    and quickly loses force and dies away.

NERO

    I hold this love the greatest cause of life and source[55]
    of pleasure: by it humanity is saved

from extinction, being ever and again renewed
by welcome Love, which soothes the fierce beasts.
May this god should hold the marriage torch for me   570
and by its flame join Poppaea to my bed!

SENECA

The people's anguish could scarcely bear to look
upon this union, nor would holy piety permit it.[56]

NERO

Shall I alone be barred from action open to all?

SENECA

The people always make greater demands on a ruler.

NERO

I want to test whether this rashly formed favor[57]
will leave their minds, when my power has broken it.

SENECA

Rather be mild and listen to your citizens.

NERO

Rule is a failure when the mob directs its leaders.

SENECA

When its petitions are denied, the mob is rightly grieved.   580

NERO

So is it right to extort what prayers cannot obtain?

SENECA

It is harsh to refuse.

NERO

But wrong to compel an emperor.

SENECA

Let him concede voluntarily.

NERO

But rumor will call him beaten.

SENECA

Rumor is fickle and foolish.

NERO

But even so damns many.

SENECA

Rumor fears the eminent.

NERO

But blames them nonetheless.

SENECA

It will easily fail; let your deified father's merits
and wife's youth, virtue and modesty break your will.

NERO

Cease finally to remonstrate, I find you too tedious.
Let me have license to do what Seneca disapproves of.
590 I too have long frustrated the people's prayers.
Since in her womb she bears my pledge and progeny
What stops us naming tomorrow for the wedding?[58]

DAY 2

(Around dawn. In comes the ghost of Agrippina.)

AGRIPPINA

I burst the ground and strode from Tartarus[59]
brandishing a Stygian torch in my bloody hand
for the criminal wedding:[60] let Poppaea marry
my son lit by these flames, which the avenging hands
and anger of his mother will turn to grisly pyres.
Among the shades, the memory of my impious murder[61]
stays ever with me, weighing upon my shade,
600 still unavenged: the boat, that deadly recompense
paid for my services; the reward for giving empire,
that night when I wept over my wrecked ship.
I would have wished to mourn my slain companions
and my cruel son's crime: no time was granted tears,
but he doubled his huge wickedness with more crime.
Slain with the sword, defiled with wounds within
my sacred household, I exhaled my suffering spirit
—just rescued from the deep! But even with my blood I failed
    to quench
the loathing of my son; the fierce tyrant rages

against his mother's name, wants to wipe out what he
 owes me,   610
shatters my statues and inscriptions carrying my memory
throughout the world—the world which my ill-fated love
gave to the boy to rule, to turn out as my punishment.
Even dead, my angry husband persecutes my shade[62]
and attacks my guilty face with flaming brands.
He presses, threatens, blames his death upon me,
his son's grave as well, and demands his murderer.
Now spare me:[63] he will be yours. I ask only a little time.
The avenging Erinys prepares a worthy death
for the impious tyrant, lashes and shameful flight   620
and punishment to surpass the thirst of Tantalus,
the dreadful toil of Sisyphus, Tityos' vulture
and the wheel that whirls the limbs of Ixion.
Though he may build with marble and proudly cover
his palace in gold, though armed companies
guard their leader's door, and the world he drains
send its vast riches, though Parthians supplicate
his gory hand, though kingdoms bring him wealth,
the day and time will come for him to atone
for his crimes with his guilty life, to bare his throat   630
to enemies, abandoned, ruined, and destitute.
Unhappy me, how low my toil and prayers have fallen!
How low your madness and the fates swept you, crazy son,
to make your mother's anger agree to such great evils,
your mother, who was murdered by your crime?
If only before I brought you to birth, little child,
and nourished you, wild beasts had torn apart
my entrails![64] You'd have died free of crime
and consciousness, innocent, and my own,
clinging close to me; you would see forever,
in the calm abode of the dead, your father and forefathers,   640
men of great renown, who now will suffer shame
And lasting grief from you, evil boy, and me
who bore such a son. Why do I linger

to bury my face in Tartarus, ill-omened wife,
stepmother and mother for my kinsmen all.

(*Later that morning.*)
(*Octavia and the Chorus enter.*)

OCTAVIA

Spare your tears on this city's festive
and joyous day,
lest your great love and support for me
stir up the emperor's fierce anger
650   making me a cause for your misfortune.
This is not the first time my breast endured
such a wound; I have borne heavier.
Today will put an end to my suffering, even if by my death.
I shall not be compelled to look upon
my savage husband's face,
or to enter the bedchamber I loathe
of that slavewoman.[65]
I shall be not wife of Augustus but sister;
if only fearsome punishments
660   and the fear of death can be averted.
But can you, recalling your dread husband's crimes
poor fool, hope for this?
Long reserved for this bridal bed
you will fall as an ill-omened victim.
But why do you often look back at
your ancestral home, your face soaked with tears?[66]
Hurry to make your way from this house,
leaving the king's bloody palace.

CHORUS

See now the day so long suspected
670   has dawned, so often bruited by rumor:
Claudia has left, driven from vile Nero's bed,
which Poppaea now occupies victorious,
while our loyalty and grief, slow to act,
delays, checked by oppressive fear.

Where is the power of the Roman people
that often vanquished glorious leaders,
and gave laws in the past
to our undefeated country
and the rods of office to worthy citizens,
ordaining war and peace, and   680
humbled savage tribes, and
clamped captured kings in prison?[67]
See on all sides Poppaea's likeness gleams,[68]
painful to our sight, next to her Nero!
Let violent hands cast to the ground
features too closely resembling our mistress,
drag *her* from her lofty couch
and quickly attack with inimical flames
and missiles the savage emperor's palace

(*The next morning.*)

NURSE

Where are you rushing, panic-stricken, from   690
your husband's bed, my child? What hiding-spot do you seek,
with such a frightened face? Why are your cheeks wet with
    tears?
Surely the day we sought with prayers and vows
has dawned; you are joined in marriage to your Caesar
with the bridal torch, he whom your beauty beguiled.
And Venus, mother of Love, devoutly worshipped
and greatest deity, has given him bound to you.[69]
O how lovely and magnificent you sat on the couch
reclining in the palace.[70] The senate wonderstruck
looked on your beauty when you gave the gods   700
incense and sprinkled the holy altars with thankful wine,
your forehead covered with the fine bridal veil,
while he, the emperor, close by your side
strode exalted amid the citizens' glad omens,
showing joy in his proud demeanor and expression.
Just so did Peleus welcome Thetis as his wife[71]

as she emerged from the foaming deep; whose marriage
men say the heaven-dwellers thronged to celebrate
710   and every sea-god with united praise.
What cause has suddenly transformed your gaze?
Tell me what your pallor and your tears announce.

POPPAEA
Dear nurse, I am disturbed by a grim, fearful nightmare
from last night, my mind is muddled, I'm bereft of my
    senses.
For when the happy day and vault of heaven
gave way to gloomy stars and night,
I relaxed in sleep, held fast in Nero's embrace.
But not for long did I enjoy peaceful repose,
for I thought I saw a mournful crowd
honoring my wedding:[72] the Roman mothers,
720   with streaming hair uttered wails of grief,
and amid the often dreadful sound of trumpets
my husband's savage mother with threatening brow
shook a torch spattered with blood, and while
I followed her, compelled by vivid fear, the earth
suddenly split open with a vast chasm
before me. Plunging in it headlong, I beheld
my bridal bed and wondered at it: I sank
upon it wearily. Then I see my former husband coming
with a great mob escorting him, and my son.
730   Crispinus hurries to seek my arms and bestow
the kisses he used to give me; then Nero
burst excitedly into my chamber, and buried
his savage sword-blade in my husband's throat.
At last my immense terror shook off my dream,
a dreadful trembling shook my face and limbs,
and struck my heart, but fear blocked my speech,
which now your trusty loyalty has brought forth.
Ah me, what are the shades of the dead threatening?
What is the meaning of my husband's blood?

NURSE

Whatever the wakeful mind deliberates, 740
a holy, swift, and secret consciousness
recalls in sleep. Are you amazed you saw
your husband, bed, and chamber when you were in the arms
of your new groom? Do those beaten breasts
and streaming locks alarm you? Octavia's divorce
brought on their wailing, within the holy house
of her brother and her father's ancestral home.
That torch which led you on, raised in Agrippina's hand,
signifies a name made lustrous, ushered by envy.
The home of ghosts below promises the marriage bond 750
of your eternal dynasty will last. Since your emperor
buried his sword in a throat
he will rouse no wars but sheath his steel in peace.
Gather up your courage, regain joy, I beg;
drive off your fear, and go back to your bridal chamber.

POPPAEA

I'm resolved to seek the shrines and holy altars,[73]
to sacrifice victims and beseech the gods' goodwill,
to expiate the threats of this night's dream,
and turn this panicked terror onto my foes.
Make vows for me, nurse, and with pious prayers 760
adore the gods above, to cancel present fear.

CHORUS[74]

If babbling gossip tells truly the Thunderer's
deceits and pleasant dalliances—
that once he lay on Leda's breast,
disguised in wings and feathers,
and once bore Europa as a fierce bull
across the waves, his loot
—he soon will leave behind the stars
he rules, seeking your embrace, Poppaea,
preferring it to Leda's, 770
and to you, Danaë, to whose amazement

he once flowed in tawny gold.
Sparta may boast her nursling's beauty,
the Trojan shepherd of his reward,[75]
yet she will outshine the face of Tyndarus' child,
the face that stirred up dreadful wars
and surrendered Phyrgia's kingdom to the soil.
—But who runs up at a fear-struck pace,
what message does he bring in his breathless haste?

MESSENGER

780   Let every soldier celebrating in the emperor's home[76]
defend the palace threatened by the people's anger.
See, panicked captains draw their cohorts up
to garrison the city, but the furor rashly started
does not retreat in fear but gathers strength.

CHORUS

What insane rage drives their purposes?

MESSENGER

The crowds are stricken with devotion to Octavia
and they run wild and do huge outrage.

CHORUS

What do they dare to do, and why? Explain.

MESSENGER

They plan to restore Claudia to her divine father's home[77]
790   and her brother's bed, her proper share of empire.

CHORUS

The bed Poppaea now holds, by mutual pledge?

MESSENGER

This caused the obstinate support that burns their spirits
and rashly drives them headlong into folly.
Whatever images stood gleaming in bright marble
or in bronze, bearing Poppaea's likeness,
lie shattered at the mob's hands and overturned
by savage iron; they drag away the scattered limbs,
hauled off by nooses, bury and trample them underfoot
in shameful ordure. They mingle their bestial actions

with words that my fear suppresses.   800
They plan to surround the emperor's house with flames,
unless he yields his new bride to the people's rage,
and in defeat gives back her home to Claudia.
So that Nero hears of the civic riot from my lips,
I won't delay to carry out the captain's orders.

CHORUS

Why do you stir up fierce wars in vain?
Cupid wields unconquerable arrows.
He will smother your fires with his flames
as he has often quenched the lightning,
drawing down lovesick Jove from the sky.   810
You will suffer wounds and pay
grim penalties with your blood.
The hotheaded god is not slow to anger
nor does he let himself be ruled.
He ordered ferocious Achilles to pluck the lyre,
he crushed the Greeks and crushed Atrides,
overthrew Priam's kingdom and demolished glorious cities.
Now too I shudder at what his mind intends,
that violent force of the merciless god.

NERO

O, too reluctant are our soldiers' hands,   820
too long-suffering my anger after such an outrage:
proof being that citizen blood hasn't quenched the torches
kindled against me, and death-laden Rome is not soaked
in the blood of the people for bringing such men to birth![78]
Now it is not enough to punish such deeds by death,
the people's impious crime has earned far worse.
That woman to whom the people's frenzy subjects
me, my always suspect wife and sister still
must yield her life's breath for my pain at last,
quenching our anger with her blood.   830
Let the city's buildings soon collapse in flames I've set,
let fires and ruins crush the guilty people

along with shameful need, savage starvation, and grief.
The monstrous crowd rejoices, spoiled by the benefits
of our era; ungratefully it fails
to understand my clemency or endure my peace,[79]
but for this reason is swept along by restless bravado,
for this reason driven headlong by its own rashness.
It must be tamed by suffering and always constrained
840   by a heavy yoke, so that it dares not try again any such deed,
or raise its eyes to meet my wife's sacred face.
It will learn, when broken in by punishment
to obey in fear its emperor's authority.
But I see approach the man whose rare loyalty
and faithfulness made him my camp's commander.

PREFECT

I bring report that the people's frenzy has been checked
by the execution of a few rash adversaries.

NERO

And *that's* enough? Is that how a soldier listens to his leader?
You *check* them? Is this the vengeance I'm due?

PREFECT

850   The impious leaders of the riot have died by the sword.

NERO

What of the crowd that dared to attack
my household with flames, to give their emperor laws,
to drag my beloved wife from our bed,
to violate whatever it could with unclean hand
and vile claims? Have they escaped the proper penalty?

PREFECT

Shall anger decide the penalty for your citizens?

NERO

It will decide what time will never erase.

PREFECT

Let your anger be tempered but not our fear.

NERO

The first to expiate my anger will be she who earned it.

PREFECT

Name who it demands, so that my hand spares no one. 860

NERO

It demands my sister's slaughter and her wicked life.

PREFECT

A frozen trembling binds me, I'm seized with horror.

NERO

Do you hesitate to obey?

PREFECT

Why condemn my loyalty?

NERO

Because you spare the foe.

PREFECT

A woman can have this name?

NERO

If she takes on crimes.

PREFECT

Does anyone charge her guilty?

NERO

The people's madness.

PREFECT

Who can control the crazed?

NERO

Whoever could stir them up.

PREFECT

No one could, I think.

NERO

A woman whom nature gave a mind inclined to evil
and equipped her heart with cunning to do harm.

PREFECT

But not with force.

NERO

So she wouldn't be invincible,
but so that fear would crush her sickly strength,
or punishment, which though late will crush this criminal
guilty for so long. Away with advice and petitions,
fulfill your orders! Bid her be taken by boat
far from here to a distant shore and executed
to ease at last the swollen anger of my heart.

CHORUS

O deadly is the people's love to many,
and ill-omened!
It fills the sails of your boat with favorable wind and carries it
far;
then the same wind dies down, and
abandons you on the deep and savage sea.
Their poor mother lamented the Gracchi,[80]
whom the huge love of the people,
and too passionate support, destroyed,
though of glorious birth,
famous for piety and faith and eloquence,
brave of heart, keen in the law.
Fortune gave you too, Livius, a similar doom:
Neither his rods of office protected him nor his own home.
The present sorrow prohibits
offering more examples. Just now the citizens
wanted to restore her
to her father's palace and brother's bed;
now they can witness her dragged away
weeping in misery, to punishment and death.
It is good to hide in poverty, content with a humble roof;
Storms strike lofty houses often
or fortune overthrows them.

OCTAVIA

Where are you dragging me? What exile
does the tyrant or his queen command—   900
if she's mollified and grants my life,
won over by my many sufferings?[81]
Or if she plans to add slaughter
to my sorrow, why begrudge me
death in my own land, cruel woman?
But there is no more hope of survival:
Unhappy me, I see my brother's ship;[82]
in this boat, in which his mother
was once conveyed, I, too, his pitiable sister,
now cast out from marriage, will be carried!   910
Now piety has no divine power,
there are no gods,
but grim Erinys rules over the world.
Who then can properly bewail
my ill-fortune? What nightingale can match
my tears with her laments?
If only the fates had granted me,
poor woman, her wings.
Carried off afar, I would escape my sorrows
on swift wing, the grim assemblies of mortals   920
and fierce slaughter.
Perched alone on a slender branch
in a solitary grove
I could pour out a melancholy protest
from my plaintive throat.

CHORUS

The human race is ruled by the fates,
and no man can promise himself anything
stable and lasting, since time tumbles us
through shifting reversals—time, that we must always fear!
Let precedents strengthen your mind, the many

930   which your royal house has endured.
How has fortune been more savage to you?
I must recall you first, child of Agrippa,
mother of so many children,[83]
married to Augustus' son, and wife of Caesar,
whose name shone brilliantly throughout the world,
who so often delivered from her heavy womb
guarantees of peace.
Soon you suffered exile, lashes
and savage chains, burials, mourning,

940   and after long torture, death at last.
Livia,[84] happy in marriage and in her sons
to Drusus, rushed to heartless crimes
and her own execution.
Julia followed her mother's fate:
after long years, she was killed with a sword blow,
though with no charge against her.
What license was ever denied your mother, Octavia,[85]
who ruled the emperor's palace,
dear to her husband and powerful in her progeny?

950   And yet she was made a subject to her slave, and died
by a grim soldier's weapon.
What of the princess who deserved to hope
for deification, Nero's mighty mother?
Was she not first done violence
by the deadly hand of sailors,
and then fell slashed at length by the steel,
the victim of her savage son?

OCTAVIA

    See now the fierce tyrant sends me too
to the sad shades and spirits of the dead.
960   Why do I linger in vain, poor woman?

(To the soldiers.)

Hurry me to my death,
whoever Fortune has granted power over me.

I call the gods to witness—fool, what are you doing?
Do not beg mercy from the gods who hate you.
I call to witness hell and the goddesses of Erebus,
crime's avengers, and you my father,
worthy of such a death and punishment.
Death on these terms I do not hate.
Rig out the ships, set sail for the seas,
and let the steersman seek with the winds   970
the shores of Pandateria.[86]

CHORUS

Gentle breezes and light Zephyrs
who once conveyed, hidden in heavenly clouds,
Iphigenia,[87] snatched from the altars
of the savage virgin goddess,
carry this girl too far from her grim penalty,
I beg you, to Diana's temple;
Aulis is kinder than our city, as is
the barbaric land of the Taurians:
there sacrifice is made to divine powers   980
with the slaughter of foreigners;
Rome rejoices in citizen's blood.

Notes

Seneca and His World

1.   See John G. Fitch, *Seneca's Anapaests: Metre, Colometry, Text and Art-istry in the Anapaests of Seneca's Tragedies* (Atlanta, 1987). For Zwierlein's reviews of Fitch's method, *Gnomon* 60 (1988) 333–42; *Gnomon* 62 (1990) 692–96.

Medea

Introduction

I thank the University of Chicago Press for permission to reprint, in altered form, a section from chapter 5 of my book *The Mirror of the Self: Sexuality, Self-Knowledge, and the Gaze in the Early Roman Empire* (Chicago, 2006).

1.   Ulrich von Wilamowitz-Moellendorff, *Griechishe Tragoedien*, vol. 3 (Berlin, 1919), 162. For an excellent discussion of Senecan metatheatri-cality in general, see Littlewood (2007).

2.   As Fitch and McElduff (2002, 25) point out.

3.   Christopher Gill (1987, 32) puts it well when he writes, "Medea . . . reinforces her resolve by self-allusion; at the same time, her words de-rive some of their impact from more or less overt allusions to other speeches of self-incitement earlier in this play or in earlier versions of Medea. . . . This process is clearest, and most potent, in the use of the personal name."

4.   Seneca bids Lucilius, essentially, to become worthy of himself (*Letter* 20.1) and reminds him that it befits the wise man not to fear ills; cau-tion is appropriate to such a figure, but not fear (*Letter* 85.2.5). See *On Clemency* 1.5.3.

5.   See, for example, *The Phoenician Women* 202, *Hercules on Oeta* 1482, and *Oedipus* 879. On *dignum*, see also Fitch and McElduff (2002, 30).

6.   At times it is Seneca, instead, who seems to speak in the tones of his tragic characters. Fitch and McElduff (2002, 38–39) discuss the ap-

propriation of heroic language (rather than Stoic language) for heroic deeds.

7. Fitch and McElduff (2002, 37) agree: "When Medea speaks of her own *animus* as superior to external Fortune (150, 176), her *sententiae* could be quoted with approval by a Stoic." See Seneca at *On the Shortness of Life* 5.3: "What can possibly be above a man who is above Fortune?"

8. On this topic, see especially Star (2012).

9. Seneca was well aware of the difficulty of speaking truth to power; see *On Benefits* 6.32. On the whole dynamic of the sage speaking to the tyrant, see Littlewood (2004, 15–56).

Medea

The first draft of this translation benefited greatly from the reviews of my fellow members on the Chicago Seneca Board and from a painstaking reading by Liz Asmis, Elaine Fantham, and the anonymous press reviewer. Many thanks to all. Throughout, I have used the edition of H. M. Hine (2000). His apparatus criticus lists the major variants to be found in the manuscript tradition and the conjectures printed in his text. My translation is also indebted to that of J. G. Fitch, ed. and trans, *Seneca: Tragedies*. 2 vols. (Cambridge, MA, 2002–4). Note on meter: I have not attempted to reproduce Seneca's iambic trimeter in spoken passages, nor the varied lyric meters of the choral odes and Medea's magic song (740–848). Instead, spoken passages are in blank verse while song is represented by an approximation of hexameters.

1. Juno and Hymenaeus. Lucina presided over childbirth; she is sometimes identified with Juno, sometimes with Diana/Eileithyia. See Ovid, *Fasti* 3.243–58 on the origin of the women's cult of Lucina.

2. Medea descends from Titan, the Sun; he is her grandfather. Hecate is associated with the moon and with magic.

3. "A spouse more loyal": that is, more loyal than Jason. Hades remained faithful to his abductee, Persephone.

4. A summon to the Erinyes or Furies.

5. Medea already knows, it is clear, that Jason plans to marry the daughter of Creon, king of Corinth, to escape the vengeance of his pursuer, Pelias' son Acastus from Iolcus. Medea and Jason's original plan to stay in Iolcus was ruined when Medea persuaded Pelias' daughters to boil their father alive, thinking it would make him younger.

6.   Medea is not at this point thinking of infanticide but rather that the way her children will turn out will be punishment enough. The statement could also be a metaphor for an idea.

7.   This range, between the Black and Caspian seas, was associated with particular harshness and inhospitability.

8.   The river Phasis rises in the Caucasus and flows down to the Black Sea.

9.   Jupiter and Juno.

10. Possibly Pax, Venus, or amalgamation of the two.

11. Hymen.

12. Hesperus, the evening star, often accompanied weddings, which were generally held in the evening; but in the morning its appearance signaled the end of the night.

13. Dionysus/Bacchus.

14. The manuscripts suggest a two-line lacuna here.

15. Phasis as a region included Colchis, Medea's home.

16. Lyaeus, the thyrsus-bearer is Dionysus, invoked in his capacity to free humans from worry.

17. So that she could kill him, the way she killed her own brother Aspyrtus.

18. Literally "the Pelasgi," who often stand in for the Greeks as a whole.

19. Which Medea did in order to slow down her father's pursuit—he had to stop to pick up the pieces of his son.

20. The promontory Malea.

21. Like the armed men who grew from the dragon's teeth Jason sowed in Colchis.

22. The Argonauts.

23. Zwierlein (1986) deletes 242–43, but Hine (2000) retains them. Medea's meaning here is that if she had not helped Jason, the fire-breathing bull he had been sent to tame might have wrought havoc on the Greeks themselves.

24. Five stars in the constellation Taurus.

25. The brightest star in the constellation Auriga.

26. Ursula Major, also known as the Plough and the Big Dipper.

27. Tiphys, the helmsman of the ship Argo.

28. The Symplegades.

29. Reading *arces* with Hine (2000) for *astra*.

30. Scylla.

31. The Sirens, whose beautiful song lured sailors to their death.

32. This line reduplicates that of Fitch.

33. Tethys, a sea-goddess, mother of oceans and water nymphs.

34. Pindus is a mountain on the border of Thessaly; Nysa is the Indian mountain where Bacchus was born.

35. Following, with Hine, Zwierlein's conjecture (in "Weiteres zum Seneca Tragicus [I]," *WJA* 3: 149–771, at 160) of *patruam* for *parvam*.

36. I have produced the same translation as Fitch.

37. So called because Phrixus and his sister Helle escaped on the golden-fleeced lamb to Colchis, though Helle fell into the Hellespont on the way. The next line refers to the unsleeping dragon who guarded the actual fleece.

38. Line 477 is considered spurious and is omitted here and in Hine's text.

39. Some texts have *exilium* (exile) for *exitium* (death).

40. Creon and Acastus.

41. The text, which is corrupt, reads *nos confligere*; I accept the conjecture *conflige*.

42. Second, after the sky, Jupiter's realm, but before Hades, Pluto's realm.

43. Phaethon, of course, who drove the chariot of his father the Sun but lost control of it.

44. Using pine from the sacred groves of Mt. Pelion to build the Argo was not an auspicious start.

45. Aquilo is another name for Boreas, whose sons were Zetes and Calais.

46. Periclymenus, who changed into a bee but was killed anyhow.

47. His wife Deianeira lined his robe with a philter of the mixed blood of

the hydra and the centaur Nessus, which she thought would make him love her again. It turned out to be a flesh-eating poison.

48. Ancaeus was an Arcadian who joined the hunt for the Calydonian boar.

49. Idmon was the seer on the Argo; Mopsus, who is mentioned next, also had prophetic powers.

50. Lines 658–59 have been transposed to after 660 following Zwierlein's edition. I have supplemented the suspected lacuna with Hine's *pro suo gnatus*, originally suggested by Zwierlein.

51. The father of Palamedes, who was killed by the Greeks at Troy for alleged treachery.

52. Admetus, king of Pherae.

53. As if Pelias, too, was risking the dangers "of the sea" in the cauldron in which his daughters foolishly boiled him.

54. The constellation, which circles the Lesser Bear and extends toward the Greater.

55. Another constellation, said to represent a man holding a snake.

56. The monstrous snake killed by Apollo; he assaulted Leto, mother of Diana and Apollo, as she was giving birth.

57. In Sicily.

58. Avoiding the geographical confusion in the original; see Hine 2000, ad loc.

59. In southern Thrace.

60. Modern Jhelum, a tributary of the Indus.

61. The province of Baetica in Spain.

62. Ixion and Tantalus were both in Hades for attacks on the gods and on their own family members.

63. The fifty daughters of Danaus—all but one—killed their grooms on their wedding night.

64. A reference to Hecate.

65. Reading *horruit* with Markland for *floruit*.

66. A snakelike monster who attacked Jupiter and was imprisoned by him under Mt. Etna.

67. Nessus gave Deianeira a supposed potion that contained poisonous blood; she spread it on her husband Hercules' clothing. On Althea, Meleager's mother, see note at 644.

68. This refers to the moon; Trivia is another appellation for Hecate.

69. A Cretan goddess associated with Diana. The clashing of cymbals was said to counteract witches' control over the moon.

70. Mulciber, the god Vulcan.

71. The idea that the Chimaera's goatish midsection breathed out flames on its own (rather than from its leonine front) seems to represent a misunderstanding of *Iliad* 6.181–82.

72. Megaera, one of the three Furies, apparently heading for Medea.

The Phoenician Women

Introduction

1. This is John Fitch's conclusion in his important 1981 study of certain metrical and linguistic features in the plays of Sophocles, Seneca, and Shakespeare, which inform the dating of the plays.

2. Indeed, this is what the French tragedian Robert Garnier does in his close imitation of the *Phoenician Women*, called *Antigone ou La Piété*, by adapting a choral ode from Seneca's *Oedipus*.

Phoenissae

For my translation I have used the editions of Fitch and Zwierlein: J. G. Fitch, ed. and trans, *Seneca: Tragedies*. 2 vols. (Cambridge, MA, 2002–4); O. Zwierlein, ed., *L. Annaei Senecae Tragoediae* (Oxford, 1986).

1. A mountain, site of Oedipus' exposure as an infant.

2. Actaeon was punished for seeing the goddess Diana when she was bathing by being turned into a stag and torn to pieces by his own hounds. See *Oedipus* 751–63.

3. Agave, mother of Pentheus, king of Thebes, who with her sisters and other female followers of Bacchus ("Bacchants" or "maenads") tore her son Pentheus to pieces in a Bacchic frenzy. See *Oedipus* 616–18.

4. Zethus, son of Antiope, helped his mother get revenge on Lycus and his wife Dirce for torturing her; Dirce was tied to a bull and dragged to death on Mount Cithaeron.

5. Ino, sister of Semele, after being driven mad by Juno for boasting about Bacchus, jumped to her death in the sea with her child. Ino's cliff was perhaps on the road between Megara and Corinth, on the southern extension of the Cithaeron range. Seneca here follows Ovid (see *Metamorphoses* 4.416–530).

6. Labdacus was a king of Thebes and the father of Laius, hence Oedipus' grandfather.

7. Eteocles.

8. Polynices has mustered an army from Argos to help him win back Thebes from his brother Eteocles.

9. The sun.

10. The Evening Star.

11. Deleted: "To deny death to one who wants it is to kill him."

12. Deleted: "I'll embrace the fires, I'll make the funeral pile flare."

13. A river in Boeotia.

14. The monster who oppressed Thebes by killing anyone who could not answer her riddle, until Oedipus' arrival.

15. Thebes: the "Assyrian king" is an obscure way of referring to Cadmus, son of Agenor, king of Sidon, which in ancient history had been part of the Assyrian empire. See *Oedipus* 712–23.

16. When Cadmus arrived from Sidon, he killed the dragon that guarded the spring at the future site of Thebes.

17. The spring close to the city of Thebes.

18. Seneca broadens his catalogue to include places not far from Thebes. Eurotas was a river flowing through Laconia; Sparta, the birthplace of the twins Castor and Pollux, was a city in the Peloponnese.

19. Elis was a state in the Peloponnese; Parnassus was a mountain in Phocis associated with the town of Delphi; Boeotia was the region that included the city of Thebes.

20. Oedipus as Jocasta's husband was the son-in-law of Jocasta's father, but as her son he was the grandson of her father.

21. The part of the underworld reserved for the punishment of the wicked.

22. I adopt Fitch's emendation of *haeret* to *haesit*.

23. She means that it is not heroic to embrace death simply if one wishes to escape life.

24. The Latin personifies the crops as Ceres.

25. Presumably *Terra*, the Earth.

26. Dis, king of the underworld. For Oedipus' death-wish, see *Oedipus* 926–34.

27. That is, among the living.

28. He refers to his victory over the Sphinx.

29. "The god" is Apollo, whose oracle predicted Laius' murder by his own son. See *Oedipus* 34.

30. Literally, "my existence uncertain."

31. Other editors print this as a question not a statement.

32. The hands of Eteocles and Polynices, the sons of Oedipus and Jocasta.

33. The blood of kin.

34. Eteocles. The brothers had pledged to rule alternately.

35. Polynices.

36. Polynices is in exile at Argos where he has made an alliance with the king, Adrastus, by marrying his daughter.

37. Thebes is exhausted from the Sphinx's depredations, from the plague that has come with Oedipus' pollution of the city, and now from the conflict between Eteocles and Polynices.

38. The Latin word here translated as "natural love" is *pietas*. Seneca has used the root earlier to denote appropriate familial affections.

39. An allusion to Leander swimming the Hellespont (the Dardanelles) to reach his lover, Hero. But instead of offering to swim the narrows, Oedipus offers to cross the entire body of water, in effect offering to undertake something impossible and certainly suicidal.

40. The volcano Etna.

41. Hercules stole from the golden apples from the garden of the Hesperides.

42. Like Prometheus.

43. The brother is Polynices.

44. Aeschylus (in *Seven against Thebes*) and Euripides (in *Phoenissae*) both explain that the seven companies of Polynices' army are assigned to attack the seven gates of Thebes. Seneca assumes his audience knows this.

45. The verb "acknowledge" (*agnoscere*) has a technical sense in Latin, denoting a father's formal recognition of a child as his own.

46. This item must form the climax to Oedipus' crazed catalogue of crimes that he urges his sons to commit. At first sight, the Latin appears to mean "give weapons to your mother." That would be an anticlimax. Given Oedipus' desire for an act that fits his (incestuous) marriage-bed, it must denote the sons attacking their mother. Thus Frank (1995) in her edition. Fantham (1983, 65) takes the final step and proposes that this is sexual assault by the sons on their mother. If that is correct, the language is strained, but not unparalleled.

47. Accepting Fitch's emendation of *eruat* to *eruet*.

48. Polynices had recently married the daughter of Adrastus, the king of Argos, in accordance with an oracle (see Euripides, *Phoenissae* 409–23, Statius, *Thebaid* 1.395–497); Seneca does not mention the oracle.

49. The Thebans are descendants of Cadmus, the founder of Thebes. See *Oedipus* 29–30.

50. Literally, "by the interposition of a mother."

51. Seneca's use of the Roman word for standards, *signa*, indicates that he conceives of this as civil war; similarly so in Lucan, *Civil War* 1.6–7.

52. This remark implies that Antigone has already attempted to plead with her brothers. No fragment of this episode survives.

53. Jocasta imagines three large winged creatures that might convey her from the battlements to the battlefield; all three were notoriously malevolent creatures: the Sphinx (a winged monster with human head and lion's body), the man-eating Stymphalian birds from Arcadia, and the winged Harpies, which were sent to punish Phineus, king of Thrace, after he had offended the gods: they prevented him eating by fouling his food.

54. The Parthians, who ruled an empire in Asia Minor, were famous for their mounted archers, giving rise to the expression a "Parthian shot" meaning an on target shot delivered while retreating. The Romans were famously worsted by the Parthians at the battle of Carrhae in 53 BCE.

55. *Una in manuscript* A; *unam in* E. *Una* has the warriors acting as one against Jocasta; *unam* ("me alone," which I have adopted) would emphasize Jocasta's courageous isolation on the battlefield.

56. Inachus was a river god and the first king of Argos.

57. Deleted: "Shoot this belly, which gave my husband brothers." The line spoils the development of Jocasta's thought and the climax of 450; it appears to be influenced by *Oedipus* 1038–39.

58. Reading *donate matrem pace* for the unmetrical *donate matri pacem*.

59. Literally, "Do you fear your mother's good faith?"

60. Because Eteocles caused the dispute by refusing to cede power to Polynices.

61. Literally, "under the strike of crime."

62. Jocasta's "your" is plural: though she is addressing Polynices, she thus implies that Eteocles is responsible too.

63. The crime of brother fighting brother is not unprecedented: the city was founded from the soldiers who sprang up from the dragon's teeth sown by Cadmus and immediately engaged in hand to hand combat.

64. Amphion, with Zethus, was the founder of Thebes; he built the walls by the power of song. See *Oedipus* 611–12.

65. I follow Frank in punctuating so that *victor* belongs with *haec saxa franges* and not *hinc spolia auferes.* Jocasta is here imagining what Polynices might do *after* his victory.

66. Seneca gives Jocasta a catalogue of places where Polynices might find a

kingdom to rule. The places listed are all in western Asia Minor (modern Turkey), starting with Lydia, moving to Phrygia, then Caria and Mysia.

67. A mountain in Lydia, famous for its wines.

68. Pactolus is a river in Lydia famous for carrying gold in its waters.

69. This winding river gives us the English word "meander."

70. Though all the manuscripts have Hebrus, the principal river of Thrace, the emendation Hermus must be correct, as it is another Lydian river.

71. In Mysia; a peak in the Ida mountain range.

72. The river near Troy, also called Scamander (see *Iliad* 20.74).

73. Cadmus, the founder of Thebes, was later turned into a serpent for killing the dragon who guarded the spring at Thebes.

74. The manuscripts assign the roles to Polynices and Jocasta, but this makes no sense, since one of the speakers is clearly a power-hungry and ruthless ruler. Division between Eteocles and Jocasta, with references to the still present Polynices, works better.

75. Eteocles is probably addressing Polynices here.

76. Jupiter, as the creator of the world and the god of kings and kingship.

77. The manuscripts are divided between *ista* (which I translate as "that") and *ipsa* (which would need to be translated "actually").

78. At this point the play comes to an abrupt end.

Phaedra

Introduction

1. On Seneca's originality vis-à-vis these models, see Grimal (1963).

2. As has been noted by several scholars, Seneca's play shows above all the influence of Ovid's *Heroides* 4, in which Phaedra writes a love-letter to Hippolytus. From Ovid he takes Phaedra's psychological struggle between the twin forces of *pudor* (chastity) and *furor* (erotic frenzy), her sudden desire to become a hunter like Hippolytus, and her ill-judged hope that her advances will prove welcome to Hippolytus. See esp.

Littlewood (1994, 269–301); and Coffey and Mayer's (1990) introduction to the play in their edition.

3. For an excellent discussion of nature and control, see Boyle 1985.

Phaedra

Except where noted, I have used J. Fitch's Latin text from J. G. Fitch, ed. and trans, *Seneca, Tragedies*. 2 vols. (Cambridge, MA, 2002–4); I have also found the Lawall-Kunkel commentary and edition helpful (Wauconda, IL, 1982). In general, I have translated all iambic senarii with iambic blank verse; other meters are represented in the English by hexameters. My thanks for the feedback of my fellow board members and the University of Chicago Press's anonymous referee.

1. The founder and first king of Athens. The Latin here may either be the subject of the imperative *ite* (Go, Cecropians) or a genitive with *montis*, as Fitch takes it to be.

2. Probably to be identified with Mt. Parnes in northern Attica.

3. An ancient deme in Attica, northwest of Athens.

4. The Rhipaean (also Ripaean, Riphaean) mountains were a range in Scythia; as Hippolytus is not in Scythia, the adjective simply means "extremely cold."

5. Ilisos is a small river flowing from Mt. Hymettus into the Bay of Phaleron.

6. Acharnae was the largest deme in Attica.

7. Bees from this mountain in Attica were said to have taken honey to feed the baby Zeus/Jupiter in Crete.

8. One of the twelve towns of ancient Attica.

9. A promontory at the southernmost tip of Attica.

10. An area in northwest Attica.

11. Of the dog breeds, Horace identifies the Spartan and the Molossian (from Epirus) as "the shepherd's dangerous friends" (*Epodes* 6).

12. That is, Diana.

13. The Araxes runs between modern Iran and Azerbaijan. The Ister or Hister refers to the modern river Danube.

14. Gaetulia was the North African home of a warlike Berber Libyan tribe. The lions of the region were believed to be especially fierce.

15. Lines 62–63 are deleted by Fitch.

16. The Sarmatians were a Slavic people dwelling in ancient Scythia.

17. The Hyrcani were a tribe on the Caspian Sea.

18. Following Fitch's transposition of 69–72 (he in turn following the earlier editor Leo).

19. A sea-god, the son of Oceanus and Tethys, and father of the Nereids.

20. The "suitor" is Pirithous, king of the Lapiths. Theseus owed him a favor, and agreed to help him abduct Persephone, wife of Pluto, god of the underworld. The attempt failed, and while Theseus was eventually freed by Heracles, Pirithous was left in the underworld.

21. The rites referred to here are the Eleusinian mysteries, over which Pallas Athena presided. Both Poseidon and Athena were competitors to be the patron of Athens; Athena offered olives, Poseidon salt-water, and the king Cecrops chose Athena's gift.

22. That is, the fake heifer in which Pasiphae was hiding. Phaedra here draws a contrast to herself—her love is hopeless—and also to Hippolytus, who is incapable of falling in love.

23. The Latin *Mopsopia* refers to Attica. Daedalus is still being referred to here.

24. The Minotaur.

25. The sun-god, Phoebus Apollo, told Vulcan/Hephaestus that his wife Venus/Aphrodite was sleeping with Mars/Ares; Vulcan caught them in the act and chained them.

26. For a description of these peripheral peoples, see Herodotus 4.62, 72; 4.93–94; 4.103. The Getae consisted of several Thracian tribes; the Scythians were a nomadic people of Iranian stock; the Tauri inhabited the mountainous regions of southern Crimea.

27. An instantiation of the god Mars as "the strider."

28. Venus is called Erycina in the text after a mountain in northwest Sicily where one of her temples was located.

29. Following Fitch's choice of the correction *texta* for *tecta*.

30. Theseus kidnapped Antiope, a queen of the Amazons. In one version of the myth, they marry and she fathers Hippolytus before being abandoned in favor of Phaedra.

31. The text names Pirithous, whom Theseus is currently accompanying to the underworld to help with kidnapping Persephone.

32. That is, Minos did not punish Ariadne for eloping with Theseus before the latter married Phaedra.

33. Following Fitch's juxtaposition of 261.

34. Like Fitch, I delete line 264 because it is unmetrical and only found in manuscript E.

35. Double, because he is thought of as both sweet and violent.

36. Lines 279–80 are found only in manuscript E and are deleted by Fitch.

37. The two constellations Cancer and Ursa Major. The latter is named the "Parrhasian bear" here to refer to Callisto, an Arcadian nymph (Parrhasia was a region within Arcadia) who was raped by Jupiter and then transformed by his jealous wife into a bear; Jupiter later turned the bear and her son into the constellations Ursa Major and Ursa Minor.

38. Presumably like Jupiter, who took on different appearances as he wooed various women.

39. Europa, whom Zeus/Jupiter took to Crete on his back.

40. Diana, the moon-goddess, who took a break from driving the chariot of the moon because she was in love with the mortal shepherd Endymion.

41. Hercules, who dolled himself up to please the queen of Lydia, Omphale, when he was her slave.

42. Reading *ditisque* with Fitch for *ditique* in the EA manuscript. The "rich sand" is a reference to the gold-bearing Pactolus River.

43. There is a short lacuna in the text here. I have supplied the sense of the verb "lay."

44. The Nereids are sea-nymphs, daughters of the sea-god Nereus.

45. The "Lucanian beasts" are elephants.

46. Lines 377–78 were deleted by Leo and Fitch and are omitted here.

47. A mountain range in southern Turkey.

48. That is, the threads of silkworms.

49. Leo and Fitch delete this verse.

50. The River Tanais (now the Don) and Lake Maeotis, also known as the sea of Azov. See note to 715 below.

51. The Black Sea.

52. Hecate, Diana, and Luna are three manifestations of the same goddess, one in the underworld, one on earth, and one in the sky.

53. A reference to Endymion again.

54. Reading *cursus* with Leo and Fitch for manuscript A's *luxus*.

55. Alpheus and Lerna are rivers near Olympia and Corinth respectively.

56. The text followed here reflects Axelson's emendations.

57. Lacuna after 509 suggested by Fitch following the earlier editor Peiper; I do not include a lacuna.

58. After Medea killed her children and fled from Corinth, she married Theseus' father Aegeus, then tried to kill Aegeus in order to secure the succession of her son Medus (whose father may or may not have been Aegeus).

59. The Syrtes were treacherous sandbanks off the north coast of Africa.

60. Tethys was a sea-goddess, the wife of Oceanus and the mother of many major rivers. Here she seems to be used by metonymy for "the western seas."

61. In Thessaly.

62. This is the same translation of this line as that of Fitch, as are the translations of 633 and 662.

63. The press reviewer notes that *cadere in* is a legal expression "for falling within the scope of."

64. Line 642, *penitus medullas atque per venas meat*, only occurs in manuscript A and is omitted here.

65. Perhaps a reference to Ariadne, daughter of Minos.

66. Ariadne again, who lead Theseus out of the labyrinth.

67. Medea. She had tried to poison Theseus himself earlier, when he came as a guest to Athens, where she lived with his alleged father Aegeus—after the events described in Seneca's play, when she is still with Jason.

68. The modern sea of Azov, north of the Black (Pontic) Sea.

69. Corus, the northwest wind.

70. Reading *temperans* in 755 with Fitch following Axelson for *territans* in manuscript EA.

71. Bromius and Liber are both alternative names for Bacchus. Seneca alludes to an alternative to the usual version, Ariadne leaving Bacchus for Theseus, rather than being abandoned by the latter.

72. The order of the lines is uncertain here. I do not follow Fitch's transposition in this case.

73. Cyllaros is the horse of Pollux in Vergil (*Georgics* 90) and of Pollux in Ovid (*Metamorphoses* 12.408).

74. Castor excelled as a horseman and his twin Pollux as a boxer.

75. Triptolemus was a king of Eleusis who presided over the sowing and milling of grain. He was credited with inventing the plow.

76. Phlegethon (*flaming*) is one of the five rivers of the underworld.

77. Reading *Aegaeae* with Fitch and Axelson for *Actaeae* in manuscript EA.

78. Colchian Phasis: a river in Colchis, the home of Medea on the Black Sea.

79. The north wind.

80. Literally "necks," referring to the stars in the constellation that form the lion's neck.

81. A promontory on the island of Leucas in the Ionian Sea.

82. *Numine Epidauri dei*: the god Asclepius had a sanctuary at Epidaurus.

83. An outlaw killed by Theseus. He was famous for robbing travelers and then throwing them off the "Scironian rocks."

84. Theseus overcame both the bull of Marathon and, of course, the Minotaur.

85. That is, as a father who has killed a son.

86. There is a lacuna in the text at 1045; supplement by Fitch.

87. Literally, more lamentable than Avernus, a lake near the entrance to the underworld that gave off fatal exhalations.

88. Yet another murderous bandit killed by Theseus. Sinis would tie his victims to pine trees bent to the ground, then release them, either splitting the victims in two or sending them airborne.

89. Theseus also killed Procrustes, a criminal who invited guests to spend the night then killed them by stretching them or cutting off their legs to fit the size of his iron bed.

90. A cave in Sparta believed to be an entrance to the underworld.

91. Tityus was a giant who tried to rape the goddess Leto. As punishment, he was tortured in Tartarus by two vultures who fed on his liver by day; it grew back by night.

92. That is, Ixion, the father of Theseus' friend Pirithous, was a king of the Lapiths who raped a cloud-shape he thought was Hera. Zeus had Hermes bind him to an eternally-spinning wheel of fire.

93. Reading *animosa* with Fitch.

94. Mopsopia is an ancient name for Attica.

The Trojan Women

Introduction

1. Lines 124, 164, 166, 205, 254, 681, 760, 764, 787, 813, 1126, 1169.

2. For example, in our play (162–63): "Happy is he who died in battle and brought / the world in ruins with him as he went."

3. The phrase J. Romm (2014, 75, 176) uses twice of the tragedies.

4. *Pumpkinification* 12 vis-à-vis *Trojan Women* 108, 130f., with the introduction to A. J. Keulen's 2001 edition, p. 9.

5. Ibid.

6. On the dynamics of power and vision in this play, see Benton 2002.

7. For a wise reading, with further parallels, see Trinacty 2014, 40–44.

8. The word itself, or an equivalent, occurs at key points. See 282, 289, 1086, 1106.

9. As Brecht does in his own "epic" theater. See M. Esslin, *Brecht: The Man and His Work* (Garden City, NY, 1971), 137.

Troades

Thanks are due to Shadi Bartsch and the University of Chicago Press's anonymous reader for their suggestions. The text is from O. Zwierlein's Oxford Classical Text, *L. Annaei Senecae Tragoediae* (Oxford, 1986), including his variations from the line order of the manuscript throughout.

1. Specifically, Neptune and Apollo, who built Troy's walls.

2. Rhesus, a Thracian king who supported the Trojans during the Trojan War.

3. Memnon; see 239–42.

4. Penthesilea, queen of the Amazons.

5. Priam, elderly king of Troy.

6. A dream in which, rather than giving birth to Paris, she gave birth to a firebrand.

7. Ulysses.

8. Diomedes.

9. Hidden in the Trojan horse.

10. Adopting Bentley's conjecture. Ajax raped Cassandra, the daughter of Priam and Hecuba. In the post-Iliadic tradition, Cassandra was known for predicting the future, but always in vain.

11. Achilles' son; oblique in the Latin.

12. Paris, of Athena, Hera, and Venus, before the war.

13. Paris, near Amyclae, in Sparta, seducer of Menelaus' wife, Helen.

14. The translation at this point follows Fitch's 2002 edition.

15. Rhoeteum was a city in northwest Troad, bounded to the south and west by the river Simoeis.

16. First by Hercules himself in Priam's youth, then by Philoctetes during the war; see 718–35 below.

17. Killed at his altar, as described at 44–54.

18. Trojan shore.

19. "Elysian" refers to the fields of the blest in Classical afterlife.

20. About to embark on the Trojan War, the Greeks were detained by Diana at Aulis until, on Calchas' instructions (352–70), Agamemnon sacrificed his daughter Iphigenia, as described in Euripides' *Iphigenia at Aulis*.

21. His mother Thetis being a sea nymph.

22. Achilles was from Phthia in Thessaly.

23. Cycnus; see Ovid, *Metamorphoses* 12.70–145. The reference to white plumage may either be to his purported fair hair, or to his metamorphosis into a swan.

24. The river of the Troad, also called Scamander, which Achilles fought (*Iliad* 21).

25. Youngest daughter of Priam and Hecuba; see Ovid, *Metamorphoses* 13.339–480.

26. A kind of merman, usually singular, in Neptune's train.

27. Nestor, king of Pylos.

28. Achilles' mother, Thetis, dressed him as a girl to prevent his conscription in the Trojan war; when Ulysses presented the girls with girlish gifts and weapons, Achilles outed himself by preferring the latter; the rest of the line appears to refer to the choice of Achilles—namely, dying young with immortal glory or living out an indistinct old age.

29. Achilles wounded Telephus in Mysia; when the wound would not heal, he later allowed rust from the original spear to be applied to the wound as sympathetic medicine.

30. Eetion, king of (Greek, not Egyptian) Thebes, and father of Andromache.

31. Compare Achilles' own account of himself in Ovid, *Metamorphosis* 12.108–112.

32. Briseis and Chryseis from Chryse: girls captured and exchanged by Achilles and Agamemnon in the conflict that begins the *Iliad*.

33. Island near the Hellespont/Dardanelles.

34. Possibly the Aegean island off Euboea where Achilles hid.

35. The famous island, near Troy, off the coast of Asia Minor (Turkey).

36. Trojan city; mentioned in *Iliad* 1.37–38.

37. Boyle (1994) writes *ad loc*: "river in Mysia at the battle of which Ach. wounded Telephus (see 215n). The catalogue of places comes full circle."

38. King of the Ethiopians of the far east and son of Tithonus and Aurora, whose grief is also described.

39. The Latin has *exemplum*.

40. Penthesilea; see 12 above.

41. That is, as well as the captive girl Briseis Agamemnon originally took away from him—the impetus for Achilles' rage in *Iliad* 1.

42. The Latin has *vitium*, whence English "vice" (as opposed to virtue), but also (as here) simply "weakness, defect, failing, etc."

43. Achilles, here by his patronymic.

44. Gronovius suggests the loss of a line after this. Pyrrhus seems to be suggesting that Agamemnon is opposed to the sacrifice of Polyxena because he wants her for himself.

45. When Achilles allowed Priam passage and hosted him in retrieving his son's body.

46. When Achilles withdrew from battle after the altercation over the women, Agamemnon beseeched him through the embassy of Ajax, Ulysses, and Phoenix.

47. Pyrrhus' birthplace.

48. A reference to Aegisthus.

49. Some commentators think 341 spurious; others connect it with 340 on the basis of the comparison of families that Pyrrhus would here make, with his own divine lineage connecting him to the sea, while Agamemnon's infernal relations are all too famous (see previous note).

50. Pyrrhus' mother was Deidamia, the daughter of Lycomedes. Achilles was "not yet a man" because he was disguised as a girl on Scyros.

51. Achilles' mother, sea nymph.

52. Achilles' paternal grandfather and famous judge in the underworld, and son of Jupiter.

53. Probably alluding to Iphigenia and Chryseis; compare *Iliad* 1.69–72.

54. Compare *Iliad* 1.106–7.

55. The winged horse of Bellerophon, born from the blood of Medusa, was proverbially fast.

56. The sun.

57. Here synonymous with the moon.

58. A promontory on the southernmost point of the Peloponnesus where a cave was supposed to lead to the underworld.

59. The three-headed hellhound of myth.

60. Her son, Astyanax.

61. Another name for the underworld.

62. In *Iliad* 16, Patroclus borrows the armor of Achilles and is mistaken for him.

63. These lines contain an unmistakable allusion to the moment in Vergil's *Aeneid* when Andromache enjoins Aeneas' son to remember dead Astyanax before the foundation of Rome, the second Troy (3.489–90): "O only remaining image of my Astyanax! / Like this did he move his eyes, like this his hands, like this his face." Seneca's fragment about absent friends bears comparison (*De Amicitia*, 59.6, ed. Dionigi Vottero [Bologna, 1998]): "Let us suffer no friend to be away from us; let us turn him back from there into our souls; let us offer the future to ourselves; let us call back the past: 'Like this did he move his eyes, like this his hands . . .' Let us make a distinctive image in our soul, one taken from life and not blurry and silent: 'Like this did he move his eyes, like this his hands . . .'"

64. See 1 above.

65. Priam.

66. Hector.

67. Ulysses.

68. The injunction of Calchas' prophecy.

69. Agamemnon's son.

70. Another reference to the sacrifice of Iphigenia at Aulis: see 165 above.

71. Reading *ustis* with manuscript A.

72. Reading *timens* with Fitch for *tumens*.

73. Ulysses' son.

74. Astyanax.

75. A reference to Priam "buying" back Hector's body from Achilles.

76. Respectively: Penelope, Laertes, and Telemachus.

77. Than his father Laomedon, who cheated Hercules and Apollo of the pay promised for building Troy's walls.

78. See 137, 824–25.

79. Probably Palamedes.

80. See lines 38–40.

81. Reading *melius* with Fitch for *medios*.

82. A purification ceremony, usually that performed by the censors in five year periods at Rome.

83. Keulen (2001) *ad loc*: "the words aim to evoke Rome's oldest dance, that of the Salii . . . the very rare word *saltatus* is also used by Livy when he reports the inauguration of this rite by Numa."

84. Keulen notes that the word *oscula* ("kisses") is used only of family exchanges in Seneca's plays.

85. As elsewhere (40, 414, 992), Andromache strongly identifies the attributes of Hector's death with herself.

86. Olympus, Ossa, and Pelion.

87. A valley between Olympus and Ossa, perhaps more famous in Roman poetry than in Greek.

88. A Thessalian port.

89. Towns in northern, western, and south-eastern Thessaly, respectively.

90. In southern Thessaly, the home of Achilles.

91. In southern Thessaly, at the foot of Oeta (see next).

92. The bow of Hercules, from Mt. Oeta, was later acquired by Philoctetes; see 137, 718–35 above.

93. Fantham (1982) *ad loc*: "The town of Olenos is reported as uninhabited by Strabo (10.451); it was devastated subsequent to the Roman defeat of Aetolia in 89 BCE, so Seneca's epithet is anachronistic."

94. In south Aetolia; the "maiden goddess" is Diana.

95. Troezen, in the northeastern Peloponnese.

96. Mountain in Thessalian Magnesia.

97. Homeric hero: see *Iliad* 2.756–59.

98. See further *Iliad* 4.219, 11.832; also Seneca, *Hercules Mad* 971.

99. On the south coast of Euboea and famous for marble.

100. Another Euboean town, whose strait is called Euripus.

101. In the Aegean, near Cos.

102. Near Sicyon.

103. Enispe was in Arcadia, on the Pelonponnesus.

104. Island near Thessaly.

105. Near Athens and site of the Persian defeat at sea in 480 BCE; the meaning of "the real Ajax" is unclear, and the editor Scaliger suspected a lacuna before the line.

106. Aetolian city.

107. Keulen (2001) ad loc: "a river of Thessaly, discharging itself into the Peneus without mingling with it, but floating on its surface like olive-oil. It was considered a branch of the Styx; see *Iliad*, 2.751."

108. "Old-man" because of Nestor; see 1.213 above.

109. Cities of the Peloponnesus.

110. Helen.

111. Grandfather of Agamemnon and Menelaus.

112. A mountain and island in Ulysses' kingdom, Ithaca.

113. Ex-husband, Menelaus.

114. The contest staged in the hills in which Paris, then a shepherd, judged Venus (Aphrodite) more beautiful than Minerva (Athena) and Juno (Hera).

115. Fitch (2004, 53) writes: "Helen's phrase 'forgive Paris' implies that Paris is the cause, but can be forgiven because Pallas [*sic*] gave Helen to him (921)—and, of course, because he is a Trojan. Both in the wording of 920–21 and in *ignosce Paridi* Helen shifts the blame from herself, but at the same time skillfully avoids blaming Paris, because she claims to be loyal to his memory (908f.) and is addressing his sister-in-law."

116. Polyxena.

117. Calchas; see 351.

118. Cassandra is excluded, according to Keulen, because she is not attending Hecuba. Or she is conveniently forgotten to heighten the pathos.

119. Pyrrhus.

120. Agamemnon.

121. After the death of Achilles, Ulysses outdebated Ajax for his weapons.

122. Presumed an interpolation.

123. Leo suspects a lacuna after this line.

124. Reading *trahit* with manuscript A.

125. Threatened by their stepmother Ino, the siblings attempted to escape from Boeotia to Asia through the sky on the back of a golden ram; Helle, the sister, was unsuccessful and fell into the part of the sea thereafter called the Hellespont.

126. Deucalion, who, with Pyrrha, survived the flood that Jupiter sent to destroy humanity, as described in Ovid, *Metamorphoses* 1.

127. A line or more appears to have been lost here.

128. The metrically incomplete line effectively mirrors Astyanax's incomplete life. One suspects that Seneca is modelling on Virgilian technique and taking Virgil's incomplete lines as deliberate. Whether Virgil's incomplete lines were, in fact, deliberate or reflect lack of finish is another question.

129. People of proverbially "barbarian" cruelty.

130. Busiris was an Egyptian king who violated rules of guest-friendship by killing his visitors.

131. Diomedes of Thrace had horses that ate human flesh.

132. This and 1147 are thought to be interpolations.

133. Death.

Octavia

Octavia

I use the A manuscript tradition for this translation and will note when I adopt modern conjectures.

1. This prayer addressed to Octavia's mother Messalina and father Claudius does double duty as mourning and self-exhortation ("come now" introduces her own emotional condition, while "I must bewail" begins the narrative of her family's ruin by the interlopers Agrippina and her son Nero). An act of family mourning would normally take place at the altar in the innermost shrine of the palace, but Octavia's circumstances are completely abnormal and could be staged as if she had come into the open to escape them. We might compare the elegiac lament of Euripides' Andromache, the enslaved wife of Pyrrhus, or the opening of his *Medea* where Medea's nurse in the preceding events, then in dialogue with the *paidagogus*, reveals Medea's emotional condition.

2. "Seaborn Halcyons": Ovid's Alcyone was turned into a seabird when she mourned her beloved husband. "Pandion's daughter": similarly Procne and Philomela, daughters of King Pandion of Athens, were turned into a swallow and a nightingale to lament the death of Tereus and Procne's child Itys.

3. On Octavia's mother, Messalina, and her self-induced downfall, see the introduction. The author alludes to rather than narrates her behavior, which would distract from the moral superiority assumed for the house of Claudius.

4. In Greek mythology the Erinyes were spirits of the underworld who avenged the murder of kin. Roman poets applied to the antithesis of marriage and murder the notion of an Erinys taking on the role of the *pronuba* (matron of honor) in order to bring the marriage to ruin.

Agrippina, the new stepmother, is this destructive Erinys. Seneca and his contemporaries were influenced by Ovid's narrative of Tereus and Procne in *Metamorphoses* 6, where Tereus' lust for his sister-in-law perverted his originally honest marriage to Procne. See also 263.

5. While Julius Caesar mounted two short term raids on southern England, across the ocean (i.e., the channel), the unheroic and unmilitary Claudius began his principate with victorious campaigns bringing these tribes under Roman control.

6. Marriage is only a source of evil in the mindset of this play, but it builds on a long tradition of wifely treachery against husbands; compare, for example, 164–65 below with Catullus 64.397–406 or Ovid's *Metamorphoses* 1.146, which unusually combines treacherous husbands and wives. Latin *coniunx* ("spouse, yokemate") denotes either partner, and throughout the play the word is stressed to denote both the villains and the victims of these marital offences.

7. The Latin has *Tyrannus*. This is the play's first reference to Nero, who is only exceptionally named (see 250). Part of the texture of this introductory act comes from identifying the historical figures only by their position in the family. Note in particular the nurse's allusion in 45–46 to Octavia as "sister and likewise bride."

8. The "son" and his "brother": the relationships are both the artificial product of Nero's adoption as son of Claudius and brother of young Britannicus.

9. Electra, daughter of Agamemnon murdered by Clytemnestra, survived under duress, and her monologue on this theme opens Sophocles' *Electra*. But she had a hope of vengeance for her father because she had helped her brother escape; in the play he returns in disguise, then kills both Clytemnestra and her lover.

10. "The shadow of a mighty name" echoes Lucan's description of the failing Pompey (1.135), but its purpose is different: she sees herself as a ghost of her noble family.

11. Until now the nurse has been unaware of Octavia; there are no cross-references between their previous speeches. If this were to be staged, it would be possible for the two women to be unaware of each other while each standing stage front, but the nurse's words imply she hears Octavia's voice from within. In any case, Boyle (72n) is mistaken to

invoke the rolling platform (*eccyclema*) to explain Octavia's reentry. The platform is only used for climactic moments, such as the opening up of Agamemnon's inner room to reveal his and Cassandra's slaughtered bodies. The beginning of *Octavia* is no climax, indeed there will be two more scenes with an equal claim to reveal the interior of Nero's bedchamber as first Octavia, then Poppaea leaves it.

12. "Menial" (*famula*) (here and at 194 and 657) is used for domestic slaves; to an empress it might seem that all citizens were mere subjects/slaves. Octavia's other term of abuse for Poppaea is *paelex*, concubine, again a term recognized in Roman law, but not in normal use.

13. I follow Ferri (2003b), who in turn follows Zwierlein, in translating Lipsius' emendation of *morte* (death) to *sorte* (position, lot in life).

14. The Latin has *paelex*; I use the strongest term of abuse in current use to refer to Poppaea.

15. An allusion to Nero's murder of Agrippina (the "Stygian boat" is intended to take her to the underworld via the river Styx). But this "gift" occurred in 59, three years before the play opens.

16. This is Junius Silanus, another member of the dynasty, to whom Claudius had betrothed Octavia; but Agrippina wanted him dead and disgraced so she could marry Nero to Octavia. See Tacitus, *Annals* 12.3–4 for the false charge of incest with his sister used to destroy Silanus: the language represents the man's suicide as a ritual sacrifice.

17. It is Agrippina who is called "victorious," as if the family were a battleground between the Claudians and the Julians.

18. The house itself is a scene of conflict; as the avenging Erinys enters, Piety takes flight. This is the first allusion to the Hesiodic myth of ages; the spirit of family devotion is compared to Justice, also called the Maiden or Astraea in the longer version of this myth (see 397 below), who flees the earth.

19. Octavia returns to her brother Britannicus, also Nero's victim, whom she has just described in her dreams (115–24).

20. Tacitus (*Annals* 13.17) and other sources report that Agrippina wept at Britannicus' funeral; he had been her protégé and hoped for counterpoise to the domination of Nero. But Agrippina is changed from villain to victim by her death; there are traces of both aspects in the play,

and the chorus at 309–76 will fully transform her into the brave and wronged victim of her murderous son.

21. She alludes to the new pregnancy of Poppaea, Nero's mistress; if she gives Nero a son it will doom Octavia to death like her own brother.

22. The people's love for Octavia is a dubious asset. They will only hasten her doom, by rioting against the new marriage.

23. A reference to Nero's infatuation with the freedwoman Acte.

24. The parallel with Juno is based on the fact that like Juno/Hera, natural sister of Jupiter/Zeus, Octavia has become both Nero's sister (by adoption) and wife. The nurse takes over the analogy cited by Catullus 68.138–40; like Juno she must endure her consort's infidelities, but Juno's forbearance helped her maintain her wifely status.

25. According to myth Jupiter seduced Leda as a swan, Europa as a bull, and Danaë as a shower of gold. The women were rewarded; Leda's sons the Dioscuri were alternately divine and mortal, Semele's son Bacchus became a god, and Alcmene's son Hercules was welcomed to Olympus with his wife Hebe, in some myths daughter of Juno, making him her son-in-law.

26. "Augustus" here denotes Nero by the honorific title of his great-grandfather Octavian/Augustus.

27. This figure of comparing human changes to *adunata* (combinations impossible in nature) is common to Latin love poetry from Virgil's *Eclogues* onward.

28. A comet was seen as symbol of a change of ruler or similar disaster; there were several at the end of Claudius' reign and during Nero's time. Boötes, "the oxherd," denotes the constellation of the plough.

29. Typhon was the evil monster produced by the earth in Hesiod's *Theogony*.

30. Not her human father but Jupiter, who punished offenders against the gods with his thunderbolt.

31. "Intruder" is literally a grafting of an alien species onto a fruit tree. In this line the author names the emperor Nero for the first time. Being the son of L. Domitius, he was himself a Domitius until his adoption gave him the name Ti. Claudius Nero.

32. Messalina was known to be promiscuous, but her ruin came when as Claudius' wife she publicly celebrated her marriage to C. Silius.

33. "Claudius' child . . . pledges of peace": Octavia matters to the people of Rome because she is the rightful emperor's child; at the same time she has value as the vehicle for a male heir to the line. Latin saw children as *pignora* (guarantees) whether of parental love or the perpetuation of the family.

34. The title "Augustus" had been given to Nero as emperor. Like Juno, sister and wife of Jupiter, Octavia is both Nero's wife and his sister, although his adoption into her family necessitated the artificial procedure of adopting her out of the family in order to avoid technical incest. Her father Claudius was "deified" as *Divus Claudius* and given a temple (with Agrippina as priestess!) after his death.

35. It is common for choral odes to introduce a contrasting myth (or in Rome legend) of the past to cast light on the evils of the present. This contrasting section recalls the founding of the Roman republic when the son of King Tarquin ("Superbus") raped the chaste wife Lucretia, and she summoned her father to avenge her violation and suicide. But "Maiden" stands for Virginia slain by her father in an honor killing in 451 BCE: Our author has first introduced the later "charter myth" of liberation from tyranny, when Virginia was killed by her father to save her from becoming the slave and so sexual property, of the villainous Decemvir Appius Claudius (in 451 BCE, Livy 3.44–48), before moving back in time to Lucretia (300–302) and the usurpation by Tarquin and his wife Tullia of his father-in-law Servius' throne; Tullia drove over her father's murdered body in the "Street of Crime," *Vicus sceleratus* (Livy 1.48; for Lucretia, see Livy 1.58–60).

36. Neither the ancient myths of republican liberty nor the lustful nature of Tarquinius' and Appius' crime properly match the nature or motives of Nero's murder of his mother, the main theme of this chorus from 310 to 337. But the author's narrative closely follows the source used by Tacitus (*Annals* 14.5–8), including her command to Nero's agent Anicetus to strike her womb, because it had given birth to such a son.

37. Negative *in-humata*, "without a burial." To be drowned at sea denied the body the last rites of kinsmen and the religious security of burial in the earth (*humare*).

38. Many of the details of this shipwreck scene echo Ovid's narrative of Ceyx's drowning in *Metamorphoses* 11.490–560.

39.　How does the audience know that this is Seneca? From the beginning its language and thought is his. And by 380 and the allusion to Corsica, where Seneca was exiled for eight years, the character is echoing some of the thoughts of, for example, his early Consolation to his mother Helvia (especially *Consoluations to Helvia* 20). In Stoic thought the wise man escaped from worldly cares by contemplating either the universe above and beyond the world or his own inner mind.

40.　Night's changing cycles; I follow Zwierlein's text based on Gronovius' emendation of *sortis*.

41.　"The final day . . . gaping void . . . heaven's collapse": this evokes the Stoic theory of *ekpurosis*, by which the universe would be consumed by fire when it needed renewal, and the constellations would fall into the void of chaos. (See *Thyestes* 832–23 and Lucan I.72–80.) Ovid begins his *Metamorphoses* with this chaos, which is then resolved into its separate elements by a kindly deity.

42.　In Virgil (*Aeneid* 8.319–58) early Italy knew a golden age, *Saturnia regna*, when Saturn ruled before he was overthrown by his son Jupiter. Seneca is reverting to the Roman variations on the Hesiodic myth of the five ages drawing on elements from the divergent narratives of Virgil, *Georgics* I.112–49; or Ovid, *Metamorphoses* I.89–150. Typical are the definition of the golden age by its lack of evils like war and fortified cities and the invention by man under the pressure of Jupiter's hardships of new skills like fishing, hunting and fowling, and ploughing, as symbol of agriculture, which can be construed as good or as an evil violation of the earth's flesh (*viscera*); worst of all was mining for gold and iron, producing warfare, greed, and luxury "that worst of evils." The word comes closer to lustfulness than mere self-indulgence, and it dominates the last lines before Seneca is interrupted by Nero's approach. But unlike the earlier historians (Sallust in particular) and poets, Seneca does not add Ambition to Greed and Lust (*luxuria*). Ambition had become too dangerous.

43.　The maiden associated with justice in 397 introduces a fuller version of human civilization expanded from the nurse's brief allusion in 160, which returns by ring composition to the opening theme of maiden now driven out by the vileness of the modern age (422).

44.　Following Fitch's edition, including line 412 *bis*, but not the supplement proposed by Zwierlein.

45. Rome's victories over Greece, Asia and its hinterland, and Egypt made her rich with spoils, which were seen as the cause of moral decline and greed leading to civil war.

46. These one-line aphorisms in this fruitless debate feature keywords bandied back and forth as if in a tennis match. Seneca's claim that a ruler should seek the love and respect, not the fear, of his people can be found extensively in his *On Clemency*, addressed to the new emperor Nero in 55 CE, and in a similar debate between the tyrant Atreus and his courtier in *Thyestes*.

47. Nero answers Seneca's model Augustus with a version historically far nearer the truth. For fifteen years after forming the triumvirate with Antony and Lepidus, Octavian was ruthless in eliminating the republican survivors (in the proscriptions); they were outlawed and escaped assassination only by flight into exile. In 42 CE, combining with Antony, he defeated Brutus and Cassius at Philippi in Macedonia, thus winning control of the eastern empire which he initially entrusted to Antony. Seneca emphasizes the civil slaughter, giving less prominence to the battles (see separate notes below).

48. A reference to the proscriptions (from *proscribere*, "post a public notice").

49. "Philippi" introduces the Macedonian campaign against the republicans ending in the first pitched battles of the civil war (42 BCE); the waters of Sicily denotes the naval warfare conducted by Octavian against Sextus Pompey, ending in Pompey's defeat at Naulochus in 36. "The Nile" stands for the miserable outcome of Antony and Cleopatra's defeat at Actium (31 BCE), when the Egyptian squadron turned tail and headed for home, leaving victory for Octavian, Agrippa, and Apollo, Octavian's divine patron. Nero's account of the battle and its turning point echoes Virgil's description of Actium in *Aeneid* 8.679–714.

50. With manuscript A.

51. "Granted divinity by his son's unique devotion" could as well be Ovid's tribute in *Metamorphoses* 15 to Octavian's own piety promoting his father Caesar to be Divus Julius, but Nero has leapt forward a generation to the end of Augustus' principate, when he in turn was promoted to Divus Augustus by his adopted "son" Tiberius.

52. "My dynasty." As Augustus founded the dynasty of his competing

Julio-Claudian descendants, so Nero speaks of his still unannounced descendant, the child Poppaea is carrying; Seneca instead argues for Nero's Claudian wife. From 551 Nero openly glorifies Cupid, god of desire and Poppaea as his love match.

53. Nero describes his mistress Poppaea as exceeding all three goddesses in the judgment of Paris, though the myth had him prefer Venus to Juno and Minerva because Venus promised him Helen.

54. From 553 to 571 Nero moves to the traditional theme, praising the universal power of Love, represented as young Cupid, armed with burning torch and arrows. This was a topos of lovers and advocates of love in Greek and Roman comedy, revisited, for example by Seneca in *Phaedra* 195–203 and the whole debate between nurse and Phaedra. But it had also become an educational exercise for young Romans to set out why Love was depicted as a young god with wings and burning torch (see Propertius 2.12 and Quintilian 2.4.26). It was perhaps part of this exercise to celebrate Love's conquest in all three realms, overcoming Jupiter ("master of the skies,") the sea-god Neptune, the god of the underworld (Hades, who abducted Persephone) and the moon-goddess (Endymion).

55. This invokes the Epicurean Venus, the life force hymned by Lucretius in *On the Nature of Things* 1.1–40.

56. "The people's anguish" is a turning point, as Seneca introduces the factor that will direct the outcome of the tragedy: the people's love for their emperor's daughter and popular gossip around the palace. Nero rejects each argument, alleging as final claim that the people are praying for an heir to the dynasty and Poppaea is bearing that child. (It was in fact a girl, who was deified by the senate but lived only four months.)

57. Following manuscript A.

58. The change of subject from 590–91 suggests that a line has been lost identifying Poppaea as the subject of "she bears." Such a line, or even two, could soften the clumsy effect of this casual announcement. It should go without saying that imperial marriages were not arranged at twenty-four hours' notice (Poppaea had been Nero's mistress for three years already). The absurdity is reinforced when we read/hear that there were many statues of Poppaea alongside Nero on the wedding day (see 682 below). But dramatic time is kept short and concentrated, despite the incongruity.

59. The opening words identify the speaker as a ghost; compare Tantalus' ghost speaking the prologue of *Thyestes* and Thyestes himself opening the prologue of *Agamemnon*. Seneca's dramatis personae report the appearance and speech of ghosts in *Troades* (Achilles; the appearance of Hector to Andromache is a hallucination) and *Oedipus* (Laius in the Nekyomantia), but apart from Tantalus' prologue only Agrippina speaks with no addressee (except the apostrophe to the dead Claudius at 618): she curses, reproaches, and prophesies in a dramatic void, though we may construe Poppaea's terror and flight in the next scene as the effect of Agrippina's apparition.

60. Agrippina identifies with the Erinys, acting as *pronuba* at the forthcoming wedding (as at her own wedding in 153–61 and 262–64). The three weddings (Claudius–Agrippina, Nero–Octavia and Nero–Poppaea symbolized by the bridal bed (*thalami*) are the source of all the dynastic evils.

61. The rest of her denunciation is focused on her son and his treachery in contriving her death, first with the theatrical collapsing ship, then in her own home on land (see 309–75 above). To this she adds his willful destruction of the honorific statues commemorating her services (608–11). But 611 *mortis metu* cannot mean, "on pain of death." I translate Buecheler's emendation *matris metu*, from fear of his mother.

62. In Hades the dead persecute the dead, but Agrippina herself invokes against Nero the penalties of the classic sinners in Hades who offended against the gods: Tantalus, Sisyphus, Tityos, and Ixion.

63. "Spare me" addressed to Claudius, her victim, who can seek revenge in the underworld. 619–31 foresees both Nero's extravagance in power (the golden house; the submission of Tiridates of Armenia), and his miserable flight and death. The details are close enough to the historical narratives (for which we must rely on Suetonius and Dio, since Tacitus' *Annals* do not go beyond 66) to suggest that these lines were written after Nero's death in 68 CE.

64. The last section of her harangue, moving from curse and prophecy to poignant regret that Nero had reached birth, shows a surprising and pathetic originality.

65. "Slavewoman" echoes her earlier abuse of Poppaea at 187 (*paelex*) and 194 (*famula*).

66. "Why look back?": cf. 671 "Claudia has left . . ." It seems that only now (after the wedding and its consummation) is Octavia leaving the palace; yet Poppaea is already within at 690–91 when the nurse reproaches her with fleeing from her bedchamber.

67. This is the nearest the author comes to evoking the politics of the republic, where the Roman people legislated, elected, and determined the decisions of the state on war and peace and foreign victory.

68. The Romans of the republic did not erect public statues of living women (Cornelia, mother of the Gracchi, had died before she was given a statue). But under Augustus, Livia and the other imperial women were honored with statues in the Hellenized empire. The bases survive today of statues honoring Nero and Poppaea as consorts, one formally dated to the year of their marriage. See B. C. Rose, *Dynastic Commemoration* (Cambridge, 1997), 21 and 22. But Nero's flouting of tradition is intensified by the supposed instant organization of the wedding ceremony.

69. These lines confirm that Poppaea is now formally married. "Devoutly worshipped" translates Birt's correction, adopted by modern editors, for a corrupt manuscript reading.

70. The nurse's speech stands in for a physical description of the ceremony; the groom escorts the bride from her home to his palace (703–5), she sacrifices in her new home (700–702), and then is seated at the public banquet (699–700, out of sequence, since this would occur last in the public ritual). Such physical accounts of contemporary ceremonies were developed by Ovid in his exile and later poetry; see *Fasti* 1.71–88 and *Letters from Pontus* 4.4.23–42, a natural antecedent of such descriptions in dramatic recitation. Parades of all kinds were also incorporated in stage productions, but the wedding in *Octavia* is specifically outside the drama.

71. To enhance the description of the wedding the nurse recalls (with "men say") Catullus' great poem 64, celebrating the marriage of the mortal Peleus and sea-nymph Thetis, when the gods still attended the weddings of mortals; "Each sea-god" represents the divine *Thiasos*, or parade of sea-gods, honoring Thetis.

72. Like Octavia, Poppaea has had a dream. Like Octavia, she dreams of kin, but her ex-husband and son were still living at the time, though they would die in 66 as victims of Nero's violence. The ambiguous text must refer to Crispinus, killed by her husband Nero in a chronological

inversion as an adulterer. The nurse's "interpretation" is obviously false, as we are shown when scared Poppaea and her nurse end their scene by planning a religious act, praying for the gods to hold off the things they fear. But the text of 761 is unsatisfactory, and Helm's conjecture (which is translated here) can only be a stopgap.

73. The nurse's soothing interpretation does not persuade, and the women, like Octavia and her nurse in their corresponding scene, go into the palace to perform expiatory sacrifices. As noted, 761 is corrupt and beyond certain correction.

74. Here and later at 806–19, the chorus should be seen as a different group from Octavia's sympathizers; these are supporters of Poppaea, perhaps wedding guests.

75. That is, Helen, further described in the sequel.

76. Reading *exultat* with manuscript A.

77. Like the editors Ferri and Boyle, I understand the transmitted *divi* in the text as "of the god" (divine Claudius), in keeping with the stress on Octavia's family or household gods. The Latin text of this line is closely echoed by 803, which may be a deliberate echo.

78. Nero's second scene (820–76) follows the themes of his argument with Seneca, with 25 lines covering his anger of the Roman people and 30 (846–76) covering his hatred for Octavia. He answers the prefect's dutiful report with thirst for his citizens' bloodshed and the demand for Octavia's execution: the compressed final section combines accusations against his "sister" with general denunciation of women, and modern editors assign 867–68 to the prefect, answered by Nero's outburst on woman's evil nature, and the order for her assassination in exile.

79. Both "benefits" and "clemency" echo Seneca's ideology of imperial responsibility, explained in his *On Clemency*, dedicated to Nero in 55 CE, and *On Benefits*, which stresses the reciprocal obligation of gratitude to the emperor from his citizens.

80. Tiberius and Gaius Sempronius Gracchus (tribunes in 132 and 122–21 BCE) were popular reformers whose legislation threatened the propertied classes. Each was killed by political mobs, but the fame of their mother—a daughter of the great Scipio—ensured that letters and statues attributed to her perpetuated the legend. Livius Drusus, an ancestor of Augustus' wife Livia, was tribune in 91 BCE. His murder that year led to the Social War.

81. This can only be understood as heavy irony: exile is seen as a gracious concession.

82. Nero's deadly vessel, the ship contrived to sink and cause Agrippina's death.

83. "Mother of so many": Agrippina the Elder, daughter of Agrippa and Julia, Augustus' daughter, wife of Germanicus and mother of three sons and three daughters, including Agrippina the Younger, Nero's scheming mother.

84. This Livia was the wife of Tiberius' son Drusus, seduced by Sejanus, and subsequently exiled. But the identity of her daughter Julia is uncertain.

85. "Your mother": Messalina, wife of Claudius and mother of Octavia and Britannicus, forced to commit suicide after her flagrant public "marriage." "Made subject to her slave," refers to Messalina's death at the orders of her ex-slave Narcissus.

86. Pandateria was the place of exile of Augustus' daughter Julia, and would now be that of Octavia, until her murder.

87. Iphigenia, sacrificed by her father Agamemnon to appease the winds holding the Greek fleet at Aulis, was, according to Euripides' *Iphigenia among the Taurians*, rescued by Diana and spirited away to the Tauric Chersonnese, where it was her duty as priestess to sacrifice strangers. When her brother Orestes was driven there by a storm, she was able to rescue him and escape with him to Greece.